CAN DO!

HOW TO ACHIEVE REAL PERSONAL CHANGE AND GROWTH

Ben Tiggelaar

CYAN

mc **Marshall Cavendish**
Business

First published in 2007 by:

Marshall Cavendish Limited
119 Wardour Street
London W1F 0UW
United Kingdom
T: +44 (0)20 7565 6000
F: +44 (0)20 7734 6221
sales@marshallcavendish.co.uk
www.marshallcavendish.co.uk

and

Cyan Communications Limited
119 Wardour Street
London W1F 0UW
United Kingdom
T: +44 (0)20 7565 6120
F: +44 (0)20 7565 6121
sales@cyanbooks.com
www.cyanbooks.com

A CIP record for this book is available from the British Library

ISBN-13 978-1-904879-73-2
ISBN-10 1-904879-73-X

Typeset by Phoenix Photosetting, Lordswood, Chatham, Kent

Printed and bound in Great Britain by
TJ International Ltd, Padstow, Cornwall

To Ingrid, Maria, Isabelle, Emma and Bernice

"The major problems facing the world today can be solved only if we improve our understanding of human behavior."

Burrhus Frederic Skinner (1904–90)

"If you want to truly understand something, try to change it."

Kurt Lewin (1890–47)

Contents

Introduction

If you want, this can turn your life upside down...

Change isn't easy.

Change costs thought, energy, and time. Anybody who has ever tried to change something important in their lives or who has ever been involved in company change will agree.

And yet...

And yet we can still change. Every person has the potential to change their own behavior. And through this we can have a deep influence on the quality of our own lives and on the lives of others.

What's more: if we understand how behavior change works for ourselves, then we are better able to address change *together with others*, for example, in companies. Don't misunderstand me: I have no illusions about becoming "perfect." What's more, I place large question marks against what many people consider "success." But I do not doubt that, by changing our behavior, we are capable of achieving important aims.

- Behavioral change can have enormous influence on our *private lives*, for example, on our life expectancy. At the end of the 1970s, the American *Centers for Disease Control* published research that showed that more than 50 percent of all deadly diseases were connected to the *behavior and lifestyle* of the deceased.
- Behavioral change is an under-exposed subject within *professional life*, for example, in managing organizations. Many company change plans fail because they concentrate far too much on technique, or intangible matters, and not enough on the *concrete daily behavior* of customers and employees.

◆ Behavioral change can also have a major influence in *society*. The way we treat each other in the neighborhood, in the shop, and in traffic determines to a large degree the quality of our daily lives. Behavioral change can have a considerable impact on our lives and on those of others, but – as I have already said – it is not easy.

To be honest, everybody should learn something about human behavior and behavioral change during their education. Many people today undertake their attempts at change with dubious insights and deficient techniques. There's room for improvement.

In everyday matters relating to money or the weather, we want people to be exact. Financial and meteorological advisors who simply follow their gut feeling and read tea leaves cannot expect to be taken seriously.

But when it comes to *change* (and to my mind, that's considerably more important), then we go looking for salvation in the strangest places. The shelf in the book store holding books about change and personal development has turned, in the last few years, into something you'd find in an old curiosity shop.

When I started working a few years ago on the *Basic Change Method* – and that is the method that is central here – I laid down three rigid demands. The method had to be:

(1) very effective;
(2) easily usable by everybody;
(3) based on accepted scientific research.

In the last few decades, a lot of innovative, interesting research has been undertaken by behavioral scientists into the effectiveness of change techniques. The *Basic Change Method* is a *synthesis* of scientific insights in that field. (I have included a scientific explanation where you can read which theories and models form the basis for this approach.)

Perhaps you are scared that it is all going to be very complicated. Let me reassure you. Personal behavioral change is, in my experience, about as difficult to learn as riding a bicycle, or looking after three small children on your own for a week. Not easy if you look at it from a distance, but everybody can learn to do it. As long as you think it important enough.

Let me close with a promise... Change may not be easy, but once you have absorbed the information in this book – by reading, considering, and especially by putting it to the test – you will have greatly increased your capacity to help both yourself and others to attempt change, whether large or small. In an effective and positive way.

Even if you have some experience in the field of change, then I would still estimate that each stage within the *Basic Change Method* (there are three) will double your capacity for change. And that can turn your life upside down. I speak from experience...

A summary

If you are in a hurry, then here's a summary for you. The *Basic Change Method* is a combination of the most effective insights from cognitive psychology and behavioral psychology. Thanks to its fundamental character, this approach lends itself to many types of change:

◆ Individual change *and* collective change.
◆ Applicable in private life, professional life, and society.

The *Basic Change Method* has three tenets:

(1) change is primarily concerned with realizing new behavioral habits;
(2) new behavioral habits demand management of behavior intentions and of change situations;
(3) change happens in different phases and requires attention, energy, and time.

The *Basic Change Method* consists of three stages: Get Real, Make Plans, Take Action:

1. GET REAL: Formulate goal-oriented and concrete behavioral intentions.
Determine which future results are really important and translate these accurately to personal changes in habit behavior in the present.

2. MAKE PLANS: Thoroughly prepare the most difficult change situations.
Develop a plan for activating the desired behavior within the most difficult change situations, using powerful stimuli and counter-behavior.

3. TAKE ACTION: Begin, measure, and reward the desired behavior.
Measure daily at first the behavior and only later the results of the behavior. Ensure immediate and regular personal rewards for everything that goes well.

At the end of this section you will find the *Basic Change Method* in its totality in a simple flow-chart. As you read this book, you may find it handy to refer to this chart, so that you know exactly where you are in the process.

A dozen awkward words

The *Basic Change Method* uses, wherever possible, normal, recognizable words. But, occasionally we can't avoid using technical terms. Below are definitions for 12 words that could cause confusion:

(1) Intention: a conscious intention; a mental resolution for the future.
(2) Behavior intention: a conscious, rational resolution to display certain behavior in the future.
(3) Situation: the direct circumstance within which somebody operates/finds themselves. Consists of physical elements, events, and the behavior of other people.

(4)   Change situation: the direct circumstances within which a person wishes to display a certain behavior.

(5)   Antecedent: a stimulus within a situation, that triggers a certain behavior. Stimuli can take the form of events and the behavior of other people.

(6)   Behavior: everything people do. There is "external" behavior (movement and speaking) and "internal behavior" (thinking and feeling).

(7)   Consequence: a stimulus within a situation that is triggered by a certain behavior. Stimuli can take the form of events and the behavior of other people.

(8)   Conditioning: a learning process in which behavior is influenced by stimuli within the situation in which one finds oneself.

(9)   Positive reinforcement: the application of consequences that a person finds pleasurable and thus reinforces desired behavior.

(10) Negative reinforcement: the threat of consequences that a person finds unpleasant, and thus reinforces desired behavior.

(11) Punishment: the application of consequences that a person finds unpleasant in order to discourage undesirable behavior.

(12) Counter-behavior: supporting behavior that ultimately helps one to display the desired behavior even in difficult change situations.

The Basic Change Method

Main points

a) Change is primarily about realizing *new habit behavior*.

b) Stimulating new habit behavior requires management of *intentions* and *situations*.

c) Change takes place in different *stages*, and costs a lot of *attention, energy*, and *time*.

GET REAL: *Formulate goal-oriented and concrete behavioral intentions*

Determine which *future* results are really important and translate these *accurately* to *personal changes in habit behavior* in the *present*.

| A. Investigate what is possible; make use of your mind and feelings. | B. Determine what end results are desirable; make use of your mind and feelings. | C. Translate these results to measurable, personal change in habit behavior. | D. Check all the previous points against applicable forms of self-deception. | E. During this change, ask the help of somebody you can really trust. |

MAKE PLANS: *Thoroughly prepare the most difficult change situations*

Develop a *plan* for activating the desired behavior *within the most difficult change situations* using powerful stimuli and *counter-behavior*.

| A. Determine which change situations will most negatively affect the desired behavior. | B. Investigate which stimuli in these change situations hinder the desired behavior. | C. Think of extra stimuli and counter-behavior that will activate the desired behavior. | D. Make a concise step-plan: warm-up and start; several intermediate steps, and a follow-up. | E. Make clear agreements about the execution of the plan, both with yourself and with other people. |

TAKE ACTION: *Begin, measure and reward desired behavior*

Measure daily at first the *behavior* and only later the *results* of the *behavior*. Ensure immediate and regular *personal rewards* for everything that goes well.

| A. Ensure a daily confrontation with the most important elements of the plan. | B. Measure daily only the desired behavior and only later include the results. | C. Ensure that for everything that goes well, there is a regular and immediate personal reward. | D. Don't give up if something goes wrong, but take one step back and persevere. | E. Keep on regularly measuring behavior and results, according to your plan. Adjust if necessary. |

Part 1:
How change really works

I really don't know what questions you may have as you start this book. Are you thinking about individual, personal change? Or are you, together with your colleagues, about to face a big challenge at work?

This book deals with both sorts of change, and more...

Life is all about change. Prosperity and poverty can alternate. Jobs and companies come and go.

Many changes are set in motion by events outside our control: nature, the economy, society. But there is one thing that we can continually influence: our behavior. We can decide – alone or together with others – to change our behavior:

◆ You can decide to look for a new job, or to start your own business.
◆ You can decide to improve your family life.
◆ You can bring about change in your work environment.
◆ You can decide to initiate a social change.
◆ You can decide to find a better balance between work and private life.
◆ You can decide to live more healthily.

Often a change in circumstances is the trigger for our desire to make a change in behavior. Something happens that appears to us as a threat or a promise:

◆ We reach an age that has a special significance for us, and this causes us to evaluate our life.
◆ We have an addition to the family, and this means a change in the responsibilities we have.
◆ Our company suddenly faces strong competition from abroad, which means we must drastically adapt our service.

Change is not simple. But everybody can *learn* to change his or her own behavior. Tens of millions of people make such changes on their own each year.

Generally, though, we do less than half of what it really takes to bring about change. That is true in our professional lives, in our private lives, and as members of society. The intention is there, but we miss the knowledge of change techniques. That is why change fails and why we hear people sigh that they really *want to change,* but that it simply doesn't work. The explanation is roughly as follows. Although a part of your behavior is directly governed by your intentions, a significant part is made up of automatic patterns that are largely governed by your immediate circumstances. And as long as you don't have these automatic patterns under control, then real change remains extremely difficult. There are, of course, other reasons, but this is the most important.

What is interesting is that we are dealing here with *fundamental characteristics of human behavior,* that are applicable to changes within companies and just as applicable to changes in your personal life; they are applicable to changes that you bring about on your own and those you realize together with others. In this part of the book, you will be introduced to several principles in the field of behavior change. We will first look at the foundation of change: how changing one aspect of behavior works for an individual. Then we take a look at the question of how changes occur when more people are involved.

This section has three chapters:

I. Do: the missing link between plans and results
Why so many change exercises fail; how both intentions and situations govern our behavior; the dynamic balance between our planned behavior and our automatic behavior.

II. The Basic Change Method: starting points for real change
The three pillars supporting the Basic Change Method: the importance of habits; the role of intentions and situations; and the gradual progress of most changes.

III. Individual behavior as a component for collective change
Large changes, such as those in organizations, consist of many "small" individual changes. Leadership is all about the art of putting yourself in someone else's place, and how groups can influence our behavior.

Chapter 1

Do: the missing link between plans and results

Children are an impromptu course in psychology. I am the proud father of three daughters, and I do not exaggerate when I say that, during the last few years, I have learned more from them than they have learned from me. I have, for example (again), learned that it is fun and sensible to try out new things regularly.

During childhood, everyone tries out the craziest things. In that period we act primarily according to our feelings and learn things at an incredibly fast rate. After that, our self-consciousness begins to assert itself and all at once we start seeing risks in very normal things, such as climbing a rope, riding our bike without using our hands, and climbing the highest trees.

Children prefer to do things that they can't do yet. This helps them learn quickly. Adults prefer to do things that they do well. That's why they learn so slowly. Adults also constantly worry about losing their health, possessions, status, and other securities. Children simply don't have time for things like this.

People who want to change can learn a lot from children. If I am at all uncertain or a little apprehensive about new things, I just look at my three daughters. They're prepared to take a chance...

What are we going to do?

"Change is an inevitable part of our lives. And in business, it is an essential element" wrote Warren Bennis, the American management guru. But no matter how inevitable or important change may be, it is not easy.

Why don't people simply *do* what they want? Why do we so often fail to achieve the changes that we aim at, in our work, in our private lives, in our company? What is the reason for this?

Pretty fundamental questions. After all, a large part of our lives revolves around growth and change. If we understand how this works and become good at it, then it can have important consequences for our private life, our professional life, and the way we function in society.

In this chapter we look at three subjects:

1. Why most ideas about change don't work. *Why do we so often fail to put into practice those changes that we truly desire?*

2. Two approaches: intentions and situations as explanations for behavior. *Is behavior largely the result of conscious choices we make ourselves? Or do we spend our time automatically reacting to stimuli from our immediate surroundings?*

3. The dynamic balance between planned and automatic behavior. *How intentions and situations frequently determine our behavior simultaneously.*

1. Why most ideas about change don't work

Perhaps the following is familiar to you. It is Sunday evening, you've enjoyed the weekend and with an eye on the new week, you make a number of resolutions:

- ◆ You are going to make this a top week at work.
- ◆ You are going to show your children more patience and actually listen to them.
- ◆ You will show your partner that you are still very much in love.

◆ And you can add your own resolutions to the list.

Before you know it, it's Friday evening. It has been a hectic week with a whole lot of unexpected events and loads of things that you can't even remember. You conclude:

◆ The week was very much like all the weeks before.
◆ You were often short-tempered with your children and didn't really pay them very much attention.
◆ You and your partner were both much too tired to show exactly how much you mean to each other.
◆ You had some other resolutions, but you've completely forgotten what they were.

Recognize any of this? Undoubtedly, you will have asked yourself how it is possible that we often don't do what we want to do and aren't really happy with the things we actually do. Is this due to our environment? Do our colleagues, bosses, partners, and children set out to frustrate us? Or are we the ones who are simply incapable of doing anything? Why do so many of the changes – both small and large – that we would like to bring about fail?

There are dozens of reasons that could be offered, but I will restrict myself here to the three most important ones.

We focus too much on results and not enough on behavior

Many people daydream about things they would like to achieve: success in work and private life, living without financial worries, getting fitter, and losing weight. You will almost certainly have your own wishes – just as I have mine.

Often it doesn't take much effort to dream about the desirable results. It does, however, take a lot more effort to determine *what behavior* is required in order to achieve this result. And let's be honest: it's a lot less fun.

9

Research into the relationship between intentions and behavior shows that our resolutions will only be turned into action if they are very specific. If we want to move from a silent wish to a resounding result, then we need to know exactly what actions are necessary for this, at which time, in which situation, and (perhaps) with whom. Many popular approaches to change, both for corporate life and for personal change, concentrate on formulating the desired results and not on formulating the desired behavior. This means that we generally do not take any action, or often take the wrong action, and only occasionally take the right one. Behavior is the missing link between planning and results. Behavior is not just a component of change; behavior is change!

We often only manage one side of our behavior

I should have said *that*, I should have done *that*. You know that feeling. We go back to the shop with that "color-fast" crimson blouse that, after two washes, has become a light pink, or with that "whisper-quiet" vacuum cleaner that is causing a disturbance two houses away. And although we are quite determined to get our money back, we let the salesman get away with giving us a credit note or, worse still, we actually believe his story and end up taking the things back home with us. We left home with a clear resolution, but in the shop things turned out different to what we had expected.

Our behavior is not simply determined by our conscious resolutions, but also by a whole range of stimuli from our surroundings. In many cases, these stimuli trigger automatic behavioral habits that make us feel assured and comfortable.

At home, it doesn't seem at all difficult to tell that arrogant salesman the truth. But once we are in the shop, the arrogant salesman turns out to be a very charming lady and what's more, our nextdoor neighbors are also in the shop. These stimuli lead completely automatically to more polite and less assertive behavior. Shakespeare described it beautifully: "That monster, custom, who all sense doth eat."

In change, most people only think about their intentions and not about the situations in which old habits have to be overcome and new resolutions have to be turned into action. Often these methods help us arrive at good new resolutions, but we encounter all sorts of problems in putting them into practice. It is just like cycling into a strong headwind. We often think we can solve matters by applying *even more willpower*, but rather than doing more of the same, we will have to learn to work differently on change.

Only by learning to "manage" our intentions *and* the behavior situation, can we hope to change successfully and with pleasure: with the wind at our backs. This is a crucial issue and we will return to it repeatedly.

We are impatient, and work without structure or timetable

Perhaps you stopped smoking, perhaps you started your own business, or perhaps you have recently moved. How easy was that? Most people know from their own experience that real change is not easy. They know that change often takes place little by little and demands a lot of time. That is also true of any positive change that we want to make. And even more so when we want to change with other people.

Many months will have passed from the moment we have our first definite ideas about a new home to the actual removal. During those months, the change becomes gradually more real and more attractive. Often years will have passed from the moment you decide to stop smoking to the moment that you are finally "smoke-free."

Change is not easy and seldom happens as quickly as we would like. You should assume that a significant change – including preparations – could take around a year.

And yet over drinks and in company, people talk so easily about it. Not words, but deeds; simply get on and do it – that's what they often say. It sounds attractive, but rarely leads to results. It is a question of *doing*, but there's nothing *simple* about it.

Most change plans that people make do not take into account the stage of mental preparation that we need if our change is to be successful. If, for example, we don't take enough time to determine what we really want, then the chance of successful change is minimal.

For many change operations within companies, this often means that projects that were initially thought very important are suddenly scrapped when things get a little difficult. Apparently, the need for change was, in retrospect, less urgent than initially suggested.

2. Two approaches: intentions and situations as explanation for behavior

Have you ever asked yourself what processes are responsible for our behavior? Is our behavior conscious, planned, and proactive, or is it unconscious, automatic, and reactive? Is our behavior driven by our conscious intentions, or are we slaves to stimuli from our direct surroundings?

The answer to this question is extremely important for the way we approach change.

The discussion about the causes or our behavior has been raging in the psychological world for many years. There are various directions in this science, each looking in a different place for the cause of human behavior. The two most important directions are the *cognitive school* and *behaviorism*.

These different schools are adhered to both by psychologists who specialize in individual behavior and by those who are more interested in group behavior.

Cognitive psychology: the intention approach

Cognitive psychologists are concerned with *conscious, intellectual, planned behavior.* They maintain that our behavior is determined by conscious processing of information, self-reflection, and the development of propositions for the future: *intentions.*

Cognitive psychology emerged in the 1950s, and was based on the ideas and research of people such as Noam Chomsky, Leon Festinger, Icek Azjen, Martin Fishbein, Albert Ellis, and Aaron Beck.

According to the *theory of planned behavior* developed by the leading American psychologist Icek Ajzen, behavioral intentions are in turn determined by four factors:

◆ The results that we expect from our behavior. For example: what is in it for me if I telephone two potential clients for my company every day? Does it ultimately give me a good feeling and is it good for my company?
◆ Our estimation of the opinions of important people. Will my friends and employees think it is a good idea for me to do this?
◆ Our estimation of our own plans. Do I think I am capable of executing this plan?
◆ And our actual abilities. Do I have the capacity and opportunity to do this?

People who adhere to this approach largely believe that we must try to realize change in others through communication, for example, in discussions or with information and education programmes.

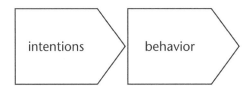

The cognitive approach: intentions direct our behavior

Self-managed behavior change is achieved, they maintain, through willpower. And you can build up this willpower by setting targets and making clear plans for your change. Much use is made of this approach to change in information campaigns and advertising.

- Most advertising commercials let us see that a product is good for us, that it produces important results, and gives us a good feeling. Example: clean washing or good relationships.
- Other ads show us that other important people make use of a particular product. Use is made of people with whom we would like to be associated. Isabelle Rosselini tells us which make-up we should use and Michael Schumacher tells us which car we should drive.
- Finally, a lot of commercials show us that our new behavior (for example, buying a new product or using one) is very simple. You can do it too, is the message. All you have to do is pick up the phone or drop by.

Behaviorism: the situation approach

Behaviorists are more concerned with *observable behavior*. According to them, our behavior is not at all determined by willpower, by conscious, future-oriented intentions; instead, it is *first and foremost* determined by *stimuli from our immediate surroundings*, by the situation.

Behaviorism arose at the beginning of the previous century and was largely based on the ideas and research of people such as Ivan Pavlov, John Watson, and Burrhus Frederic Skinner and later, more practically oriented behaviorists such as Joseph Wolpe, Ogden Lindsey, and Aubrey Daniels.

Situation stimuli – events or things done or said by other people – lead, according to behaviorists, to the *automatic* playback of one or more learned or congenital *behavioral programs*.

- The stimuli in the surroundings were divided into *antecedents* (stimuli that trigger behavior) and *consequences* (stimuli that are triggered by our behavior). For example: the traffic light turns green (antecedent), we put our foot down (behavior), and our car drives off (consequence).

◆ We learn through *trial and error* that in certain situations, antecedents, behavior, and consequences belong together. In this way, we develop a whole range of behavioral programs. The programs range from technical actions, such as typing at a computer, to social actions, such as politely joining the queue at the supermarket checkout on Saturday afternoon. There are some programs that we do not need to learn; they are passed on to us at birth.

People who adhere to this approach believe that you must realize behavior change in yourself and in others by encouraging the desired behavior and discouraging undesirable behavior by means of *reinforcing* or *punishing* stimuli from the direct surroundings, *immediately prior to* or *immediately following* the occurrence of the behavior:

◆ An example of employing antecedents (stimuli that trigger behavior) is the use of vivid warnings on cigarette packets. Every time smokers go to light up, they are confronted by this message.
◆ An example of using consequences (stimuli that are triggered by our behavior) is the bonus system in many companies. If you perform exceptionally well or reach a certain target, then you are given an additional financial reward, in the hope that you and others will achieve similar results in the future.

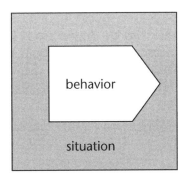

The behaviorist approach: situation stimuli direct our behavior

Research: Saying one thing and doing another

What we think and say we would do in certain situations some-times gives little indication of what we *really* would do. One of the first researchers who proved this through research was the American Richard LaPiere. Between 1930 and 1932 he researched racial discrimination. He accompanied a Chinese couple on their journey through the United States. During that journey, they visited 251 restaurants, hotels, and other establish-ments. When they entered these places, LaPiere kept himself in the background. In this way, he was able to observe what hap-pened, and his presence had no influence on the behavior of the managers. All in all, the couple were refused service on just one occasion.

Half a year later, LaPiere sent a letter to the managers of all the establishments, with a question: would you serve people of Chinese descent as guests in your business? One hundred and twenty-eight people replied to the letter. Of these, 91 percent said no, one said yes, and the rest said that it would depend on the circumstances.

That last reply was ultimately the one closest to the truth. Expressing a certain attitude or intention in a survey is one thing. But when two well-dressed, polite Chinese people arrive at your reception desk and request a room, then that is apparently some-thing completely different.

One of the lessons that can be drawn from LaPiere's research is that the general opinion people have about subjects bears little relationship to the behavior they will show. If an attitude or intention is to have any predictive value, then it must be more accurately defined.

LaPiere, R. T. (1934). "Attitudes versus Action." In: Social Forces, 13, 230–37.

3. The dynamic balance between planned and automatic behavior

In the previous section, you read about two different approaches in psychology. One approach maintains that our behavior is managed by consciously developed resolutions: intentions.

The other approach maintains that our behavior is largely auto-matic, is induced by events within the direct surroundings in which we find ourselves: situation stimuli.

The next question is: *which is true*? Are people primarily creatures that consciously choose what they do? Or are we creatures who constantly react to all sorts of stimuli from our surroundings?

The interaction between intentions and situations

It is my conviction that both are true and that the influence of intentions and situations is constantly in a state of *dynamic balance*.

Happily, I am not the only one who thinks this way. Researchers and practising psychologists are increasingly convinced that inten-tions and situation stimuli *together* explain the greater part of our behavior. Our behavior is active, planned, conscious, and driven by

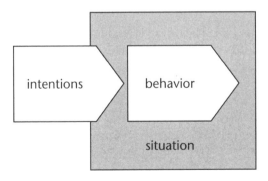

A combined approach: intentions and situation stimuli together direct our behavior

our intentions: our plans for the future. And *at the same time*, our behavior is reactive, unconscious, and is largely driven by direct circumstances; by the situation in which we find ourselves at a given moment.

Some actions are only partly planned and largely automatic, such as using a computer program that we are very familiar with. Or introducing ourselves to other people. To stay with the use of the computer: we consciously choose what we want to do – for example, saving a particular text document – and after that, we automatically follow the "save document" pattern, in which we play back almost without thinking a series of learned and frequently rehearsed actions.

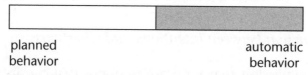

planned
behavior

automatic
behavior

Planned and automatic behavior are in a constant state of dynamic balance

Behavior becomes more automatic the more it is rehearsed or practised. But also when our planning side doesn't know exactly what to do. Uncertainty (which can be caused both by too much, as well as too little information), stress, and lack of time guarantee automatic, reactive behavior.

Just think of panic situations in traffic. I was once told that, in emergencies, I should pump the brake: that means rhythmically applying the brake to ensure that the wheels do not block and send you into a skid.

But when, a few years ago, one of my wheels went off the road at 120 kph and I went into a skid, my automatic half applied the brake as hard as it could. I span round three times and ended up on the verge, totally stupefied by what I had just done. It is the sort of event that makes people say after it has happened: "I didn't know what I was doing," or "That wasn't what I meant to do."

planned   automatic
behavior   behavior

Some behavior is largely automatic and only marginally planned

Some actions are largely planned and only marginally automatic, such as a job interview. Behavior that we do not often show and for which sufficient information and time is available is particularly suitable for the cognitive planned approach. Incidentally, pro-active, planned behavior costs us more energy that purely automatic, reactive behavior. So when our minds can get away with automatic processes, then that is what they will do in most cases.

planned   automatic
behavior   behavior

Some behavior is largely planned and only marginally automatic

It has taken you a lot of time and trouble to learn much of the behavior that you now show automatically. It is often said that before we can become *unconsciously capable* of something, we have to go through the stage of being *consciously incapable*. Many people recognize this. If I think back to all that bungling that I did during my first driving lessons, it is a mystery to me that I can now drive hundreds of kilometres in a day without really thinking about it. Once behavior has become automatic, it is extremely difficult to prevent it. Automatic behavior can – particularly if it leads to a direct result that I experience as pleasant – become almost *addictive*.

Breaking old habits and learning new ones – and that is, after all, a fundamental aspect of change – is something we often experience as a difficult and sometimes even painful process.

19

QUESTION & ANSWER

Q: *Why must we concern ourselves with behavior? Surely it's results that count?*
A: It's ultimately about results, that's true. But if you are unable to translate your aims, wishes, and desires into actual behavior, then you will never achieve the results. A few other reasons for concentrating first on behavior and only later on results:

◆ You often have to *wait* a long time for results.
◆ Results often depend on several people, behavior is *your individual* contribution.
◆ Results often depend on all sorts of *external circumstances*.
◆ Anyone who carries on showing the "right behavior," will *eventually* achieve results.
◆ What's more, placing too much emphasis on results can lead to *undesirable behavior*: imitating, copying others, beginning just before the deadline, faking results, manipulating figures. The stock exchange scandals of recent years show what placing an emphasis on (short-term) results can do to companies.

Q: *What about our personality? Doesn't that play a role?*
A: Personality is a term used in psychology to show how individual persons *generally* act and interact with other people and the world around them and how they differ in that from other people. Personality is primarily a descriptive term that includes a number of behaviors. We can use this to a certain extent to predict future behavior, but not to explain or change it.

It is important that we realize that the influence of intentions and situation stimuli differ from person to person. Some people have strong willpower that makes them less receptive to influences from their direct surroundings.

Q: *Is planned behavior always better than automatic behavior?*
A: No, certainly not. Automatic, intuitive behavior can sometimes have very positive results; think of the passer-by who,

20

without hesitation, jumps into the river to save a child. Often, such people say that they didn't think and just acted.

Q: Is planned behavior the product of our mind and automatic behavior the product of our emotions?
A: No, that isn't the case. Emotions play an important role in *both processes*. Both our conscious choices and our automatic reactions are aimed at getting a "good feeling." Planned behavior has to result in a good feeling in the long term. Automatic behavior is frequently directed at achieving a good feeling right now. Bad emotions also play a role in both sorts of behavior. In our judicial system, we have both manslaughter (a more "automatic," reactive action) and pre-meditated murder (a planned, intentional action).

ASSIGNMENT

You learn most when you have to find things out or try them out yourself. That is why you will find a short assignment at the end of every chapter in this book.

These assignments are about you personally. If you really want to learn something about change, then you have to find out how change works in you.

I would advise you to keep your answers and observations together in one place. On the website www.tiggelaar.com you will find a notebook specially intended for this in which you can write down the answers to all the assignments. You can, of course, use your own notebook.

And now the assignment for this chapter.

Analyze your own behavior in terms of "planned" behavior (intention-directed, conscious, controlled) and "automatic" behavior (situation-directed, unconscious, automatic).

- ◆ Think, for example, back to this morning, when you got up. Which actions were intention-directed and which were directed by the situation?
- ◆ Analyze a number of actions about which you are dissatisfied. To what degree is that behavior intention-directed and to what degree is it situation-directed?
- ◆ What conclusions do you draw from your analysis?

Chapter 2
The Basic Change Method: starting points for real change

My attic is filled with memories of all sorts of whims I've had. Recently, I came across a complete taekwondo outfit. I bought it one day when I decided that this was the sport for me. But, after a few weeks' training, I discovered that taekwondo wasn't about breaking bricks through the middle (an ability I would have loved to have mastered in a few training sessions in order to impress my wife), but more about combining movements. Quite honestly, it was really rather like a dancing lesson. Not my biggest hobby. To cut a long story short: taekwondo turned out to be less my sport than I had thought it would be…

The memories of my foray into taekwondo country taught me something. If you want to do something new that entails a lot of effort, time, or money (or, as in the case of taekwondo, all three), then it is sensible to take a closer look at things in advance. Second, it shows that important changes, just like martial arts, almost always revolve around new habits in behavior. You have to practise the steps and movements in taekwondo over and over again until you can carry them out unconsciously and automatically. Only then will you be able to impress you partner by knocking out a dangerous mugger in the middle of the night with your little finger.

For some time now, I've known that change almost always takes place in stages. That is why I still have my taekwondo outfit. Perhaps I will be ready to do it a few years from now.

What are we going to do?

In this chapter, we will look at the three starting points for successful change. They form the foundation for the approach to change that is central to this book: The *Basic Change Method*. So this is obligatory reading.

The *Basic Change Method* is an approach in which a large number of current insights into change from the modern psychological and behavioral sciences are bundled together. With the word *Basic*, I want to stress that the method is both well founded and no-nonsense. On the one hand, there are many *change professionals*, for example, in corporate life, who will be able to take advantage of the method. On the other hand, you have to be able to apply the *Basic Change Method* in your own life without having to have studied psychology.

I will therefore try not to tire you with all sorts of obscure technical terms. Here and there, I won't be able to avoid using "real" psychological terms, simply because there is no everyday word for them. But in every case, you can rest assured that they will be followed by a clear, simple explanation. The three starting points of the *Basic Change Method* are the following.

1. Change is primarily about realizing new habit behavior. *What is behavior and why is habit behavior so important?*

2. Stimulating new habit behavior requires management of intentions and situations. *Why planned behavior and automatic behavior are both important for changing habits.*

3. Change takes place in different stages, and costs a lot of attention, energy, and time. *We deal with the different factors that play a role in behavior change.*

1. Change is primarily about realizing new habit behavior

In the previous chapter, you read that change is ultimately always about behavior. Even the most far-reaching change in an organization always begins with one change in one individual. What's more, most changes in organizations are designed to influence the behavior of other people: clients, employees, or financiers.

Once more, behavior is not an aspect of change; behavior is the change. The English poet Matthew Arnold wrote, "Behavior is three quarters of our lives, and therefore is our greatest concern."

What is behavior?

What exactly do you we mean by the term "behavior" that appears so often in this book? To put it at its simplest: behavior is what every single person does. In this book, we place the emphasis on the "external" behavior of people, and make a distinction between:

◆ motor behavior (movement);
◆ and verbal behavior (speaking).

The advantage of this external behavior is that it is easily and objectively observed. That is particularly useful if we want to realize change together with other people. For example, in a club or a company. Change demands in almost every case some form of external behavior.

In addition, we can also talk of "internal" behavior in people, and we can make a distinction between:

◆ cognitive behavior (thoughts);
◆ and emotional behavior (feelings).

This inner behavior has the disadvantage that it is not generally easily and objectively observed. For ourselves, if is often difficult to observe and analyze our own thoughts and feelings. It is much more complicated for other people. On the other hand, we all know that thoughts and feelings play an important role in our daily functioning.

25

In virtually every change, our inner behavior plays a part. We must at the very least *resolve* to change something (thoughts). In most cases, we will want to change because we are *unhappy* with the current state of affairs (feelings). We expect that a certain change will make us satisfied.

From inside to outside

It is sometimes possible to make ourselves feel better by simply changing our thoughts. But in most cases, it is important that we don't stop at inner behavior. If you wish to change something in the social and physical reality (a better relationship, a new job, a new house, financial success), then it won't be enough to concentrate on thoughts and feelings. Such changes also demand motor and verbal actions. We have to take action that is both seen and heard.

If you want to realize changes that are noticed by other people (for example, your family members, colleagues, customers), then you will always have to move from the inside to the outside.

I admit, it doesn't sound special at all... an open door. But be honest: aren't there a whole lot of changes that have existed for some time in your mind and your feelings? Changes that you think are really important, but which, for one reason or another, you simply can't turn into "external" behavior. In other words: you think about it, but you don't do anything about it. I know that I do that quite often. The great majority of changes never get further than "inner behavior." And no matter how comforting it may be to cherish exalted thoughts and emotions, other people only notice anything if you turn them into *observable deeds*. And you yourself will often only see the results of your ideas and plans at the moment you put them into action.

People are successful in their work, their relationships, and in other fields *not* because they are so much more brilliant than you or me. The most important difference is that they are better able to turn their thoughts and emotions into external behavior. I will keep on repeating it throughout this book: *behavior* is the missing link between plans and results.

The importance of habits

Now we are going to make it even more complicated. Doing something once doesn't really help things very much at all. The most effective changes are changes in *habit behavior*.

Of course, most people only get married once, but maintaining a good marriage is a full-time job. Of course, we do not change jobs or company every year, but performing well is a full-time job. A few more examples:

◆ Companies do not grow by being friendly to clients *now and again*, but by *always* striving for complete customer satisfaction.
◆ You don't improve your health by taking a single walk. You have to make sure you get enough exercise every week.
◆ It may be a one-off decision to change the computer system in a company, but if you want to learn to use it properly then you, as manager, will have to work on creating new habits.
◆ Your family life doesn't improve by visiting Disneyland once a year, but by frequently letting the people around you know how much you appreciate them and love them.

2. Stimulating new habit behavior requires management of intentions and situations

Generally we don't even do *half* of what is necessary for behavior change. Most people, who want to change something, try to do it purely through willpower. Willpower is, however, just one element in a change; we have already discussed this. Our daily life is a constant interaction between, on the one hand, *planned, conscious, intention-directed, future-oriented behavior* (from inside to outside, if you like) and, on the other, *automatic, unconscious, situation-directed, reactive behavior* (from outside to inside).

Even within a single action, these two things interact with and complement each other. As I type these sentences, I am consciously thinking about what I want to say, but my fingers are moving automatically over the keyboard.

Interaction between intention and situation

Sometimes, our intentions are at cross-purposes with the situation stimuli. We may want to do one thing, but the situation gives off such stimuli that we do something completely different:

◆ You want to spend your time working on an important plan for your company, but e-mails and telephone calls distract you the whole day long.

◆ You have made a resolution to eat less, but when they serve up your favorite food, your automatic "let's enjoy it" program takes over. Regularly our automatic pilot makes us unconsciously fly away from our intentions, away from our conscious resolutions. When intention and situation are regularly at cross purposes with each other, then this can lead to frustration and feelings of stress. I compared it earlier to cycling into the wind. On other occasions, our intentions and the stimuli from a situation actually strengthen each other.

◆ You have decided to eat more healthily and when you arrive in the supermarket you are surrounded by stimuli from the surroundings that strengthen your resolve; you see special offers on free-range meat and on organic fruit and vegetables.

◆ You decide to help your elderly neighbor by mowing the grass for her. She is so obviously happy with what you have done that you decide to help her with other chores around the house.

When intention and situation stimuli together drive your behavior, then this gives you a pleasant feeling. It is just like one of those miraculous bicycle trips when you have the wind at your back on the way there and, as you start to ride home, the wind shifts and is in your back yet again. If our intentions and the situation stimuli reinforce each other, then change becomes easier and more enjoyable.

The true art of successful change is that we manage intentions and apply situation stimuli that together stimulate the desired behavior. This is what makes the change method discussed in this book unique, and we shall return to it on several occasions.

The one-sided approach to behavior

You will notice that, in daily life, most people tend towards a certain side when managing behavior. In our Western society, with its tradition of rationality, this is by and large the side of conscious intentions:

◆ Many corporate advisors believe that you should discuss at length with your employees any new plans you have before putting them into operation. They are only fully satisfied when everybody has agreed to cooperate.

◆ Many policy makers attach considerable importance to good information. If something has to change in the motorists' driving behavior, then they make television commercials in which they explain why you should always wear a safety belt or why you should maintain a proper distance.

◆ Many parents think it is extremely important that their children understand *why* certain things are allowed or forbidden. They spend a lot of time discussing with their children what is desirable and what is not. No matter how valuable these opinions may be, they influence only a part of our behavior. The other part is governed by the direct stimuli from our environment. And in many cases, those situation stimuli contradict our intentions. We will stick to the previous examples:

◆ Employees can all say "yes" to a new way of working, particularly if management applies pressure in that direction. But if, for example, the new software is disappointing (as almost always seems to be the case), then they will quickly revert to the old, trusted habits.

◆ Motorists who watch a commercial on TV about bad driving habits may very well nod in agreement and tell themselves that

29

in future they will do things differently. But if, when they get into the car the next day, they find they are late for an appointment, then they will once again drive too quickly, forget to put on their seat belt, and not maintain a proper distance from the car in front of them.

◆ We can make our children believe many things consciously (not drinking, not smoking), but when they go out with their friends, the influence from the direct social situation is very strong. All young people know that smoking is bad for you, and yet thousands take up the habit every year.

Work on behavior from two sides

Both intention and situation direct our behavior. These two influences are in a dynamic balance with each other: *whatever is not directed by our intentions is directed by the situation and vice versa.*

If you want to change behavior – whether your own or other people's – then it is essential to include both aspects in your approach!

One of the most frequently made mistakes in change – both in our private lives and in companies – is that the direction we receive from our intentions is diametrically opposed to the direction we receive from the behavioral situation. In most cases, the situation stimuli win out over our intentions. Our automatic responses defeat our conscious resolutions and our willpower. The head wind becomes too strong, and we stop our bike ride. One last illustration. In many companies and institutions, it is desirable that people do not spend more than they have in their budget. Sounds logical. We try to influence each other's intentions by sending e-mails and holding discussions. The direct work situation, however, sends different signals when we try to do our best and work within budget. Our colleagues don't like it one little bit if there is no budget for their plans or for new machines or new cars. And at the end of the year, things really hot up: the people who stay within their budget get *less* for the coming year; and those that have gone over budget get *more* for the next year. Ultimately, in many companies, situation-directed, automatic behavior wins over intention-directed, planned behavior.

Research: DIYers do it in stages

The American researchers James Prochaska, John Norcross, and Carlo DiClemente carried out some revolutionary research in the 1980s into voluntary, planned behavior change, particularly with so-called "self-changers" – people who had implemented important behavior changes in their own lives. One part of the research was under the leadership of Prochaska, and involved comparing several hundred different therapeutic approaches. Prochaska and his team came to the conclusion that all these different approaches were based on just a handful of basic change processes. Change processes, by the way, that we deal with in this book. An additional part of the research involved the team producing more than 50 studies in change behavior, involving several thousand people. The conclusion was that most DIYers made unconscious use of the same basic change processes. But that change, since it lacked structure, often involved trial and error.

Prochaska and his team concluded that change generally takes place in five stages:

(1) the stage prior to contemplating change
(2) contemplating the change
(3) preparing for that change
(4) the action
(5) the maintenance.

According to the researchers, it is important that change programs follow these five stages. Most change programs, however, are, according to them, far too short and concentrate far too much on action.

In many change programs – for example, aimed at stopping smoking – it appears that under 20 percent of the people were ready for action.

And over 45 percent of the patients that seek psychotherapeutic help give up their treatment before it is completed. The researchers believe that this is because the treatment does not match the stage in which patients find themselves.

Prochaska, J. O., DiClemente, C. C. and Norcross, J. C. (1992). In Search of How People Change. Applications to Addictive Behaviors. In: American Psychologist, vol 47, no 9, 1102–14. American Psychological Association. Prochaska, J. O., DiClemente, C. C. and Norcross, J. C. (1994). Changing for Good. New York: Avon Books. Prochaska, J. O. and Norcross, J. C. (1999). Systems of Psychotherapy. A Transtheoretical Analysis. Pacific Grove: Brooks/Cole Publishing.

3. Change takes place in different stages, and costs a lot of attention, energy, and time

You could compare personal change to a theatrical performance in which you are the writer, the director, and the leading character.

First of all, you will have to write a script for the change. Next, as director, you will have to rehearse the most important scenes. And only then can the premiere take place, the first of a long run of successful performances.

Change in companies has something similar to these stages, except that here there are frequently several writers, a number of directors, and a whole case of actors and extras. (No wonder that some change projects end up in total chaos!)

Get Real, Make Plans, Take Action

Change takes place in a number of stages, each of which requires thought, energy, and time. If you want to realize an important change then you must expect – just as you would if you were writing, directing, and performing in a new stage play – that it can take anything up to a year.

In order to keep things simple, the *Basic Change Method* has three stages, each of which is related to the most important elements that play a role in change. These three stages, by the way, largely include the same elements that were identified by Prochaska and his colleagues in the research we have just described.

The three stages are:

◆ *Get Real*: formulate target-directed and concrete *behavioral intentions*.
◆ *Make Plans*: thoroughly prepare the most difficult *change situations*.
◆ *Take Action:* begin, measure, and reward the desired *behavior*.

Let us look at each of these stages in greater detail.

◆ *Get Real:* we must know what we really want and what changes in behavior are necessary for this. In this stage, the emphasis is largely on becoming aware of what we can do and what we want to do. It means accurately formulating our aims and behavioral intentions. Your role in this stage is comparable to that of a playwright.

PHASE	FOCUS	ROLE
Get Real	intention	writer
Make Plans	situation	director
Take Action	behavior	actor

The three stages in the Basic Change Method*: Get Real, Make Plans, and Take Action*

- *Make Plans:* we have to ask ourselves in which concrete way we are going to realize the desired behavior change. The emphasis in this stage is largely on anticipating behavioral situations and creating powerful stimuli that encourage the desired behavior. From inside to outside. That sounds rather complicated, but don't worry: the following chapters will explain step by step how this works. Your role in this stage is comparable to that of the director.
- *Take Action:* in this stage, we actually put our plans into action. We rehearse new behavior and then put it into practice. Measuring behavior plays an important part in this stage. We look at the results later on. Your role in this stage is comparable to that of an actor.

Why do we want to change?

You will understand that, *prior* to the *Get Real* stage, a whole lot of things can happen. After all, our desire to change has to come from somewhere! Often, this desire for change is stimulated by events in our immediate surroundings or by the behavior of other people. This acts as a *promise* or a *threat* and stimulates the desire to change.

A few examples:

- A good friend who you haven't seen in a while has lost 30 lbs and apparently now plays sport twice a week. You think: if he can do it, so can I. Back at home you get on the scales for the first time in months – and yep, your suspicions prove right: something will have to change. Less food, a healthier diet, and more exercise.
- A new colleague tells you that her relationship has improved immensely during the past year. Now that she has accepted a new position, she has made new agreements at home about who does what in the housekeeping, including the upbringing of the children.
- The economy is in recession and the company you work for has to re-organize. Costs have to be reduced in order to ensure the continuity of the company. Your job is threatened, and that's worrying. On the other hand: you always wanted to work for yourself. A few weeks ago, a former colleague asked you whether you would like to work on an assignment together.

PROMISE	EVENT	THREAT
"Finally – the world is at my feet"	You've completed your training and are looking for a job	*"Nobody is really waiting for all those unemployed…"*
"A new, happy stage in my life"	The first new member of the family	*"How can I combine this with a busy job?"*
"If she can do it, then so can I"	A good friend has lost 25 lbs	*"I really must pay more attention to my weight"*
"Now is the time to start my own business"	Your job is suddenly under threat	*"How on earth am I going to pay the mortgage?"*
"Time to check the balance work vs relaxation"	Recently, you've often felt ill in the weekends	*"A little more, and I will have a breakdown"*
"At last more time for me and my partner"	You're getting close to the age of retirement	*"How will others think of me in the future?"*
"I will be more assertive, so this doesn't happen again"	A saleswoman puts you in your place	*"Soon everybody's going to be walking over me"*
"Now I can expand my business"	Your company has more customers than it can handle	*"Everything's going to get into an enormous mess"*
etcetera…	*etcetera…*	*etcetera…*

Impulses for change: events that can be seen as a promise or a threat

Often, the things that make us want to change come about totally unexpectedly. They appear as an important opportunity or as a problem. Perhaps there has always been a silent desire to do something, but it requires something to happen to activate that desire.

Several years ago, the actress Michele Pfeifer said in an interview: "I had a teacher who said one thing to me: 'I think you have talent.' And I have never forgotten that. At that time I never really thought I would become a famous actress. And yet, during my first years in the film business, that remark gave me a lot of confidence."

Attention, energy, and time

If the impulse is already there, then we can make use of the *Basic Change Method* to give shape to our wishes. In my experience, it is generally the *Get Real* and *Take Action* stages that demand attention, energy, and time.

The *Get Real stage* is all about setting your targets and formulating a conscious resolution. Most people require quite some time to decide what they really want and then to determine what behavior that will require. Sometimes this will take a few months. You know the feeling: when you first start actively thinking about what you really want, then during the first days – and often even the first weeks – you will often change your mind. It is a search that takes time and energy.

In the *Make Plans stage* we have to analyze which stimuli in which situations trigger an automatic behavioral response and how we can stimulate the desired behavior in practice. I personally find this the nicest stage. In this stage, you have already fairly accurately defined your change desires and you can now concentrate fully on how your own behavior actually works. In the *Make Plans stage* – just as in the *Get Real stage* – you can get to know a lot about yourself and about human behavior in general.

The *Take Action stage* is all about putting our behavioral plans into action. Most changes revolve around developing new habits. Habits that will lead to the realization of your ambitions.

A few examples:

- If you want to be fitter, then exercise will have to become a daily or weekly habit.
- If the company wants to increase its turnover, then contacting new and existing customers must become a daily habit.
- If you want more pleasure from your relationship, then you will regularly need to do enjoyable things together. Developing new habits can take months. Certainly, when we want to break old habits and put new ones in their place. That means that we have to give up old certainties (in the form of daily routines) and develop new certainties to replace them. That all sounds rather unpleasant, but since we first concentrate on behavior and only later on results, it is quite possible to get through all this in a pleasant way. This doesn't mean you have to wait for months before you get any positive news. In fact, you will notice progress from day one. First in behavior and then in results.

QUESTION & ANSWER

Q: Isn't it rather too simple to believe that one change approach works with everybody?
A: In some things, we people are much more alike than we often like to admit. Human behavior can be described as a combination of future intentions and stimuli from our direct environment.

In this book, most of the ideas in this field are offered in the most accessible way possible. The basis for this approach, however, is rooted in decades of psychological and behavioral science research. At the back of the book you will find a short scientific justification and a list of references.

Q: Why would a change take a year? Isn't that a bit over the top?
A: In most cases, it is over the top to think that changes in behavioral habits can take place any quicker. I know: there are change gurus around who in just a few minutes can release people from all sorts of fears and phobias. But if you don't suffer from any particular phobia, but want to make concrete changes in your private life or your work environment, then this approach isn't really any good for you.

A year is a safe bet. If the changes that you envisage take place a lot quicker, then that's a bonus. In reality, there are more than enough changes that actually take a lot longer than a year.

ASSIGNMENT

It can be fun to study people or organizations that have been able to implement real change. Perhaps in the past you have also put into practice some important changes. Choose one change that appeals to you and that you know something about, and analyze it.

When you make the analysis, keep in mind the following:

37

◆ What were the intended results and what behavior did they require?
◆ In what way was the new desired behavior stimulated?
◆ What stages did the change process pass through?
◆ What lessons can you learn from this?

Write down your conclusions in an exercise book (you can obtain one free of charge on the website www.tiggelaar.com) so that you don't lose them.

Chapter 3

Individual behavior as a component for collective change

To be honest, I only really understood the term "empathy" when my eldest daughter got her swimming certificate. It's fascinating how you can learn an important life lesson on a weekday in the local swimming baths!

As I stood on the balcony of the swimming pool, looking down at the way my daughter was standing there, together with other seven-year-olds, waiting to jump into the water, I suddenly saw myself standing in that very same place almost 30 years ago. I wasn't only able to replay those images of that event in my head, I really felt exactly what I had felt all those years ago. A remarkable experience.

When we got back home and started celebrating her certificate, my daughter told me exactly what she had thought about and how she had felt before she jumped in the water. It was an exact copy of what I had felt.

This experience helped me understand what empathy really is: I could really project myself into the feelings of somebody else and, as it were, look round. At the same time, I realized that on all previous occasions when I had assured somebody that I understood exactly what they felt, that I had exaggerated somewhat.

I readily admit that I have not been blessed with enormous empathic talents. But now that my children are reaching an age about which I have tangible memories, then I find that I can now more often feel what they are feeling.

The disadvantage is that the older they get, the less likely they are to accept that somebody so much older actually understands what they are feeling.

What are we going to do?

Perhaps you are not so much interested in making changes in your personal life, but more in handling change in your work situation. The *Basic Change Method* is equally useful in both areas. The behavior of other people is also driven by a combination of intentions and situation stimuli.

It is my absolute conviction that knowledge of personal behavior change is of great importance to change management in organizations. If you are able to understand how change works for you, then you will be much better able to help others to change. "He who would govern others first should be the master of himself," wrote the English playwright Philip Massinger.

In this chapter we will be looking at the most important elements of change in others.

1. Important collective change consists of many "small" individual acts. *Thinking in terms of groups and whole organizations is often less effective than approaching change from an individual perspective.*

2. Leadership: the art of placing yourself in the skin of others. *Leadership is all about the insight we have into the behavior of others and our ability to influence both future intentions and direct situations.*

3. The effects of groups on behavior change. *Groups often make us change our behavior. This can be both advantageous and undesirable for change.*

1. Important collective change consists of many "small" individual acts

Collective changes are very much like jigsaw puzzles. You know approximately what the final picture will look like, but first of all, each of the individual pieces has to be fitted into its proper place. The pieces are the individual behavior of all the people who are involved in the change process. They are each connected to the other pieces, but still they all have to fit into their right place.

Sometimes it is about completing a very small puzzle: a simple change within the family, such as eating together more frequently. Sometimes it is about achieving a turnaround in a company. Then it's a jigsaw puzzle with more than 1,000 pieces. From a distance, these may seem two totally different challenges; if you look closer, however, you'll see that the pieces are very similar.

Small building bricks

No matter what the change is you want to make with other people, the building bricks are always small, individual revitalizations. But it goes even further than that: every major change *starts* with a single change made by a single person. If you are lucky or the change turns out well, others soon join in, but in some cases, people carry on a perennial lonely crusade before others follow them in a certain direction. If a family functions better, then that is all down to the small things that the various family members do day by day. They make more time for each other, they listen to each other better, they help each other in the household chores. We can sum this up in the term: "they are more considerate to each other" – as long as we remember that this is a container term. We often sweep together a whole lot of small things into one large heap, so that an outsider simply cannot discover *who* has done *what* to make the family work better.

Another example: if a company wants to achieve higher turnover, then it is essential that more individual customers buy more from the company. And if it is to achieve that, then it is generally essential that the salespeople and the customer relations staff pay more attention to each individual customer. They may very well ask these individual customers more frequently how they are. And they may very well do something extra for them as well. Such small, everyday

41

behavior can be summarized in the enormous professional term: increasing customer friendliness. But once again, by using this umbrella term, we lose a lot of information.

It is not difficult to embrace the day-to-day actions of a whole range of individuals in such a term. But for many people, it is extremely difficult to translate the term back to the detail of day-to-day reality.

Beware of large, vague terms

Speaking in broad terms or container terms is very popular. That is understandable. When everybody in the company understands what the term "customer friendliness" actually means, then it is rather time-consuming to describe each of the individual pieces of behavior in minute detail. The same is true when everybody in the family understands what it means to "be more considerate to each other." What's more, these sorts of terms have an important ring about them: people in the know understand that they cover an enormous territory. The problem with change is that we are generally about to embark on *something new*. Something we have never done before, or something that in any case we have not done for a long time. And at such a moment, it simply won't do to talk in broad, vague terms. Nobody will understand what you are talking about.

Perhaps you manage a company and think it important that your employees take the initiative. And maybe because of that you leave a lot of room for them to fill in their own jobs. I will admit that in many cases this can work well. If you work with capable people and there is no talk of change or major improvements, then it can be fine. But a moment can arrive when the results are different from those you intended and that we all think that something must change. At that moment, we *have to* immerse ourselves in the behavior of individual employees, because that is at the very heart of the change we hope to achieve. In such change, there has to be some discussion between management and employees or between

Individual behavior change is the building block of renewal in families, in companies, and in our society

the employees themselves in order to determine what this new behavior will be.

To summarize: individual behavior change is the building block of renewal in families, in companies, and in our society. Anybody who reasons and works from individual behavior change can play a vital role at these levels. Anybody who prefers to think in broad terms runs the risk of remaining superficial and vague and not achieving any concrete results.

2. Leadership: the art of placing yourself in the skin of others

The way we humans observe and interpret the world differs from one person to another. Sometimes the difference is negligible; at others, it is enormous.

If you are going to change together, then you need a common point of departure. An observation, an aim, a problem, or a feeling about which you are in total agreement before you start.

43

The most difficult lesson for leaders is that they must really learn to place themselves in somebody else's thoughts and, more importantly, in their feelings. That means that in almost every case you must first listen and try to understand the other and only then speak yourself. Let's be honest, this is not easy for most leaders.

The American industrialist Norman Augustine, former head of Lockheed Martin, said: "You often hear people saying that somebody talks too much. But to be honest, I've never heard anybody being accused of listening too much."

Influencing intentions

Once there is a common point of departure, then it is the leader's job to build on this foundation. You must use your influence in such a way that you help other people to adopt the proper behavior and thereby achieve the desired results. And for this there are (and you know this by now) two elements available. We can influence the intentions of other people and we can adapt the situation stimuli. At the very least, we have to make sure that these two elements do not conflict with each other.

It is very important for leaders that they immerse themselves in the behavior of other people. As manager – but also as educator – you will frequently have to ask yourself what tools you need to be able to influence the intentions of others. And you will have to decide what situation stimuli will lead to the desired behavior in others. Influencing the *intentions* of others can be achieved in several ways:

◆ Providing information: explain the necessity for change and why it has to happen now; explain that other people think it important; show that people are really capable of achieving this change.
◆ Give a good example yourself: show, without words, that certain behavior can achieve positive results, is appreciated by others, and is not complicated.

44

♦ Let others think about these matters: ask questions; let others formulate their own thoughts and solutions; sometimes give the others time to discover or experiment with something. *In particular, asking open questions is a simple and very powerful way to bring about change in other people.*

We often make simultaneous use of various methods for influencing intentions. We explain things *and* we ask questions *and* we act as examples. All three approaches work, but the conclusions that people make themselves often have the most lasting effect.

One thing we must be careful of when approaching collective change is that we do not put ourselves in the central position. Many leaders want to *direct* the intentions of others. That is why they will explain it all again, talk about it for a much longer time, and give even more instructions. Transmitting information to others often gives them a pleasant and secure feeling. But the effect all this has on the intentions of others is minimal. I will repeat it once again: if you want to influence the behavior of others, then it is absolutely essential that you find a common point of departure. You always have to start with a feeling, opinion, observation, and an aim about which you are all in absolute agreement. For example, that the change you discuss together is absolutely *essential*. That is the common foundation on which you can build other intentions.

Managing situation stimuli

Once the intention to change certain behavior has been formed in the other, then it is quite possible to adapt the situation stimuli *together* with him, so that this way of influencing behavior is also moving in the same direction. How you do that will be discussed a little later.

Sometimes you don't succeed in changing somebody's intentions. It could be because your interests are too different or because the other doesn't have the time or inclination to spend hours communicating with you. There are countless possible explanations.

45

It is also possible just to change the *situation stimuli* within which people function. That doesn't automatically need to be manipulation (that term is generally used for stimulating *unethical* behavior in others). I'll give a few examples:

◆ When, as a manager of a factory, you design the work situation in such a way that the workers are stimulated towards safe and responsible behavior (instead of holding a weekly sermon about the current state of play), then you are certainly not doing anything wrong.

◆ When my partner is extra friendly towards me because she thinks it is important to work on our relationship (instead of giving me as a gift a book telling me how I should behave), then I personally have no objections.

◆ When we teach our children to eat politely through punishing and reinforcing stimuli (instead of lecturing them about the rules of etiquette), then I consider this neither wrong nor manipulative.

◆ Something else: sometimes the *need* for change is evident, but colleagues refuse to believe this. You can also arrange situation stimuli for use in this sort of circumstance so that they actually *experience* the problem. For example, pay out board salaries a week later than normal in order to focus the attention on (future) financial problems. Make video recordings of angry clients and show these at a board meeting.

We must realize that the situation *always* influences the behavior of both ourselves and others. When the situation stimuli move people in a direction other than the one that you as leader intended, then it is sensible to adapt them if at all possible.

Changes in which our intentions for the future and the direct situation stimuli work together take place more easily and in a much more pleasant manner.

True leadership means choosing the proper aims and stimulating the proper behavior by creating *intentions* that people must reach and *situation stimuli* to help create that proper behavior. For this reason, insight into the way people act is absolutely essential. Often this means constantly working on your *own behavior* as leader.

Research: The diffusion of innovations

At the beginning of the 1960s, the American researcher Everett Rogers compared 400 surveys about innovation. He did the same in the 1990s, but this time compared more than 4,000 publications.

He concluded that communication between people was the most important factor in accepting innovations. People look to each other and exchange experiences about new products, new ideas, and new behavior. If innovations meet a number of criteria, then people will adopt them.

Five elements determine whether innovations are adopted:

(1) Relative advantage: we must be convinced that the innovation offers a clear advantage compared to the current situation. This advantage must match an actual, existing need.
(2) Compatibility: an innovation must fit in with our existing norms and values and easily fit in with our current behavior.
(3) Complexity: we must be convinced that an innovation is not difficult to understand and use. The more complex the innovation, the less successful it will be.
(4) Test drive: innovations are more successful if they can be tried out on a small scale.
(5) Visibility: innovations are more successful when we can easily observe the advantages others have from them.

Not everybody within a social system (a group of friends, a company, a society) readily or easily accepts innovation. Rogers distinguishes five groups that consecutively adopt innovation:

(1) The innovators: people who are always on the lookout for something new and enjoy taking risks.
(2) The early adopters: these people are interested in innovation, but don't really want to get too far ahead of the rest of the field. Because of this, this group has the greatest social authority. It is vital to involve the early adopters in change.
(3) The early majority: this group is positive towards the change, but first waits to see what the early adopters do. The early majority forms a bridge between the early adopters and the rest of the people.
(4) The late majority: this group is skeptical about the change, but lets itself be influenced by the other groups.
(5) The laggards: this last group only gets on board when it has been proven absolutely that the change is advantageous or unavoidable.

Rogers, E. M. (1995). The Diffusion of Innovations (4th edition). New York: The Free Press.

3. The effects of groups on behavior change

Most people act differently in a group than when they are on their own. What's more, different groups influence our behavior in different ways.

Anybody who did a holiday job when he or she was young will probably remember something about it. At one moment, you are surrounded by your friends, and the next you are surrounded by total strangers who speak a different language, have a different culture, and behave differently. The chance that you acted exactly the same in both sets of circumstances is remote. People who do research into group behavior define a group as two or more people who influence each other. Incidentally, the term "group behavior" is rather confusing, because people who have made a study of group dynamics state that the group as such does not show any behavior, but that it is always about the behavior of *individual persons within the group*.

Other people in the group do, however, have influence over your behavior. This is because other people can influence your intentions and form a rich source of situation stimuli. Even the way other people look at you has a direct influence on your behavior.

It is very important that you fully understand what I have written here. I will explain why. Many managers *think* they are leaders of a group, when *in fact* they give leadership to individuals within that group.

That is a big difference. You cannot influence a group, but you can influence individuals within a group. And these individuals then influence each other. And this is why it is essential for leaders that in any change process they address individuals who on the one hand are open to change and on the other have influence within their group.

Some managers do this automatically. They are unconsciously able to decide – whether through experience or talent – exactly who they should influence. For other managers it is vital that they fully familiarize themselves with the relationships within the group.

Our great readiness to adapt

One of the most important direct effects that groups have on individuals like you or me is that we immediately feel the need to change our behavior. This inclination to adapt what we say and do arises, according to most researchers, from our fear of being rejected.

Our readiness to adapt (*and our fear of rejection*) is, according to the research of psychologist David Wilder, at its greatest when we are in a group of between four to six other people who all, to our mind, think the same way. In smaller or larger groups, we are less readily prepared to adapt.

We are more prepared to deviate from the rest when we know the people very well. Good friends can sometimes agree to differ. And it helps when you are not the only one to take a different position. It is much easier to deviate in the company of somebody else than to deviate all on your own. People who deviate in a group of people they do not know so well often get a lot of attention from the group (if you really love attention, this is the way to get it: "Well, I'm not sure whether I agree with you on this"). But they lose the attention if they continue being out of step for any length of time.

From learning to doing: the transfer problem

The automatic need for people in a group to adapt what they do and say disappears like snow in the sun the moment the group is disbanded. This is another essential piece of know-how for leadership.

It is a well-known phenomenon that people who during a meeting or training session have reached complete agreement or who have become collectively enthusiastic about a new piece of knowledge revert to their old behavior once they return to their work place. The difficulty with which new knowledge is passed on to others is referred to as the *transfer problem*.

This problem can have various causes: the people in the meeting or training have temporarily adapted their behavior (as an automatic reaction to the stimuli in *that* group situation), but their intentions remain unchanged. Or their intentions and resolutions have really changed, but once they return to their old work place, they are confronted with stimuli that automatically encourage their former behavior.

If you were ever the only person from a department who took part in a training or course, then you will recognize this. When you get back to your work and want to put what you have learnt into practice (intention), you meet resistance from your colleagues (situation). This resistance, these negative stimuli from your direct surroundings, automatically result in us ending our attempts to innovate and leaving our new intention for what it is.

If you want to avoid this, then it is much better to send the whole group on the relevant course, or have a trainer come to your company, to your work place. The latter is more effective and cheaper. Many advisors and trainers may very well maintain that getting people together in a conference hotel somewhere far away from everything makes it easier for the participants to arrive at new insights and intentions. That is true. But the idea that these new insights and intentions inevitably move back to the office with the participant is a costly illusion.

Going down together: groupthink

Groups are a rich source of *situation stimuli* for our individual behavior. Thus, groups have a direct influence on what we as individuals say and do. Contact with other individuals in a group can also influence our *intentions*. These two influences mean that groups can obstruct change or encourage it.

An important obstructive effect caused by the pressure to achieve consensus is that important information or innovative ideas are missed. This process was dubbed "groupthink" by the researcher Irving Janis.

A few characteristics of groupthink:

- Not expressing your true thoughts or feelings.
- Consciously maintaining an illusion of unanimity.
- Investigating only a limited number of alternative solutions to a problem.
- Being extremely selective in looking for and applying external information.
- Speaking negatively about people outside the group.
- Rationalizing decisions that were not particularly good.
- Not developing emergency scenarios.

Janis suggests that the failure of the Cuba invasion in 1961 was caused by *groupthink* in the inner circle around President Kennedy.

On April 17 of the year in question, 1,400 Cuban refugees landed, with US support, in the Bay of Pigs. Kennedy was convinced that the Cuban army was weak, that the Cuban air force was insignificant, and that nobody would know that the US was supporting the action. After two days, the refugees were surrounded by 20,000 Cuban soldiers, their air force had sunk or chased off the American supply ships, and the US was made to look stupid on the international world stage.

A leader can break through groupthink by acting as an impartial, critical chairman; by giving somebody the role of devil's advocate; or by employing external experts. Another thing that can help is concentrating the discussion on those areas that people are uncertain about and making temporary decisions that can be reviewed at the next meeting.

Lost and alone against the group

Sometimes you have the unenviable task, as leader or member of the group, of having to exert pressure on the behavior of certain individuals in the group completely on your own. It may help to realize that many people who were ahead of their time have done the same before you. But it is also helpful if we make use of the insights that we gained from the previous chapter. In this sort of situation, it is important that you influence behavior through both intentions and situation stimuli.

◆ Try to influence the intentions of others by patiently and consistently explaining your position, asking questions, and setting a good example. Always start by trying to establish a *common standpoint* – an opinion, an observation, or an aim that you all agree about. Then show how your idea or plan is useful to the others, show that other important people are behind you, and demonstrate (if others in the group doubt you) that they are perfectly capable of executing your plans.
◆ In addition make use of situation stimuli. Our reactions to such stimuli are often much more similar to each other than our

reaction to our conscious, rational points of view. Reward people who are sympathetic to your standpoint. Do not exaggerate; it is better to use subtle body language, such as a friendly nod in somebody's direction, than to praise somebody at length for agreeing with you. Since we are all sensitive to social stimuli, this can have greater influence than the content of your argument. Address in particular those people in the group with a certain social authority. When they support your opinion, this creates a direct stimulus for the others.

QUESTIONS & ANSWERS

Q: Isn't this idea about leadership rather old-fashioned? Shouldn't we give employees greater freedom in what they do? That is much more motivating!
A: It is, indeed, generally motivating to do work that you are good at without too much interference from others. But when change is imminent, when new behavior is essential, many employees want a leader who shows the way and are prepared to accept the responsibility. At the very least we want to know what the aim of it all is.
It is the job of a company's management to define the boundaries clearly. What are we aiming at? What innovations are necessary? When should a plan for this change be ready and how should we set about making such a plan? What methods do we use?
It is sensible to fill in the details (what precisely are we going to do?) with the people who have recognized expertise in the day-to-day work.

Q: Don't all these individual behavior changes cost a lot of time? Wouldn't it be better to aim at larger groups of people simultaneously?
A: Even when you aim at larger groups of people, they all change one by one. Maybe a large number of people could change at the very same moment, and maybe the underlying social pressure plays a role, but every change remains a personal, individual change. That is why we began this book by studying individual change.

Analyzing behavior change at the level of the individual gives you a better insight into what arguments would change their intentions and what situation stimuli could be effective. Paying attention to individual differences in a group will also help you decide who you should aim at. If you don't manage this and the people in the organization who do *not* enjoy social authority are the first to embrace an innovation, then it will cost you as manager considerable time and energy to implement the change efficiently and effectively.

TIP

In the final chapter of the following section, there are numerous tips for coaching and managing change in others.

ASSIGNMENT

Think back to a recent gathering with other people: a meeting, a visit to friends, or another occasion in which you found yourself in a group. Note down what effect the behavior of others (what they said or did) had on you.

◆ What behavior had an influence on your intentions, on your resolutions for the future?
◆ What behavior resulted in a temporary, automatic adaptation of what you said and did in that situation?
◆ What lessons can you draw about leading others?

Part 2:
Get Real

Formulate goal-oriented and concrete behavioral intentions

In the preceding section, we compared personal behavior change – the most important building brick of all change – to a new play that we had written and directed ourselves, and in which we had also played the starring role. In this first stage of the *Basic Change Method*, everything revolves around your role as author of the play. What is your story all about?

From here on, this book will become more confrontational. The previous part could be considered a general review of the fundamental principles of behavior change. But from here, we are going to be talking about what you want to change yourself. In your work, in your company, in your private life....

Of course, we could read this book as an interesting manual about change in general. But it is far more constructive to apply it to yourself. I speak from personal experience. The ideas in this book have not only been tested in assignments with companies and in coaching courses with individuals, but I have also tried them out on myself. In this way, I have been able to experience personally the true value of specific change techniques.

In this section – *Get Real* – it is all about determining your intentions. Determine what *future results* are really important and translate these *accurately* to a number of *changes in behavior habits* in *the present*. My assessment is that if you carefully follow the steps in this chapter, the chance of successful change will be at least *doubled*.

If you really want something to change, but only have vague resolutions, then, using the research that we discuss in this section, it is quite likely to make your chances of success *four times as great*. In this stage of the *Basic Change Method*, there are five separate steps which we will deal with in five chapters.

I. Investigate what is possible; make use of your mind and feelings. Think about your top achievements in the past. What achievement in the past still appeals to you? It is very interesting to see what others can do, but it is much more interesting to see what you and the people around you can do.

II. Determine what end results are desirable; make use of your mind and feelings. What do you really consider important? What would you like to look back on when you are 80? And what do you need for that?

III. Translate these results to measurable, personal change in habit behavior. If you know what end result you want, what behavioral pattern does this imply? It is important to be able to write this down as tangibly as possible.

IV. Check all the previous points against applicable forms of self-deception. Our observations and interpretations are far from perfect. That means that we regularly make mistakes when faced with important choices.

V. During this change, ask the help of somebody you can really trust. Don't undertake important changes all by yourself. Get the support of somebody you trust and be perfectly honest and open with him or her.

Chapter 1

Investigate what is possible; make use of your mind and feelings

A little while ago I gave a training session to a group of ten sales people from the same company. The sales manager had enlisted my help because the turnover had fallen below expectations. According to him, the sales staff didn't have enough knowledge and marketing and sales techniques.

We started with a role-play session. Two of the ten participants sat at a table and tried to sell their products to a client. The sales manager was right: it wasn't very good at all. On the other hand, you couldn't say that they did everything wrong. After about five minutes, I asked the other participants what they had noticed. And then the thing happened that always occurs in this kind of session: in just a few minutes, more than 20 things were pointed out that should be better in the future. The sales manager in particular had noticed a large number of mistakes. He read them out from a sheet of paper.

While the people who were criticizing seemed to grow in stature (they were, after all, doing their best to carry out the assignment), you could see the two colleagues who had done the role-play shrinking in front of your very eyes as the evaluation continued. They now knew very well what they couldn't do. And what they actually could do had been temporarily totally forgotten.

What are we going to do?

Everybody has been given unique talents at birth and has developed unique skills during his or her life. If we really know these talents and skills, then we also know exactly what changes we are able to achieve. In this chapter, I would like to invite you to do three things:

(1) **Think "yes" rather than "no"**. *Focus your attention first and foremost on the possibilities that you have rather than on the impossibilities. That's the way to achieve growth.*

(2) **Surprise yourself with your *own* abilities.** *Take a plunge into your own history or into the history of the group of people with which you want to achieve change and bring to the surface achievements which still have the ability to amaze you.*

(3) **Use your mind and your feelings.** *What you felt or feel about your own top achievements is very important.*

1. Think "yes" rather than "no"

The vast majority of feedback that is given in companies, in teams, in school classes, is negative. Generally, managers and colleagues start their feedback with a compliment, but that is simply a way of opening the door to a whole litany of things that are going wrong.

Similarly, when we look at our own story, we have the inclination to focus on everything that has gone wrong, on what should have gone better, and on countless points of improvement that we really should tackle some time. But people who really want to carry out important changes should focus primarily not on impossibilities, but on possibilities.

Take a look at one of the most important illustrations in this whole book. It consists of a large circle containing the word NO and a smaller circle in it with the word YES. The meaning: anybody who, in both work and the rest of his or her life focuses primarily on the No area will undoubtedly find all sorts of things that are going well. By eliminating these one by one, it seems as if we are making progress. We close down divisions that aren't operating well and

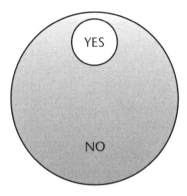

Many people are inclined to focus their attention on the NO area

punish employees who behave in an undesirable fashion. We conquer with considerable pain all sorts of bad habits in our private lives.

All this makes the NO area a little smaller, and because of this the YES area *seems* bigger. The problem is: it's an optical illusion. In reality, the YES area is still exactly the same size.

Shrinking the NO area only makes the YES area seem bigger

This approach is deadly where innovation and changed is concerned. You know that with each change quite a lot of things will initially go wrong. What's more, you feel insecure. Sometimes change is painful. If you then focus on reducing the NO area rather than expanding the YES area, then you will grind to a halt.

Focus your attention in the proper direction

The only real way to grow – both professionally and personally – is to expand the YES area. Direct your attention first and foremost on those things that are going well. In the company where you work, with your immediate colleagues, but also in your own activities and private life.

Take care: it is not about suddenly thinking of your negative points as something positive. We don't need to lie to ourselves or to other people. It is all about where you first look. Where do you first focus your attention?

Face the sunlight, and the shadow will always be behind you is an old saying. The shadow is still there, but you decide first to look on the sunny side.

You can only succeed in expanding the YES area if you ask the right questions:

– *What things went better than expected yesterday? How can we make that happen again today?*
– *What contributions that you have made to your company give you the most pride? How can we achieve more of them?*

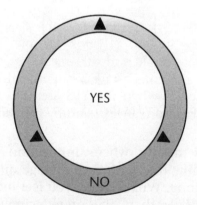

The only way to achieve real growth is to expand the YES area

And we mustn't ask bad questions such as:

- *How come things always go wrong when you lot do them? What have I done to deserve this?*
- *Why do things like this always happen to me? What have I done that I deserve to be punished like this?*

Back to the sales training that I mentioned at the start. You won't turn average salespeople into top salespeople by constantly pointing out to them the things they do badly. You only breed top salespeople by pointing out to average salespeople the small top achievements that they already deliver and by stimulating them to develop this behavior further. Any sales person who can increase top achievements from 5 percent to 10 percent will set off a revolution in his or her company. And anybody who grows from 10 percent positive thinking and acting in his or her private life to 20 percent has at least twice as much pleasure in life.

Okay. Sometimes you have to spend time on the NO area. Everybody makes mistakes and what's more you can come up against things that are really negative. Denying this is pointless. But we know that you can actually learn a lot from these things. And these learning points (think of them as tiny YES components within the NO area) ultimately deserve the most attention.

Another thing: it is quite possible that something in the NO area stops further growth of the YES area. Think about a bad habit that prevents you functioning properly: for example, you have difficulty in listening to other people and that means that your friendships and relationships all remain rather superficial. Such a concern, however, only emerges when the YES area has been growing for some time. For that reason, always start by focusing on the positive.

2. Surprise yourself with your own abilities

I don't know whether you've noticed it or not, but books about success and change often make use of the same people by way of illustration. I have read endless pages about the success of businessmen such as Bill Gates. Well-known sportspeople, such as Michael Jordan, or leaders, such as Martin Luther King, are also very popular as role models.

Of course, you can learn a lot from these people. And, of course, their stories are inspirational. But the big problem is that their stories say very little about what *you* can do.

Of course, I think it fascinating to learn that the inventor Thomas Alva Edison carried out more than 6,000 experiments before he produced a working electric light bulb. I even make use of this story in my training sessions as an example of persistence. But if you just want a few changes in your work, your company, or your private life, then it would be rather nice if they could happen a little quicker than Edison's first electric light bulb.

Achievements from the past

The first step in designing an important change is very simple: look back into your *personal* history and be amazed at your *own* abilities. Don't ask what *other* people can do. Don't look at all the things that went wrong in the past. Concentrate on a number of special achievements that *you yourself* have achieved in the past. You should pay particular attention to your *learning abilities* in the past.

◆ Have you, for example, learned to do something in the past that you originally thought you would never be able to do?
◆ Or have you, at work, somehow managed to complete an impossible task on time?
◆ Or did you, during your training, manage to solve a problem that initially you didn't even understand?
◆ Or have you taken part in a very difficult discussion, and gradually, point by point, won the argument?

If you look hard, you will find lots of achievements from your past that can still amaze you. And yet it was you who did all that!

When you work on change for a team or a company, then the same still applies. What were the exceptional achievements that you achieved in the past? What achievements still amaze you?

The essential thing is that you stop looking at what *other* people can do, and first of all concentrate on your *own* talents. Your own past achievement offers the best guarantee for your achievement in the future.

Research: Old behavior predicts new behavior, but how does that work?

Yesterday's behavior has a considerable influence on what we will do tomorrow. If we want to predict whether somebody will take the train tomorrow or the car, then it's important to know what choices that person made in the past. Very few psychologists disagree with this. But *exactly how* old behavior influences new behavior – there the opinions differ:

◆ Some maintain that old behavior primarily influences our intentions, so that we constantly make a *conscious choice* to repeat past behavior.
◆ Others maintain that old behavior *directly* – that is, without the intervention of the brain – influences our new behavior.

Every time we find ourselves in a certain situation, we automatically repeat the actions we did in the past.

Several years ago, Judith Ouellette and Wendy Wood carried out a so-called meta-analysis into this question. They collected 64 different behavioral studies and processed the results on a computer. After extensive statistical analysis, they reached the following conclusions:

- Behavior that occurs daily or weekly (habit behavior) is *directly* influenced by old behavior. If the context (the daily situations in which people demonstrate their behavior) doesn't change, but remains stable, then the influence of old behavior becomes all the stronger.
- For behavior that occurs once every six months or annually, old behavior still has an influence, but then particularly *via* people's intentions. We remember what we did in the past and largely base our resolutions on this. The intentions (that are also influenced by all sorts of factors, such as the opinions of other people) then have a strong influence on behavior. Particularly when the context is not stable, but changeable, then the (indirect) influence of old behavior is reduced.

What does this tell us?

- Behavior change is not simple. Old behavior has considerable influence on new behavior.
- If we want to change behavior that only takes place a few times a year or even less often (such as voting for a certain party in elections), then we must primarily direct ourselves at *intentions*.
- If we want to change behavior that takes place weekly or even more frequently, then it is insufficient to work on intentions. We will have to intervene in the context within which the behavior takes place: *the behavioral situation*.

Change the situation and you change the behavior. You should also realize that if, in the past, you were able to change your behavior or were able to learn something new, then the chances are that you will be able to do the same thing again tomorrow. This plays a central part in this chapter.

Ouellette, J. A. and Wood, W. (1998). "Habit and intention in everyday life: The multiple processes by which past behavior predicts future behavior." In: Psychological Bulletin, vol 124, no 1, 54–74.

3. Use your mind and your feelings

Some achievements from the past may, when viewed rationally, be very good, but don't give you any pleasure. Perhaps you have achieved something really special professionally, but in order to do that, you neglected people at home. Maybe you have won out in negotiations with a colleague or client, but in retrospect you feel as if your victory has damaged the relationship. It is important to involve your feelings when searching for achievements from the past. After all, feelings are a very important driver in your behavior. *True feelings have a magnetic force,* wrote the French author Honoré de Balzac. A change that doesn't feel good when it has taken place is one that we don't really think was worthwhile. That is also true when you look for successful past changes in your company. The figures can add up, the change can rationally be considered successful, but if nobody – clients, or employees, or financiers – feels good about it, then the change has actually failed. Of course, in such situations a good feeling in one group can be at the expense of the good feeling in another. A reorganization that saves the company can also cost jobs. But when a positive feeling isn't experienced by the person leading the change, then he or she is unlikely to attempt something similar in the future. We have the capacity to remember events as well as feelings. When you think back on your own past achievements, close your eyes and try to imagine them as visually as possible.

Then ask yourself what you feel when you see these images and write it down. If on your list of achievements you come across one that is, when considered rationally, highly successful, but has a distinctly negative feeling about it, then I would strongly advise you to cross it off the list. The achievements that give you a good feeling should be promoted to the very top of your list.

QUESTION & ANSWER

Q: Only looking at positive things? Is that sensible? Shouldn't you occasionally confront negative things?
A: Yes, you sometimes have to. If there is a positive lesson to be learned from a negative experience. And also if certain elements prevent the growth of the YES area. In that case, the NO elements have to be tracked down and tackled. Not to reduce the size of the NO area, but to ensure that the YES area can grow further.

Q: Not everybody is negative. In our company, there's quite a positive atmosphere.
A: Fortunately, there are some people who automatically look more at the YES area than at the NO area. There are, however, many people and companies that seem to direct their attention to the wrong areas.

Just try to keep track – only for a day – of how much negative feedback is given in your work environment and how much positive feedback. The American psychologist Shad Helmsletter once said in an interview that between the ages of six and 18, we get to hear 150,000 negative comments. Our parents, teachers, and other people tell us daily about around 30 things that we shouldn't, can't or mustn't do. In the same 12 years, we only get a couple of thousand positive remarks.

Q: And what if you can't trace one single good achievement in your past?
A: Anybody who has got this far in this book has at least learnt to read. That requires more effort than most changes that we face.

ASSIGNMENT

In order to know what you are capable of, it is vital that you remember a number of exceptional achievements. It doesn't matter if they took place last week or 20 years ago, whether they are professional or personal, as long as you did it yourself. I would therefore like to ask you to do the following before you start the next chapter:

◆ Think back to several exceptional achievements that you have performed in your life. Write down at least five. Ask other people in your surroundings to help you think about them.
◆ Pay attention to several special learning and change achievements from the past. What did you learn? What did you change in your life? Write down at least three such achievements.
◆ Try to remember what you thought, did, and felt during these achievements. Write this down. Ask yourself which of these special achievements give you a good feeling now.
◆ Using this list, try to sum up the talents and abilities that you possess. You can put them into the following categories:

– *Physical abilities (for example, in the area of fitness or sport);*
– *Mental abilities (for example, in the fields of learning, thinking, or creativity);*
– *Emotional abilities (for example, experiencing peace and balance, conquering grief or feeling great joy).*

On the website – tiggelaar.com – you will find a number of charts that you can use for various types of changes, for example, for collective change within organizations.

Chapter 2

Determine what end results are desirable; make use of your mind and feelings

It was during a short trip to the Canary Islands. My wife and I were celebrating our fifth wedding anniversary and our second daughter was on the way. In the few days that we were far away from our hectic daily lives, I started asking myself what my most important goals in life were. You could call it a sudden burst of responsibility, but I think that would be putting it too kindly. It also had something to do with the critical questions my wife had fired at me in the weeks before. She had asked me whether it wasn't about time for me to put all my fancy ideas about strategic and goal-directed thinking into practice myself.

I had just started my own company and I was working my butt off. During that week on holiday, I asked myself whether that was really sensible. I realized that my wife, my oldest daughter, and my unborn second child were the most important things in my life, and I realized that I was spending barely any time with them. And when I was at home, I'd walk around stressing and arguing. Not particularly constructive.

By realizing what the most important thing was, I understood that I would have to change my behavior. Not that that happened straight away. But that holiday was the necessary start.

What are we going to do?

In the previous chapter I gave you a list with a whole lot of possibilities for change. When a promise or threat from outside has fanned the desire to change, then it is important that we describe this desire as accurately as possible.

Often, people experience a major breakthrough when they are able to formulate their desires clearly. Anybody who has clear goals is able to expend their time better and experience the actions they undertake as more meaningful.

In this, it is not so much about reaching *the very top*, but rather deciding your *personal top*. Becoming everything it is possible for us to be...

In this chapter I want us to concentrate on the following three matters:

(1) **Formulate ambitious and clear end results.** *So that you know where you are going and can check whether you are still on course.*

(2) **Differentiate between different types of goals.** *There are various levels and different areas in which you can formulate your goals.*

(3) **Use your mind and feelings.** *It is not enough just to know what you want; you have to have a warm feeling about it as well.*

1. Formulate ambitious and clear end results

Often we need an external impulse to make us think about our goals in life. This is not always a pleasant experience. Not so long ago, a friend of mine had a serious accident. It was so serious that his life was in danger (later he told me that he really felt as if he had been literally given a second chance). When he came out of the coma, it seemed as if he would never again be like he was. Although later during recuperation this turned out to be untrue, his accident had turned his priorities in life upside down. His days now are totally different: he works less, and he spends more time with his family. And he does voluntary work in a shelter. After the accident, he says with conviction, that the quality of his life has improved.

This type of story – you are sure to know a couple like it yourself – sets us thinking about what our lives should really be like. Occasionally, we need a shock from outside to bring into real focus our vision for our personal future or for the future of our company.

A few reasons why this is positive:

◆ If you don't have any explicit goals, then you have no way of knowing whether what you are doing is meaningful or not.
◆ If you don't formulate goals, then there is no way of setting priorities in your schedule. It is impossible then to say "no," because everything is of equal importance.
◆ If you do not have clear goals in a company, then it is extremely difficult to delegate responsibilities. Nobody knows what they should do if unexpected choices have to be made.
◆ Your time and talents are too costly for you to be unaware how you are using them.

If you were 80...

Formulating the results you are striving for becomes easier and much more fun if you ask yourself a few questions:

(1) *Imagine that you are 80 and are looking back on your life.* What are some of the best memories that you cherish at that moment? Who were the most important people for you? What made you happy? What have you learnt? What do you leave behind? What gave your life meaning? Have you anything to look forward to? Don't be modest: what would you *really* like?
(2) *Keep on thinking that you are 80.* You remember that, on your way through life, you made a number of important changes (round about the age that you actually are at the moment). What were these changes? What problems and obstacles did you clear out

of the way? What challenges did you accept? Privately, professionally, socially? What did you learn, what have you done, what have you achieved?

These aren't simple questions, but it is very useful to think about them at an age when you still have the chance and energy to change things. (If you are already 80, then imagine you are 90!)

I regularly meet pensioners who say that in retrospect they should have done all sorts of things differently: that they were too preoccupied with their job, that they should have spent more time with their children. It is illuminating to imagine how, when you have reached retirement, you will look back on your life.

Questions for companies

You can apply the same sort of questions to companies. But if you are a businessperson or a manager, then it is better to answer the questions about yourself first, and only then the questions about your company. Your work is the service of you and the people around you, not the other way round. When you are thinking about the company, then the following questions are relevant:

◆ Imagine this: we are now five years further on and your company is on the front page of an important business magazine. You have been chosen as the most successful organization of the year. Can you describe what your company looks like then? What do you understand by success? What are you supplying? To what customers? And what sort of people are working for you? What do they do?
◆ And if you look back from that successful future to today: what are the changes that have made you become so successful? What have you changed in your products or services? And what have you changed in the way you approach your customers?

2. Differentiate between different types of goals

You can formulate goals and plans for your life on different levels and in different areas. To make things clearer and to help you understand how your ambitions and goals are related to each other, you can make use of the *growth model* (see over). It helps to imagine your life as a tree that can grow in various directions.

The growth model

The roots of the tree are a symbol for your *personal abilities*: physical abilities and skills (strength), emotional abilities (heart), and intellectual abilities (mind). We already listed these things in the previous chapter. It often takes a lot of digging before you discover your own abilities and those of other people.

The trunk of the tree represents your *life vision*. What convictions are important to you? What, for you, is the meaning of life? What do you believe in? Our life vision directs a whole range of different life areas and the way in which we use our personal abilities. Here we are talking about goals and choices for our life as a whole.

The branches of the tree form your most important *strategic goals* at the present moment. What do we want to achieve in the mid-term, in your personal area, your professional area, and in your social area? What do you want to learn? Here we are dealing with goals and choices that relate to periods of several years in your life.

When you formulate strategic goals, you can deal with *three life areas*:

◆ The private area: in which you have the role of mother, father, partner, sportsperson, reader, friend, neighbor, and acquaintance.
◆ The professional area: in which you have the role of manager, colleague, specialist, researcher, teacher, and pupil.

75

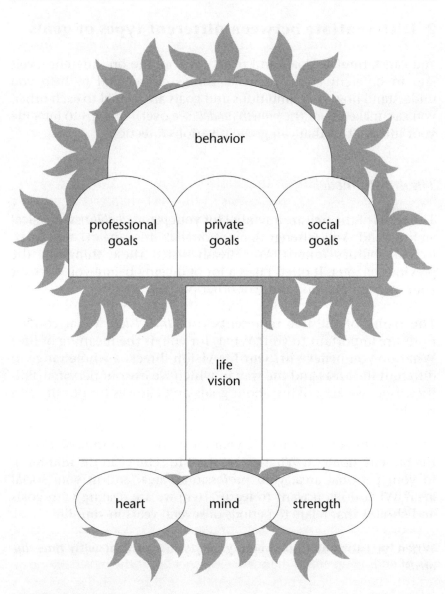

behavior

professional
goals

private
goals

social
goals

life
vision

heart

mind

strength

The growth model

◆ The social area: in which you have the role of motorist, citizen, voter, administrator, member of a sports club, voluntary organization, or church.

It is important that you do not translate your goals to just one area. It can be tempting for hard-working people to look for answers about the meaning of life primarily within the professional area. Your life is made up of various roles in several areas.

The leaves and fruits on the branches of the tree are the way you behave. We will be looking at this in the next chapter, but it won't do any harm to start thinking about it now. It is all about goals in behavior: what should you do daily, weekly, or monthly in order to achieve your strategic goals. If we have to change together with others, you have to realize that your behavior – just like the leaves on a tree – is the first thing others notice about you from a distance. The leaves and fruits tell us what sort of tree we are dealing with.

Why is this growth model important? If you set goals, define desired results, then it is good to keep the relationships between your goals in mind.

It is, for example, good to ask yourself whether your philosophy, your strategic goals, and your behavior actually match, or whether you actually work against yourself.

Ordering your wishes and goals also helps you track down inconsistencies. You can't do everything in the 24 hours in a day and seven days in a week that we have at our disposal. Anybody who wants to have a top career *and* a rich family life *and* be active socially runs the risk of ending up empty-handed. *Choose or lose* is the motto of one of my philosophical friends. Ultimately, in this book we keep on coming back to behavior. What we *do* is inextricably linked to all the other elements of the tree. The roots feed the leaves, but the leaves also feed the roots. What you *do* also strengthens your abilities.

behavior:

1. study, 8 hours a week
2. eat only vegetables, 1day a week
3. work out together, 1evening a week
4. wait before talking, each conversation
5. leave for work 10 min. earlier, each day

professional:
getting ahead
with my current
employer, finishing
a course in project
management

private:
learn to listen
better; doing
more things
together; living
healthier

social:
actively
support good
causes; driving
more carefully

life vision:

striving
for justice;
building a
happy
family life;
keeping
my faith;
treat others
the way I
would like
to be treated

heart:
compassionate;
enthusiastic

mind:
quick learner;
linguistic talent

strength:
sportive;
in good shape

An example of a filled-in personal growth model

The growth model for companies

It is not such a big step from *personal entrepreneurial behavior* to *corporate entrepreneurial behavior*. It is also important for organizations to strive for the proper match. Ordering the various goals in the same sort of growth model helps with this:

◆ **The roots** represent in the corporate growth model the people in the company: the available talent, the management, and the employees. What can they really do?
◆ **The stem** is the company philosophy: what is the aim of the organization, why does it exist?
◆ **The branches** are the most important strategic goals. Possible areas in which these goals can be found are: the *customer area* (who does the organization address, how do they deal with them?), the *products and services area* (what does the company supply and what is so unique about it?), and the *process area* (in what way do people work internally and how does this way of working profit people outside the company?).
◆ **The leaves and fruits** are the different types of behavior that those people in the company should display. Daily, weekly, and monthly. And in companies the same thing holds true: choose or lose. The best organizations do not simply know which goals are the most important for them, but also know very well exactly what they should *not* do.

Research: 35 years of targeted and useful investigation

Edwin Locke and Gray Latham, two American work and organizational psychologists, are true research veterans in the field of goals and their effect on motivation and performance. Locke has been publishing on this theme since the end of the 1960s and Latham since the middle of the 1970s. Recently, they summed up 35 years of investigation in a single, joint article. The most important results are given here.

Two core matters were constantly confirmed during research into goals:

◆ The *highest* goals lead to better performance, as long as these goals are attainable.
◆ *Specific* high goals lead to better performance than vague high goals, such as "do better".

According to the researchers, goals generally have four functions:

◆ *Goals give direction*: setting goals ensures that the attention and efforts are directed at activities that are connected to these goals and are directed away from activities that have little to do with these goals. Goals appear to have an influence not only on planned behavior, but also on automatic behavior:
◆ *Goals give energy*: high goals result in greater energy than low goals. People do not perform better just as a matter of course. Goals are frequently an essential prerequisite.
◆ *Goals have an influence on perseverance*: people can keep working for much longer if they have formulated a high aim. If we have no aim or a low aim, then we give up much sooner.
◆ *Goals stimulate the development and use of task-relevant knowledge and strategies*: people who are confronted with a new aim go out and look for ways to achieve it. We make use of existing knowledge and experience or develop new strategies – and often do both together.

Locke, E. A. and Latham, G. P. (2002). "Building a Practically Useful Theory of Goal Setting and Task Motivation". In: American Psychologist, vol 57, no 9, 705–17. American Psychological Association.

3. Use your mind and feelings

Graphs and models can sometimes seem very rational. It is, however, the intention that you also make use of your feelings when you define your goals. Ultimately, you want to *feel* better about your life, your company, and your relationships.

As individuals, we are prepared to do a lot of hard work to achieve our ultimate goal of satisfaction, happiness, and balance. Our desire to achieve a certain feeling drives a great deal of our intentions.

It is not complicated to use your feelings to determine your goals. The simplest method is to close your eyes and to imagine you are at the moment when your goals have been achieved. You will notice that if you imagine this as true to life as possible, then it will immediately evoke a feeling in you.

Now some people are able to imagine the future in *widescreen* with *Dolby surround sound*, others seldom get further than imagining the future in portable black and white with mono sound. But even if the latter is the case, you will still notice that your feelings are stimulated. Just do your best, even if you don't get further than a black-and-white television, to tune into the future station.

Don't just imagine your ultimate goals, but in particular imagine your strategic goals. Try to write down accurately what you see. *What exactly have you achieved in several years time? With whom? What date is shown on the calendar?*

QUESTION & ANSWER

Q: I don't have any of those elevated goals. Is that really necessary?
A: It's not about elevated goals. You don't have to measure your goals against those of others. It's all about what *you* consider the top. When do you feel that your talents and potential are used in the best way?

Q: Why should we look back as if we were 80? Why not look ahead from today?
A: If you think from today, then there's a big chance that your goals will remain safely in the vicinity of your current activities. It is much more sensible to get away from daily matters. In this stage it is, after all, about formulating what you really want.

Q: How many goals may you set?
A: You can at first set as many goals as you like. It is sensible *only then* to make your ordered list of strategic goals; which are the most important and most urgent, which can wait for a while.

Q: In our personal abilities you talk about heart, strength, and mind. What happened to soul?
A: Often the "soul" is considered our "core:" our deepest thoughts and emotions. These two things are included in the growth model.

Incidentally, a debate has been taking place in neuropsychology in recent years about whether the soul, that Plato once described as the *immaterial core*, actually exists. Many scientists, both religious and non-religious, are convinced that we should consider the soul as a *part of our thinking and feeling* rather than as something separate.

ASSIGNMENT

In the previous chapter, you developed an idea of your own abilities. In this chapter it is about defining your life vision and strategic goals.

This is perhaps the most important assignment in this book: an essential step in the change processes that you must not omit. Even just defining what you ultimately consider important and what concrete goals belong to this can have an enormous influence on your life.

For convenience, I will repeat in different wording the questions that I have posed elsewhere in this chapter. Take your time in answering them.

◆ Imagine that you are 80. It is a beautiful day, you are sitting in the sun in front of your house and you are looking back at your life with gratitude and satisfaction. What has given meaning to your life? What have you learned? What has made you happy? Who were the important people in your life? What will you leave to those dearest to you? And is there something to look forward to? As an 80-year-old, you do not suffer from false modesty. Don't mince your words and tell yourself exactly what was and is important in your life.

- *You may write down as many things as you like. Set aside at least an hour for this, then put away your answers for a while and look at them again later. Once more: don't be modest. If necessary, think back to those top achievements you listed in the previous chapter.*
- Read your answers to the previous question one by one. Indicate with figures, letters, or some other sign which you consider the most important. What goals were the most important in your life? What, in retrospect, were the least important? Those answers that you consider the most important are collectively your life vision.
- *Now write down this vision point by point. Write a short description of each point to show what you mean. Set aside at least an hour for this, then put away your answers for a while and look at them again later.*
- Imagine once again that you are 80. As an 80-year-old you look back to the age *that you have at this moment*. What should you change at that age in order to reach your real life goals? What problems should you solve, what obstacles should you overcome? In other words: what strategic (intermediate) goals belonged at this age to your end goals, to your life vision?

Divide your strategic goals into three areas:

- *Your private area: your relationship, your family, your friends, your relations.*
- *Your professional area: your activities, your company, your degrees, the way you function in business.*
- *Your social area: your role as consumer, as citizen, as member of association or church.*

Set your answers aside for a while and then slowly run through your strategic goals. As you are re-reading them, ask yourself the following:

◆ Do the goals in the various areas match each other? Do your philosophical and strategic goals match each other? Do your goals match the abilities you defined in the previous chapter? Or should you *first* define a number of learning goals for your private area, your professional area, or your social area?

◆ Next indicate which strategic goals are the most important at this very moment. Which problems, which challenges, are really worth your time and energy? (These goals do not need to be neatly allocated across the three areas.)

◆ Finally: define these strategic goals as specifically and accurately as possible. What do you want to achieve by when? Use figures and dates. Don't be too modern, but define strategic goals that are both reachable and challenging.

Chapter 3

Translate these results to measurable, personal change in habit behavior

Some people were perspiring and shifting uncomfortably in their seats. This wasn't how it was supposed to be. Calmly thinking together about the future; listening to a number of nice stories about trends; exchanging information… that was how it all started.

What's more: a number of inspirational strategic goals had been defined with which everybody could feel comfortable. Surely that would be enough?

But just when the meeting was about to end in a spirit of harmony, a few of those present asked for all this to be translated into action points, division of tasks, and deadlines. And from that moment, the fun went out of things.

And then that irritating chairman – the one they'd brought it for a substantial fee; what an impolite man! – he kept on asking what we were going to do now!

It's a daily occurrence in all sorts of companies: spending hours in meetings and conferences and then not taking any decisions, let alone agreeing about any action. In some organizations, "we have to have our freedom" has been elevated to a corporate philosophy. Terms such as coaching and empowerment are used as an excuse for indecision.

Of course, the non-committal exchange of information can sometimes prove useful, but the chance that this "by itself" will lead to ingenious choices and better performance is very slight. That is why it is essential to translate things into behavior. This certainly doesn't need to be dictated. But managers, employees, and advisors should have the courage to probe deeper with their questions.

It is my experience that you are only on the right track if your think you are being rather impolite.

What are we going to do?

We know from the previous chapter what our goals are. Now we have to think about how we are going to achieve them. This almost always requires a number of changes. Change to the fixed patterns in which we find ourselves, to the relationships that we maintain with others, to the way we personally function. All these obstacles that at the moment make our goals inaccessible, demand a change in our current behavior. This is an awkward chapter. That is not because it is difficult to understand the need to translate your goals into behavior, but rather because accurately formulating your behavioral intentions requires a certain amount of practice. In this chapter, I will ask you to run through the following points.

(1) **Translate your strategic goals into behavior.** *Formulate as clearly as possible what you have to do to achieve your strategic goals.*

(2) **Determine which changes in behavior are most important.** *Restrict yourself to a maximum of five interrelating changes in behavior.*

(3) **Describe the desired behavior in a measurable, active, and personal way.** *The more accurately you describe the behavior, the greater the chance that you will actually do it.*

1. Translate your strategic goals into behavior

For most people, achieving the most important goals in life doesn't happen out of the blue. It costs you quite a bit of effort. The road to your goals is littered with obstacles: relationships with others that should be better, old habits that seem to make our goals inaccessible. We can spend a lot of time regretting these things, but ultimately they will need to be solved. The American politician Jesse Jackson said: *Tears and sweat are salty, but they render a different result. Tears will get you sympathy; sweat will get you change.* Real solutions involve behavior. We will have to develop new behavior to bring our goals closer.

In the *Basic Change Method* we place the greatest emphasis on "external" behavior: motor behavior: what you do with your body; and verbal behavior: what you say to yourself and what do you say to others?

A few examples.

Imagine that the strategic goal in your professional area is to get a new and better job. It is better to formulate a *concrete behavioral intention* as outlined below:

◆ Every Saturday for the next three months, I will write at least three application letters, and after exactly five days, I will phone the addressee.
◆ In the coming three weeks, I will phone or e-mail at least one person I know well and ask them whether they know of any good job for me.
◆ Every week in the coming two months, I will take a good contact or a headhunter out to lunch in order to discuss my career prospects.

If your goal in your private area is to lose weight, so that you can lead a healthier and more pleasurable life, you will most probably have to eat less. Sounds logical, but what do you mean by "eat less?" Do you prefer to keep it vague and say: In the future, I must pay more attention to what I eat? Or do you formulate a more concrete proposal?

◆ In future, I will restrict any cooked meal to a maximum of 700 calories.

◆ In future, I will only take one helping at dinner, eat it, and then place my knife and fork on my plate and take it into the kitchen.

Behavioral goals for companies

If you are a manager in a company, then the same things hold true. You can define very challenging goals within the product, process, and customer areas:

◆ Introduce a new product onto the market within three months.
◆ Cut delivery time by 50 percent.
◆ Increase the Customer Satisfaction rating from 6.5 to 7.5 within six months.

But unless these are translated into concrete behavioral intentions (*preferably formulated by the staff in consultation with the leadership*) nothing will really happen.

◆ If a shop aims at increasing customer satisfaction, then it could be important for every employee to conclude every contact with a customer with the question – Is there anything else I can do for you? – and then to react promptly and accurately to any request.
◆ If a computer system supplier wishes to increase customer satisfaction, then perhaps it would be a good idea to offer every client a free visit (or for a fixed fee) after one week, one month, and six months to check how the system is working, and to track down any malfunctions and rectify them.

The more concrete you can formulate your behavioral intentions, the greater the chance that you will actually put them into practice.

You should realize that one change may often require *several changes of behavior*. For example, if somebody wants to start his or her own company, they may have to take a course, write a business plan, and then go out in search of clients. Conversely, a single change in behavior can have a number of results. If you learn to listen to people more attentively, then you will benefit from this in more than one area.

Research: Accurately formulated intentions work better

Intentions do not always lead to behavior. If our intentions are not accurately formulated, then frequently nothing really happens.

Researchers Andrew Davidson and James Jaccard published an article in 1979 concerning attitudes to contraception. The article clearly illustrates the need for accuracy in behavioral intentions. The research showed that the more women had specifically formulated their position on the contraceptive pill, the greater the predictive value this attitude had for later behavior.

The researchers asked married women a number of questions about contraception. The more precisely a woman was able to express her opinion, the better it reflected the actual behavior of that woman when measured at a later date.

The researchers tracked the women for two years after they answered the survey and came to the following conclusions:

◆ A positive attitude towards *contraception* resulted in a correlation to the use of the pill during the following two years of 0.083.
◆ A positive attitude towards the *birth control pill* resulted in a correlation to the use of the pill during the following two years of 0.323.
◆ A positive attitude towards the *use of the birth control pill* resulted in a correlation to the use of the pill during the following two years of 0.525.

◆ A positive attitude towards the *use of the birth control pill in the coming two years* resulted in a correlation* to the use of the pill during the following two years of 0.572.

This classic research by Davidson and Jaccard shows that our preference for a particular behavior can have considerable predictive value for what we will actually do, as long as this behavior is formulated in a specific and personal way.

Davidson, A. R. and Jaccard, J. J. (1979), "Variables that Moderate the Attitude–Behavior Relation: Results of a Longitudinal Survey," In: Journal of Personality and Social Psychology, 37, 1364–376.

2. Determine which changes in behavior are most important

I can imagine that you are enthusiastic about certain goals that you have set. And I can imagine that you want to set about things right away. Perhaps you also have an idea of what behavior changes they require. But beware of moving too quickly.

If you are after a new job, there are several possibilities. Similarly, if you want a better distribution of responsibility in the home, there are also several possibilities. You can actually *think* of more possibilities than are actually practical.

When you are working on change with several people, then all sorts of suggestions will be made. Often it is quite difficult to decide in harmony which behavior is the most relevant. Perhaps you think: let's not be difficult. If there are various behaviors that will allow me to achieve my goal, then I'll choose them all and I'll get there quicker.

Unfortunately, there's a snake in the grass. If you want to make too many behavior changes at the same time, then the chance is that

(*The correlation coefficient is a measure that shows the connection between two elements. A score of –1 shows that this connection is completely negative, 0 indicates no connection, and 1 shows that the connection is completely positive.)

you won't persevere. And that means that with all our enthusiasm we don't achieve anything.

That is true when you want to change your own behavior, but even more so when you try to achieve behavior change together with other people, for example in a company.

"If time is money, then everybody lives beyond their means," wrote the German author Ludwig Fulda. And that's true. You must realize that every behavior change demands time, attention, and effort, so don't exaggerate your ambitions.

Selecting behavior

One you have thought up a respectable number of behaviors that could help you reach your strategic goals, it is important to put them into order and make a choice.

You do this by assessing the *impact* and *feasibility* of the behavior.

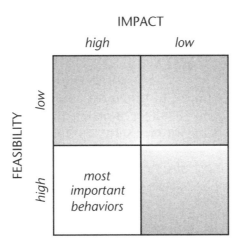

Determine which new behaviors are most important by assessing the impact and feasibility of each behavior

◆ A company that cuts its prices by half will probably be very popular with the customers (impact), but won't be able to carry on operating for very long (feasibility).

◆ If you jog for an hour every day, you will quickly improve your condition (impact), but will you be able to keep it up (feasibility)?

For each behavioral possibility, we have to ask ourselves what the impact will be: how much nearer to one or more of our strategic goals will it bring us and how quickly? Will this behavior allow us to remove an important obstacle that is standing between us and our goal? Is this a real solution to our real problem?

We must also ask ourselves whether we can actually show this behavior. Since we have already listed our abilities, we can give an answer to this question.

In addition, the feasibility of behavior is dependent on its simplicity. If you have defined a complex behavior, then split it into several simple behaviors. *I would advise you not to choose more than five behaviors.* And behaviors that preferably have some connection with each other.

3. Describe the desired behavior in a measurable, active, and personal way

This is a difficult paragraph. In almost every workshop that I give about change, it seems that a lot of people have difficulty in formulating the desired behavior precisely.

The mistake that most of them make is that they do not formulate *behavior*, but rather a *result* or a *whole collection* of behaviors.

Instead of formulating in a concrete way what they are going to do, they jot down sentences such as: achieve a better relationship, have more pleasure in my work, sell more. A simple way of testing whether the desired behavior has been formulated precisely enough is to ask the question: *What are you going to do for that?*

An example: *I am going to sell more.* What are you going to do for that? *I am going to be more active in my market.* What are you going to do for that? *I am going to phone my customers more frequently.* What are you going to do for that? *Every day I will select two customers and ring them before lunch.*

That is clear.

Some people get angry with others if, during a workshop, they are helped liked this to define their behavior in as precise a way as possible. They feel trapped. Another regular occurrence is that people are afraid to carry on asking. Scared that they will offend the other person.

But tell me honestly: if you don't want to formulate what you are really going to do for change, then how much do you really want it?
My position is this: when you feel that you have stopped being non-committal and think that things are becoming confrontational – that's *exactly* when you are on the right path. Then you experience just slightly that feeling that goes with real behavior change. That exciting feeling of exchanging old certainties for new, concrete behavior that will ultimately bring you to your goal.

It is essential that you write down your desired behaviors in such a way that they are *measurable, active* and *personal* (MAP). Only if we formulate our intentions in this way will we be able in the next stage to choose the situation stimuli that promote this desired behavior.

The MAP Checklist

Try, when you are formulating *each behavior*, to include as many of the following points as possible. Once again: the more precisely you can formulate your behavioral intention, the greater the chance that you will actually carry it out.

Measurable

◆ What sort of desired behavior is it: motor or verbal? What are we going to *do*? What are we going to say?
◆ Can this behavior be split up into a number of actions? Be as specific as possible and make sure you keep it *simple*.
◆ How often each day or week do we wish to repeat these actions?
◆ What else is measurable: the length of the action, the intensity, the quality, the scope, or the distance?
◆ At what time, in which place, and in which context will the actions take place?

Active

◆ Don't define what you are *not* going to do, but what you *are* going to do. Don't say: *"I won't put off doing my work until just before the deadline"* but: *"I will finish all assignments that come in within three days."*
◆ Don't say: *"I will stop smoking,"* but rather: *"From now on I am going to live healthily and refuse all cigarettes.*
◆ In general: avoid words such as *not, stop,* and *finish.*

Personal

◆ Who exactly will carry out the actions?
◆ Will this happen alone or together with others?
◆ Which other people are (possibly) involved?

QUESTION & ANSWER

Q: How do you choose behaviors that lead to the desired results?
A: Talk about them with other people. Read books connected with your goals. A lot of knowledge can be had for free. If we change *together with others*, for example in a company, let those people who will have to show the behavior be the first to suggest what behaviors are necessary to reach your goals. Your customers,

employees, and financiers are the experts in the field of their daily activities. Provide them with as much additional information as possible. About the goals, about how others work, and so on.

A very good way of discovering the proper behavior is to *watch others.* What do other people do (or what did they do) to achieve the goals that you are aiming at?

Sometimes you can simply observe this, at others it takes a little more effort. But you are always free to ask questions.

I got my first job – at a newspaper where I desperately wanted to work – because I phoned the recently appointed editor and asked him how he had got *his* job. Of course, he was initially rather surprised that I phoned him about that, but then he gave me a whole lot of useful tips and a few months later we became colleagues.

Q: Isn't it rather long-winded to formulate everything so exhaustively?
A: "Just get going" sounds attractive, but in a large number of cases this simply leads to half-achieved or failed changes. According to estimates, precisely formulated intentions are *two to seven times* more frequently executed that vaguely formulated intentions.

Q: What should we do when change is largely expected from others?
A: In organizations, we often only achieve results when employees and/or customers change their behavior. It is generally important to involve these groups in the plans as soon as possible. After all, *they* are the ones who will actually have to do things.

It is also important to determine what behavior on your part will help these groups change *their* behavior. The last part of this book contains a number of examples and suggestions in this area.

ASSIGNMENT

In the previous chapters, you defined your personal abilities, your life visions, and your strategic goals, and put these in order of importance. Now we are going to translate the most important strategic goals into the behavior that is required to achieve them. You should realize that several behaviors are required for each goal. On the other hand, there are a lot of behaviors that can contribute to achieving several different goals. The assignment consists of three sections:

◆ For each of your strategic goals, think up a number of *simple* behaviors that will help you reach them. What do you have to do? What do you have to learn? Which relationships will require special attention? Think up as many behaviors as possible. Look at the way other people go about achieving this type of goal.

◆ Next determine the impact and feasibility of each behavior. How effectively does this behavior work, how quickly, how many strategic goals does it support, and are you really capable of putting it into practice?

◆ Now select a maximum of five behaviors. Describe each of them in measurable, active, and personal terms.

Use the MAP checklist from this chapter. Ask yourself whether you want to attempt these behaviors simultaneously or (partially) consecutively.

Chapter 4

Check all the previous points against applicable forms of self-deception

Everybody lies. Every day. Even me! You pull in your stomach when you look in the mirror and you look for the most attractive figures when you check your administration.

We lie most to ourselves in order to reduce the tension between the world of our imagination and the world of hard reality. It is a relatively innocent process as long as we are aware of it and can laugh at it.

But sometimes, self-deception can be dangerous. I once made a bad assessment about the way things were going in a company I worked for, because I was simply too optimistic and didn't really want to pay attention to the bad news. Fortunately, I had a good bookkeeper who alerted me to the danger on time.

A good remedy against self-deception is a tip I was once given by a female director. It is derived from the way children try to get an answer out of their parents and nearly drive them mad. Whenever you make a plan, ask yourself three times "What is it good for?"

As a company, we need to grow faster.
What is that good for?
Well, we want a larger company.
What is that good for?
Well, you know – we want to grow. That's good for the company.

Why? Well – you may be right. We don't really want to grow. We're just concerned about continuity. Do we have a future in the long-term? What would happen if, say, I couldn't work? I'm worried about that.

What are we going to do?

Self-deception is an important barrier to change. Often, you can only really get started on a change process once you have seen the cold reality with your own eyes. Sometimes we have to experience a severe threat from close by.

If you have consciously exposed your self-deception, then the next question is: Am I really prepared to make the necessary investment? *Every change has its price, you do not get any discount, and the costs have to be paid in advance.*

Fortunately, we are not only capable of self-deception but also of a critical analysis of our own feelings and thoughts. Take note of three points:

(1) **Beware of phantom problems and phantom solutions.** *We waste too much time on things that are not really important.*

(2) **Beware of possible mistakes in your observations.** *Not everything that we think we observe is objective reality.*

(3) **Beware of possible mistakes in interpretation.** *There is a whole range of common mistakes in interpretation that can entrap us.*

1. Beware of phantom problems and phantom solutions

An important lesson that I have learned in my consultancy work is this: only when a client is absolutely convinced that he has a real problem that he must solve can you be of any use to him. If somebody calls in the services of a consultant under pressure from others, but does not really think the problem is real, then it can prove an extremely difficult assignment.

When can you talk of a real problem? If there is an obstacle standing between the you of here-and-now and your most important aims for the future.

◆   This can be a habit that you or other people have, or a relationship or set of circumstances that you have to change.
◆   In companies, real problems frequently revolve around circumstances and behaviors that could lead to the loss of customers, employees, or financiers.

Real problems can often be experienced by several people, not just the person suffering from them. And real problems do not offer a way of easily reaching goals in an alternative way. It is dangerous if we do not recognize real problems or view them as phantom problems.

It is less dangerous when we see phantom problems as real problems. Although in general these can cost us an awful lot of time.

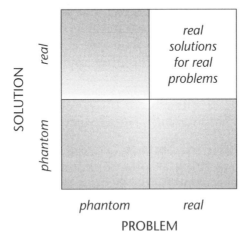

Much time is wasted on phantom problems and phantom solutions

Phantom problems

There are two kinds of phantom problems. In the first category, the obstacle you perceive standing between you and your goals is not a real obstacle at all. It is awkward but has no relationship with the goals we have formulated. A few examples:

◆ You think you do not have sufficient qualifications to make a career, yet your manager is only really concerned about your personal effectiveness.
◆ You think that the delivery time for your product is too long to make it a success, yet your customers are only really interested in the price.

In the second category of phantom problems we discover that the goal we have formulated is not really that important. We will use the same examples:

◆ In fact, you weren't really planning on making a career for yourself. You're quite happy doing the job you have.
◆ It doesn't really matter what the customers think about your products. The business is doing just fine.

Apparently, the goal we set ourselves was forced on us, either by ourselves or by others. While it was in the realm of daydreaming we were quite enchanted by it. But when we actually had to invest in achieving the goal we just didn't bother anymore.

Phantom solutions

Real solutions remove the obstacle between us our and goals. But there is also such a thing as phantom solutions. These *seem* to remove the obstacles standing between us and our goals. If all the employees in a factory complain about the corporate culture, we could install a brand-new stereo system that pumps out pleasant music all day long (true story!), but this doesn't really tackle the actual problem.

Phantom solutions are interventions that only tackle the symptoms of a problem or lead towards a totally different goal. Sometimes, phantom solutions only make things a lot worse. There are people who have negative feelings because they are overweight. The reason for being overweight is that they eat too much and exercise too little. But in an effort to escape these negative feelings for just a moment, they resort to chocolate, snacks, and savory nibbles.

Often, a phantom solution involves some sort of denial behavior: you make a new plan for the coming year; you don't change anything, just do things more efficiently. It is all about actions that give a temporary sense of certainty and rest because you do something you are good at, and that apparently has something to do with your problem.

From time to time, this isn't a bad thing. But if the brief moment of rest persuades us to avoid tackling the real problems, then it doesn't help at all.

2. Beware of possible mistakes in your observations

Our minds are extremely good at filtering information. Take the way our observation works. From all the possible stimuli that reach us from our surroundings, such as images, sounds, and smells, our brain constantly selects the things that are most relevant to us.

Your eyes register *all* images that fall within your field of vision and file these away in less than a second in what is called your sensory memory. Your brain selects from these *only those things* that at that particular moment indicate some form of danger. In this way, it protects you from an overload of stimuli that do not mean anything.

And so your brain doesn't process everything that reaches your senses. It is important to be aware of this. If you make plans for important changes, this natural process of information selection can lead to problems.

101

Habituation

The first thing that can make things difficult for your observation is something called *habituation*. Your brains largely direct their attention to those things that change. After a while, things that remain stationary no longer attract our attention; on the other hand, we no longer hear the constant tick of a clock after a certain time.

Sometimes we are faced in our private lives or in organizations with stealthy problems. Such problems gradually creep in step by step, and when we notice them, it's sometimes too late. Bad habits in the area of food and drink often develop in this way. And the same is true in relationships. Often one of the partners suddenly realizes (for example, when he or she is confronted with a strong memory of former times) that, in the last few years, love has diminished a lot *without them being aware of it.*

In companies, this sort of thing shows itself in safety behavior. Often a major accident is due to a whole list of small changes – gradually taking less care in the job – that nobody notices. Similarly, when the turnover of a company gradually decreases by small amounts, then it takes some time before the management recognizes this and takes the necessary steps.

Selective attention

A second observation phenomenon that can lay in wait for you is *selective attention*. Our attention is primarily attracted by things that have *meaning* for us.

If you are considering buying a new car and you decide on a Renault, then you will notice a lot more of these than of other brands. If you change your mind and decide on a Volkswagen, then you will suddenly notice that a lot more of these are on the roads. This is no sinister plot by the car industry, but simply a normal observational phenomenon.

A small experiment will demonstrate this. The illustration below can be viewed in two different ways. The first thing you can see is a saxophone player. The second thing is the face of a young woman. Look at it carefully. You will notice that it is impossible to see both images clearly at the same time. The *meaning* that your brain attaches to the picture *determines* what you see. Thus, to a certain extent, we see what we *want* to see. This can be risky in our plans for change.

Few people can see things as they really are. Some see only what they want to see, others what people show them, was the complaint of the French socialist Gustave le Bon.

Look carefully, what do you see?

103

Research: the aliens that never came

In the 1950s, social psychologists Leon Festinger, Henry Riecken, and Stanley Schachter anonymously joined a sect in Chicago. This group, known as the *Seekers*, was made up of more than 30 members, and was led by a man and a woman. They believed that the earth would perish in a massive flood and that the members of the sect would be saved at precisely midnight by a group of aliens in flying saucers. The aliens – given the name *Protectors* – sent messages to the female leader of the sect.

As the researchers expected, no flying saucers turned up at midnight on the prescribed day. After four hours of heated discussion about why the Protectors hadn't shown up, the leader received a message: the faith of the sect had saved the world; there would be no flood.

One problem: various members of the sect had given up their jobs and sold all their possessions. What's more, many of them had come into conflict with friends and family. This had strange consequences. Until the evening in question, few members had done very much to attract converts. But now the leaders of the sect and most of its members used all sorts of ways to convince other people.

Apparently they found it so threatening to give up their self-deception – this was the analysis of social psychologist Robert Caldini more than 30 years later – that they desperately tried to find evidence for their strange belief. Since there was no physical evidence available, they sought "social evidence" in the form of converts who would share their belief in aliens.

This form of psychological panic football shows the power of our natural tendency towards consistency. When, after three weeks, they had not attracted any new converts, the group fell apart. Most of the members of the sect never saw each other again.

Festinger, L., Riecken, H. W. and Schachter, S. (1956). "When Prophecy Fails." New York: Harper & Row. Caldini, R. (1988). "Influence. Science and Practice" (2nd edn). New York: Harper Collins.

3. Beware of possible mistakes in interpretation

Once we have observed the reality around us, we give it a meaning. We divide our observations mentally into main and sub-categories (transport – car – sports car) and in addition often attach an assessment to them (beautiful/ugly, good/bad). The meaning we give to things does not always serve the naked truth. Certainly, when those things are about our own lives. Our minds constantly make up stories that create certainty. Stories that provide some sort of structure in this complex world. Whether the reality that we create actually exists is another matter altogether.

Below, I list three common forms of self-deception that modern psychological research has brought to light. Anybody who leads change – whether in his or her personal life or in an organization – would do well to check his or her ideas and plans regularly for errors in thinking.

Mistakes in association

We often make a connection between events that we observe more or less simultaneously. This connection does not necessarily exist. If things are going badly for the economy *and* for our company, then we are likely to assume a causal connection. There can be a whole list of other causes. Scientists talk of a causal connection between events A and B when:

◆ event A precedes event B in time;
◆ there is a statistical connection between events A and B (this means that repeated observations show that there is a calculable connection between the two events);
◆ this statistical connection is not caused by event C.

Mistakes in attribution

If we are involved in a failure, we often look to the circumstances to provide a reason. If everything is going well, then we are more likely

105

to put down the success to our own efforts. If others are involved in the failure, then we are more likely to attribute the failure to people rather than to circumstances. But in all cases, coincidence plays an equally important role. Change begins by accepting responsibility for your own life.

"This is a characteristic of genuine self-knowledge: that we see more faults in ourselves than in others," wrote the German author Friedrich Hebbel.

Mistakes in consistency

Once we have opted for something then this, to a large extent, colors our interpretation of reality. People are constantly looking for confirmation of their opinions about themselves and about other people and things they consider important. This is particularly true if we have done a lot or given up a lot for a particular conviction.

This is clearly seen when we hear bad news. If, for example, there is a serious problem or fraud in the company where you work, then your first reaction will be one of disbelief or even denial, because this news does not match the image you have of "your" company. If it turns out that the news is true, only then (often slowly and gradually) will you adapt your personal image of your company to reality.

QUESTION & ANSWER

Q: Why do we talk about problems? Wouldn't it be better to talk about challenges?
A: Nobel prize winner Daniel Kahnemann has shown in several research projects that avoiding loss is a more important driver for people than making gains. This is called *loss aversion*. As a rule, an opportunity or a challenge (profit) has to be two to two and a half times greater than a problem (loss) to make us take action. Thinking in problems is thus literally more motivating than thinking in opportunities or challenges.

Q: What should we do if the problem has no solution?
A: Alcoholics Anonymous use a prayer at all of their meetings: *God, give me the serenity to accept things that cannot be changed. Give me courage to change things that must be changed. And the wisdom to distinguish one from the other.* For many people, life on earth brings restrictions that cannot be changed overnight. The only course of action here is to change the way you look at the problem. Learn from it, but don't let it ruin your life.

Another possibility: you think that you have a real problem, but that is not the case: the problem exists *only* in your head. Then you must direct the way you think towards other things: change your "thinking habits".

You can also change what you *think* by changing what you *do* and what you *say*. If at certain times throughout the day – for example at meal times – you say out loud what you are grateful for, then your thoughts will be directed at positive things.

Q: If you or the people around you don't think something is a problem, but you still want to change, will you succeed?
A: There is a good chance that the thing you attempt will come to nothing. Most people only spring into action and persist against adversity when they know they can solve an existing problem.

The difficulty is, of course, that many problems only reveal themselves after a considerable time. Perhaps it is good to imagine yourself at some point in the future.

Imagine that you are dissatisfied with the way your life or your career is going. Try to imagine what it would look like in a year if you didn't change anything. And what would happen in five years? Or in ten? Perhaps it will then become clear where the problem lies and your motivation for change will increase. When undertaking change with others, you often have to take measures to let other people experience the fact that there is a real problem.

Q: How can you easily recognize whether you are realistically thinking about the world, yourself, and change?
A: Irrational thoughts about yourself and the world around you are often characterized by being absolute and extreme. Some people are excessively positive and overestimate their abilities. Many people, on the other hand, underestimate themselves. Their thoughts are not goal-driven and often lead to negative emotions.

According to the psychologist Albert Ellis, you have to beware of the following "absolute" way of expressing things:

◆ If I made a mistake, that would be *disastrous*.
◆ I simply *can't take it* if he doesn't appreciate me.
◆ I *must* do this, otherwise I feel terrible.
◆ I feel terrible; I *should* have done that differently.
◆ I *am* simply clumsy. I *can't* do anything about it. People *are* like that.

You can combat these types of negative thoughts by asking two questions:

◆ *Where is the proof for this thought?*
◆ *What feeling does this thought give me?*

If you have a realistic image of yourself and of the world around you, you will be better able to determine which changes are really relevant. Think here about the following: change is possible, but it is generally not easy and takes place step by step. Don't be put off if it doesn't happen easily to start with, or if it takes place with ups and downs.

ASSIGNMENT

Your life is too valuable to spend time on phantom problems and phantom solutions. Look at the answers you wrote down in your previous assignments. And ask yourself what form of self-deception, as discussed in this chapter, could have played a role in the answers you gave. Rework them if necessary. As you do this, ask yourself the following questions:

(1) *Am I really 100 percent behind the goals that I have formulated?*
(2) *Do I really believe that the behaviors I have formulated will actually achieve these goals?*
(3) *Do I allow my plans to be influenced too much or too little by the people around me?*
(4) *Do I really believe I am capable of carrying out or leading the necessary changes?*

Perhaps it is sometimes a painful process, but I won't ask you until the next chapter to talk about your ideas with other people. It is sensible to answer these critical questions for yourself before revealing your plans for change to those around you. And this is particularly true if the change is one you want to achieve with other people, for example in a company.

Believe me, in the many training and coaching sessions that I hold, people nearly always need to rework some of their answers.

Once you have critically reviewed your answers and, where necessary, adapted them, write them down as follows:

◆ Write down your life vision in several clear points.
◆ Write down the strategic aims that are most important to you in the coming years, together with figures and end dates.
◆ Write down five behaviors that in the coming years can contribute to these strategic aims. Measurable, active, and personal (MAP).

Chapter 5

During this change, ask the help of somebody you can really trust

Although I am a confident person, I have to admit that, in unfamiliar situations, just like most people, I prefer to wait and see which way the cat jumps. In practice, this means I often wait and see what other people do.

When I am caught in a tailback just a short distance before the exit I need, I am not generally the first to drive over the hard shoulder. If somebody else does it (some daredevil who doesn't need social approval for his or her behavior in traffic), then I am generally the fourth or fifth car that follows his or her lead.

When I am attending a meeting and have the feeling that people are talking nonsense, I often say independently exactly what I think. Apparently, I have more self-confidence in meetings than when I'm driving a car. And apparently there are often people at such meetings that know this and wait until I intervene before joining in.

If it is an important meeting, there are, I think, few people who are completely independent. We need others to help us discover our abilities, others with whom we can discuss our goals and determine our behavior. And we also want to share our failures and successes with other people.

What are we going to do?

Change often leads to a period of uncertainty. And that is exactly when we need other people to help us to define the world and our role in it.

In this chapter we deal with the following points about social support during change.

(1) **Realize that you need other people.** *People are social creatures who need other people to give direction and meaning to their lives.*

(2) **Find somebody who can really help.** *Decide what sort of "change coach" you need and what you expect from him or her.*

(3) **Clearly agree together how you will do things.** *Coaching and managing change in others requires a special talent. Some useful tips about this.*

1. Realize that you need other people

In the film *Cast Away*, Tom Hanks barely escapes an air crash and ends up on an uninhabited island. After a while, he manages to take care of himself: he has sufficient food and builds a hut for himself. But ultimately, the loneliness becomes too much for him and he attempts – without too much success – to commit suicide.

Suicide as a result of loneliness happens a lot. People can't manage without other people. Apparently we are programmed for relationships with others.

Why are we social creatures? Needless to say, opinions about this differ, but it is widely accepted that we do not have much chance of survival as solitary human beings. We generally need other people for a whole range of basic needs, such as providing housing and food. We need at least one other person to start a family and have children.

112

Other people give us certainty

In our Western society, in which we enjoy every luxury imaginable, it is perhaps the case that we primarily need other people to give *meaning* to our surroundings and the role we play in them.

It is particularly in uncertain situations that we turn to others or watch what others do in order to decide our own stance. This searching for what we call *social proof* often has strange consequences. We sometimes read in the newspapers that somebody has drowned while there were people around who did nothing. The explanation given for this by social psychologists is that in this sort of uncertain situation, we pay too much attention to those around us when deciding what we do and are scared of showing any behavior that deviates from the norm. If too many people spend too much time looking at each other instead of thinking for themselves, then there is a big chance that the person in the water will drown before anybody takes any action.

In addition to looking to others to determine our reality, we also look to them to determine our self-image and our values. Sometimes that takes place in harmony and friendship. *A good friend is our second conscience,* according a German proverb. Friends can help us see reality and help us define the role we play in it.

Sometimes we actually rebel against people in our immediate surroundings in an effort to discover our role in the world. Just think of the way teenagers choose their music and friends in order to rebel against their parents.

Change often creates a period of uncertainty in which the help of others is very welcome. Many changes are awkward because they require us to learn new habits that will only bear fruit after some length of time. What's more, we will have to let go of some habits that in the past gave us a sense of security. Change processes in companies are particularly awkward when people have to give up existing certainties and when not everybody is (as yet) convinced of the need for this or the promise of a better future. The role of others, who show understanding and support during these changes, is of considerable importance.

2. Find somebody who can really help

When you have formulated your strategic goals, have listed your behavior intentions, and have, furthermore, checked these for any traces of self-deception, then the time has arrived for you to reveal your plans for change to the world around you. Perhaps you have already spoken to somebody about your intentions, but now it is necessary to look for a *change coach*. Somebody who helps you develop your plans further and pulls you through when adversity strikes.

Coaching, support, and all forms of supervision – even if that is just one telephone call a week – appear to be important factors for success in a change process.

We can, of course, seek help during such change periods from people in our immediate surroundings: our partner, our parents, our friends, or our colleagues at work. Change can also provide the impetus for making new friends or looking for a professional coach. Perhaps it is just as pleasant to work with somebody who doesn't know you at all and is completely unprejudiced towards you.

What type of coach are you looking for?

It is important that you know in advance what sort of help you require:

- *Are you looking primarily for a listener*: somebody who asks you questions, who lets you do the thinking, and acts as an impartial sounding-board?
- *Are you looking primarily for somebody in the same position, or a partner*: somebody who is going through the same change and doesn't simply listen but also asks you to provide a listening ear?

114

- *Or are you looking for a mentor*: somebody who has expertise in that area of change in which you are involved and knows exactly what to do in order to support you through the change you want?

You should realize that the same people can play different roles in different situations. I have been friends with a historian for many years, and he has often played the role of mentor for me. For example, in the period when I still had to develop into a trainer and writer.

Some time ago, he started his own company, several years after I had started mine. And then I was able to act as his coach and help him with questions about personnel and finance. I have always found my own change coaches in my immediate circle of family and friends. But there are, of course, any number of good professional coaches that can help you plan and execute change.

It is very important that you trust the other person. If you choose a listening coach, then you must be sure he or she is really interested in you. If you choose somebody who is in the same position as you, then you must be sure that he or she shares similarities with you. And with a mentor, you have to be convinced of his or her expertise.

I think that it is very important that you share a few fundamental starting points with each other about the change you have chosen. In a company, you will most probably prefer to choose a change manager who believes in the solution you have in mind.

And for support in your private life, for example in solving problems in your relationship, sharing views on important aspects of life is of great importance.

Research: Women, men and the difference in communication

For support during change, many people turn to those in their direct surroundings, for example, their partner. If such a coaching project is to be successful, then it is important that both people have good communication skills. They must be able to discuss relevant problems and discuss the background to some-body's behavior without reproaching each other. And that is not always easy.

Sharon Brehm, an authority in the field of relationships, collected a large amount of empirical research material that shows the difference between the way men and women commu-nicate and the problems this causes in intimate relationships. A small sample from her (very recognizable) findings:

◆ Men are apparently much worse than women at sending and picking up non-verbal signals, such as frowning, laughing, looking at the other person, and shrugging the shoulders.
◆ Men seem to be worse listeners than women, they are less good at comforting people who are distraught, and talk less about relationship matters.
◆ Research shows that when they are married, men are better able to maintain the peace and keep discussions and conflicts focused on the real problem. This can make their spouses think they are cool, disinterested, and insensitive. The above-average insensi-tivity that men show in their relationships with women plays, according to several researches, a central role in marital problems.
◆ On average, women are more likely to reveal their feelings in discussions than men. In their discussions, men are more focused on exchanging facts and achieving practical goals while women are more focused on talking about their emotions.
◆ During conflicts, women are more inclined than men to develop and show strong negative feelings.
◆ On average, women make greater use of psychological pres-sure than men to achieve their ends, such as playing on feelings of guilt.
◆ And finally, women on average reject attempts at reconcilia-tion more often than men.

Bradbury, T. N. and Fincham, F. D. (1992). "Attributions and Behavior in Marital Interaction." In: Journal of Personality and Social Psychology, vol 63, no 4, 613–628. Brehm, S. S. (1991). Intimate Relationships. New York: McGraw-Hill.

3. Clearly agree together how you will do things

If you are working together on change, whether in a company or in your private situation, it is vital that you agree a protocol, a work plan.

Some suggestions on this:

◆ Good coaches work in stages. Follow together the steps in this book. First consider together your intentions, then plan the most important change situations, and then put things into action. You must realize that you will ultimately have to do it yourself.

◆ A good coach is not a yes-man, but one who dares to pose sincere questions that set you thinking. A good coach isn't afraid of being confrontational, points out your responsibilities for your own life, and questions matters of self-deception.

◆ A good coach will try not to dictate what you should think or do. He or she fully understands that maintaining a dialog and posing questions works a lot better than giving somebody a lecture.

◆ A good coach reaches firm agreements with you. Wherever possible; put these agreements down in writing in a *change contract*. That change contract should certainly contain your goals, behaviors, and ways of supporting that behavior.

◆ A good coach does not only talk to you in a business-like way, but is also interested in how you are feeling. He or she shows sincere interest in the feelings of uncertainty that people can experience during behavior change.

◆ A good coach offers encouragement during the actual change. Sees you, phones you, goes running with you, or goes out to dinner with you. And regularly reminds you of the final goal of the change process.

◆ A good coach is patient. Helping others prepare a change process and then supporting them, though it takes at least several months.

The willingness to change in others

Of course, you may not want to change something in yourself, but rather help somebody else or a group of people who are as yet *unaware* of the need for change. For example, at work. That demands empathy, attention, and patience. You will first and foremost have to find arguments that are valid for other(s). And you can only do this if you first discover the aims of the other party. Once you know this, you can then pose questions that help the other(s) recognize the need for change.

In a company, those questions could be:

◆ How important is service to you?
◆ How important is it for you it to keep customers?
◆ How important is it for you to make sure there is a job for you in this company?

In a department, you could ask the following questions:

◆ What is the importance of this department?
◆ What does that mean in our daily work?
◆ What would we have to change to make ourselves indispensable for our customers and this company?

In a relationship, the questions could be:

◆ What do you really expect in this relationship?
◆ What are you prepared to do to make us happy together?
◆ What do you think is necessary for this?

If an empathic dialog doesn't work and there is now a real problem that demands a real solution, then – as we mentioned earlier – it is sometimes necessary to let the others experience the problem for themselves.

A manager in an MBA class told me and his fellow students about a sloppy colleague that he had been working with for ten years. His colleague was completely satisfied with the way things were going; our student was not. He had tried for years to convince his colleague that he should show more responsibility in his work. But whenever projects seemed likely to fail, he would always put in a last minute rescue to save his colleague. The class advised him not to help his colleague on the next occasion. Several weeks later, the student seemed very happy and surprised. He had told his colleague very explicitly just before his colleague left on holiday that he would no longer offer a helping hand on a project that was slowly but surely heading for derailment. And then he had quite demonstratively washed his hands of the project.

After an initial period of indecision and several moments of stress, his colleague had, at the very last moment, postponed his holiday for a week so that he could bring his project to a good conclusion.

QUESTION & ANSWER

Q: What if you are anxious about finding a change coach?
A: If you find it difficult to plan appointments with somebody else, then try to find somebody who you can telephone or e-mail. I have had several good experiences with coaching by telephone and e-mail.

The advantage of e-mail is that people have to write down in their own time their motivations, what they really want, and what their doubts are. It seems that this makes them think more carefully than when you meet each other at an appointed time and only depend on the spoken word.

Q: To what extent is the empathic approach described here necessary in a company? Aren't clear instructions enough?
A: That may be enough for small changes. And also if there is a major crisis. But for most changes between these two extremes, I have only seen bad results from such a dictatorial approach. The hard truth is that managers who regularly slam their fists on the table are laughed at behind their backs by their employees. If the

manager is around, then a lot of people will adjust their behavior temporarily, but when they are once again on their own, they will simply revert to the old way of doing things. Most people want to be appreciated and understood. Any manager who listens to his personnel will automatically get more cooperation.

According to the psychologist Carl Rogers, we can, by placing ourselves in the shoes of another, help the other to put into words desires and ideas that would otherwise remain concealed. This is beneficial to development and the ability to change.

ASSIGNMENT

Your intentions are now clear. The time has come to discuss them with somebody else (if you haven't already done this). And this brings the *Get Real* stage to an end.

First a number of questions:

- ◆ What people need to know about your plans? Who do you need to help you realize your goals? Who would be able to coach you?
- ◆ Set a date for your first discussions with your change coach. In the meantime, you can continue working on your change plan. You should realize that a discussion with a coach can often lead to redefining and focusing your intentions and plans.
- ◆ Imagine that you are cast in the role of change manager or change coach: what are the most important intentions that you have learned from this chapter about the way in which you should approach change in others?
- ◆ *Nice but not obligatory...* If you have a son or daughter of seven or older, then try to explain to him or her what you are planning to do. In my experience, this can be extremely illuminating.

Part 3:
Make Plans

Thoroughly prepare the most difficult change situations

In the previous chapters, we compared personal change to a play of which you are the author, the director, and the lead actor.

- In the *Get Real* stage, everything is about your job as writer.
- In the *Take Action* stage, which will be discussed later in the book, it is mainly about your role as actor.
- But in this stage, *Make Plans,* it is all about your role as *director*.

You are going to prepare yourself for a magnificent first night and a long run of successful performances thereafter. For this, in common with sensible directors, you will concentrate on the most difficult scenes in the play. Or, as we call that in the *Basic Change Method*, we pay attention to the *most difficult change situations*. By this we mean those situations where you know in advance it will prove difficult to apply and maintain your desired behavior.

Our assignment in this stage is to develop a *plan* for activating the desired behavior *within the most difficult change situations* using *powerful stimuli* and *counter-behavior*. Generally we do less than half of what is really necessary to achieve a behavior change; you will read more about this later. We *overestimate* the strength of our intentions. Intentions are *essential* for change, but they are not *sufficient*.

Compare this to climbing a mountain. Naturally, you must first have the intention of reaching the summit. But you know from the start that the climb won't be without difficult moments. It is important that you are prepared for the *awkward situations*. You have to have enough rope, spikes, and links with you, a compass, additional food, and a medical kit.

At the start of this book, you read that our behavior is determined by our intentions *and* by the situation in which that behavior takes place. Everything that is not determined by your intentions is determined by the situation in which you find yourself at that particular moment. We use the term "situation" to mean the *direct environment* in which you wish to exhibit the particular behavior. That direct environment consists of *physical elements* (the space in which you find yourself) and *social elements* (the people around you and the things you are doing). We use the term "change situation" for a special situation in which you wish you exhibit the new behavior you have determined.

You have also read that many changes fail because in the situations where we wish to exhibit our new behavior all sorts of things happen that *contradict* our intentions. We call these *situation stimuli* that obstruct the desired behavior. If we really want to change successfully, then we will have to actively intervene in difficult change situations.

◆ You can do that by making measures in advance that help you change the situation to your advantage (just as a climber takes his climbing equipment with him).
◆ And you can do this by training yourself in the proper procedures in difficult situations (just as a climber trains to keep a cool head in emergencies).

I will be perfectly honest: this part will cost you some effort. But let's look at it positively: if this is the first time you have studied human behavior, then you can learn an awful lot in a short time. And when

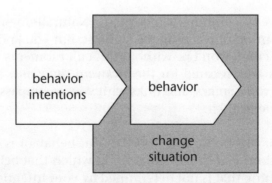

Successful change requires management of behavioral intentions and active intervention in difficult change situations

you understand how situation stimuli influence your behavior and the behavior of others, you will be much better equipped to manage effectively all sorts of changes in the future. If you have formed an accurate behavioral intention using the *Get Real* part of this book, your chance of a successful change is already above average.

In the light of the research that we discuss in this part, you can expect that your chances of a successful change – and particularly *persevering* in new behavior – will have doubled or even trebled.

The *Make Plans* stage is made up of five steps:

I. *Determine which change situations will most negatively affect the desired behavior*
It is not just our intentions that have a strong influence on the behavior we wish to exhibit, but especially the various change situations in which we wish to exhibit it.

II. *Investigate which stimuli in these change situations hinder starting and continuing the desired behavior*
What other people say and do and whatever else happens in a difficult change situation to a large extent determine our behavior at that particular moment. In many cases these stimuli can hinder our intended behavior change. Because, for example, they encourage the old behaviors that we are trying to change.

III. *Think of extra stimuli and counter-behavior that will activate the desired behavior*
Often we will actively have to stimulate the desired behavior within difficult change situations. We have three powerful techniques that we can use for this: reminders (a form of stimuli in advance); reward (a form of stimuli in retrospect); and *counter-behavior* ("extra" behavior that clears the way for the desired behavior).

IV. *Make a concise step plan: warm-up and start, some intermediate steps, and a follow-up*
A good change plan doesn't need to be a thick volume, but should contain a number of obligatory sections. These include a clearly

formulated warm-up and start; various motivating intermediate steps; and a follow-up which makes clear how we can maintain our results.

V. *Make clear agreements about the execution of the plan, both with yourself and with other people*
Often social pressure is necessary for us to come into action. Our change coach plays an important role here. But in addition, we can reach agreements with ourselves and with other people about the execution of our change plans.

Chapter 1:

Determine which change situations will most negatively affect the desired behavior

A few years ago, one of my good friends was invited for the very first time in his life for a job interview. He paced around nervously for a few days. He had always got his previous jobs through informal channels, but this time he would have to take part in a formal interview with the manager and the head of personnel of the company he wanted to work for.

"As long as they stick to factual things about the job, then I'll be okay," was his expectation, "but if they start on about personal matters or things that didn't go as they should have done, in my education and so on… well, then I get stressed out. I'm no good at that."

My friend knew in advance what the most difficult situations in the interview would be. I suggested that we practise those very situations together in advance. The day before the interview, we spent several hours training at my house. Until he was able to formulate a clear answer to an awkward question.

Several times, he got extremely angry: "What a horrible question, you don't think they're going to ask my anything like that? If they do, then…"

The following day, he phoned me from his car. He had got the job and they had asked three of those "nasty questions" that we'd practised. He was able to answer them all without blinking.

What are we going to do?

In the first part of this book – *How change really works* – you can find a lot of examples about how stimuli from your surroundings influence your behavior. In this chapter, we will go into this in more detail. We will discuss step by step the fundamentals of *behavioral analysis* and learn to use them.

Perhaps you are wondering why you need to know this or you are afraid that it will be a dry theoretical story. Let me say two things about that:

◆ The approach discussed in this section is in principle fairly simple, but it does require a change in the way you think. If you get to grips with this approach, you will better understand your own behavior and the behavior of others.
◆ Almost everybody who comes into contact with this approach and makes use of it, is amazed at its practical uses and its effectiveness in daily life and the work environment.

We start with three points:

(1) **How external stimuli direct our behavior.** *How many different types of environmental stimuli can you detect and how do they direct our behavior?*

(2) **The most difficult situations in a change process.** *What different types of situations will you encounter in the process of behavior change?*

(3) **Describing the most difficult situations.** *What stimuli and behaviors play a role in the most difficult situations?*

How external stimuli direct our behavior

Why does certain music give us goose pimples, even if we don't want it to? And how exactly do we learn to read? Why is it that, after practising for a while, we can read without thinking about letters and syllables? These

128

are processes that we cannot explain with theories about conscious thinking and planned actions in humans. We need to adopt a different approach for this.

The scientific area that studies how all sorts of stimuli effect our behavior in specific situations is called *behavior analysis*. This behavior analysis places our human behavior under a magnifying glass and looks in considerable detail at what we humans do in specific situations. The fundamentals of behavior analysis are very simple. They can be broken down into just three elements:

- There are things that precede our behavior: signals, events, the behavior of others. These stimuli in advance are known as "antecedents."
- These antecedents are followed by behavior. That behavior – you may remember it from the first part – can be divided into "external" behavior (*moving and speaking*) and "internal" behavior (*thinking and feeling*).
- And there are stimuli that follow our behavior. Once again these are events, signals, the behavior of other people. These stimuli that happen after behavior are known as "consequences."

The following three chapters deal with these three elements. If we learn to understand the way in which antecedents and consequences are connected with our behavior, we will be better able to understand and influence both our own behavior and that of other people.

Analytical research shows what you may intuitively have suspected. Consequences that we consider pleasant lead to an increase of a specific behavior. Consequences that we consider painful lead to a reduction of a specific behavior. What makes change so difficult is that all sorts of behaviors lead to pleasant consequences (for example, lazing around), but have, in the long term, negative results. On the other hand, behavior that leads to unpleasant consequences (for example, hard work) is often necessary for long-term positive results.

ANTECEDENT ▶	BEHAVIOR ◀▶	CONSEQUENCE
The telephone rings	I answer it	The caller introduces himself
My boss is shouting	I say "calm down"	He gets angrier
My son does a drawing	I express my admiration	He does another one
A guest comes in	I give a friendly smile	The guest smiles back
A colleague asks for help	I solve his problem	He is extremely grateful
My computer crashes	I phone the help desk	I spend 20 minutes in the queue
The traffic lights turn red	I brake	My car stops

Behavior analysis identifies three elements: antecedents (stimuli that trigger behavior), behavior, and consequences (stimuli that are triggered by our behavior)

First behavior, then results

In the previous section – *Get Real* – you formulated your first goals. Goals are the results that you will have achieved at a given moment. A few examples:

◆ A new job or a good business of your own, in a year's time.
◆ Better physical fitness and one stone lighter, in six months.
◆ A more assertive attitude in your business and private life, in three months.
◆ A harmonious family life, in six months.
◆ A department that works within budget and meets deadlines, in three months.
◆ Communicate more clearly with people around you, in six months.
◆ A pleasant, active life after retirement, in three months. Then you accurately translated your goals into behavior necessary for that.
◆ Write and send off two job applications a week.

- Every day before noon, phone at least one potential customer for your new company.
- Listen more and more attentively to your partner and talk less. And do it daily.
- Say what you expect of your colleagues more clearly and more emphatically, every day.
- Every day, consciously eat and enjoy three good meals a day, and don't eat anything else in between.
- Every day, take a "mini-sabbatical" of half an hour at lunch time.
- Every week, spend at least one afternoon with your (grand)children.
- Every week, go for a two-hour run.

A staircase with many steps

We will first have to learn how to manage our behavior before we can achieve results. To make things easier, you could imagine your change process as a staircase. At the top of the stairs is the *change result* you want to achieve. The various actions that you formulated in the previous section can be seen as the *steps* on the staircase.

In this section, we will direct our attention at those steps: small, simple daily behaviors which, step by step, bring us to the change we desire. Often this can take many months.

This detailed approach to each individual step is not a superfluous luxury. Many changes fail because we want to run up the stairs too quickly, often taking more steps at the same time.

As you will have noticed, we talk in behavior analysis of stimuli. That is not because we want to make things complicated, but simply to avoid confusion. If we made use of terms such as "cause" and "result," then many people would think this meant "the cause of their change desire" and "the result of their change exercise." But that's not what behavior analysis is all about.

131

Change is like climbing a staircase. Your daily behaviors form the steps which lead, one-by-one, to results

We will first of all look at the stimuli that *immediately* precede behavior and those that *immediately* follow behavior, and how these occur within a specific situation.

In the following chapters, we will deal with the "molecules" of change: small, individual daily behaviors. We will use examples such as a finger that presses a computer key (behavior) and the letter that appears on the screen (consequence or stimuli that are triggered by our behavior). Once you understand how this works, then you will be able to understand "bigger" behaviors and whole series of behaviors.

Effects of strong stimuli

Decades of behavior analytical research shows that the *stimuli directly preceding* (*antecedents*) and particularly the *stimuli directly following* (*consequences*) behavior have the greatest influence on our daily behavior.

The consequences that follow our behavior *immediately* and *with certainty* have particular influence. Consequences ensure that the behavior will occur more in the future, or just the reverse.

◆ Antecedents (stimuli that trigger behavior) can lead once or more often to behavior. If, for example, a colleague asks for our help, we will initially be inclined to give it.
◆ Consequences (stimuli that are triggered by our behavior) determine whether the behavior is repeated or not. If we experience the consequences of a particular behavior as pleasant, useful, or good, then we will display that behavior more frequently. If we experience the consequences as painful, useless, or bad, then we will stop that behavior. If, for example, helping a colleague causes us problems – we may not have enough time to finish our own work – we will be less inclined to help in the future.

A good example in our modern work environment is reading and answering e-mails. In contrast to other activities that will only lead to *later* and *uncertain* positive consequences, e-mail gives many people in a company the *immediate* and *certain* pleasure of positive consequences: being able to accomplish a simple task quickly and also perhaps win the appreciation of the people we are mailing.

How our behavior is conditioned

When consequences ensure that certain behaviors are displayed more frequently, we can talk of *confirmation* or *reinforcement* of behavior. When consequences ensure that certain behaviors are displayed less frequently, we call that *weakening* the behavior. In this way, behavior can be learned or unlearned. This learning process is known as *conditioning*. Conditioning means literally that behavior is made conditional on stimuli from the environment. Situation stimuli manage, fully automatically, a part of our behavior.

You can compare this with an old-fashioned jukebox. The button you press (the stimulus) determines which song you get (behavior). And that song is always the same unless you change something to do with the buttons or the singles that are kept in the jukebox. The operation of the jukebox (conditioning) is, however, rigid.

In change, conditioning can *promote* new behavior, but it can also *obstruct* it. That is why it is important that we understand something about conditioning before we try to change our behavior either individually or with others.

Sometimes situation stimuli push us in the same direction as our intentions. Then we have the wind behind us in our change efforts. And sometimes, situation stimuli push us in the opposite direction from our intentions. Then we have the wind against us.

2. The most difficult situations in a change process

A little while ago, my wife went on business to the South African capital, Johannesburg, the city with the highest crime rate in the world. To be perfectly honest, I was not particularly happy. Fortunately, a very experienced colleague assisted with the preparations. During these, they discussed the difficult situations in which you could find yourself. How do you react to a mugging? What about physical intimidation? And what should you do if you fall ill? Her colleague had learnt from experience that it was exactly these situations – where there is simply no time for hesitation – that you have to prepare for most.

The importance of difficult change situations

It is important in change processes that you determine in advance what the most difficult situations will be and anticipate them. To return to the example of the jukebox: in what situations would the buttons be pressed resulting in the wrong music? By preparing yourself for this and, in such situations, pressing several other different buttons, you will significantly decrease the chance of start-up problems and back-sliding. I don't know whether you have ever tried to

134

sing a different song while another is playing. All the stimuli – the melody, the rhythm, and the tempo – force you to sing along with the music playing. Except if you have your own backing – for example, a rhythm track – to support you.

The term *change situation* can sometimes cause confusion. Some people are tempted to read more into it than I intend. A change situation is nothing more than an environment in which you wish to display new behavior. Change situations include all sorts of stimuli that can influence our behavior:

◆ Physical stimuli (the space in which you find yourself, furniture, objects, the nature, sounds, light, smells).
◆ Social stimuli (perceptible behavior by others, verbal and body language).

All these stimuli can obstruct or actually encourage our desired behavior. An example: you want as a company to treat customers in a friendlier manner than before. Everybody is in total agreement. But:

◆ On the very day that we are planning to start, it is 30 degrees outside and the air-conditioning has broken down (physical stimuli);
◆ The first three customers behave very rudely (social stimuli).

Just try smiling sweetly and being friendly to your customers.

Three types of change situations

In a change process, some situations are more important than others. The situations where we expect the worst, and where we expect stimuli that will hinder us, are the most important. We can define three different difficult change situations.

(1) *Natural change situations*: for example, the way you organize your daily tasks; interaction with your partner at home; driving

in the car to work. It is in these situations that the greater part of your behavior change will have to take place. What's more, this is where you meet your family and colleagues. Together with other familiar environmental stimuli, they can form an obstacle to behavior change.

(2) *Expected problem situations*: for example, those stress moments at work; getting home later than expected; joining the tail-back on your daily drive to and from work. In such situations there is a chance that you will not carry out your behavior intentions. Situations that lead to tension and insecurity often induce (old) automatic, undesirable behavior patterns.

(3) *Unexpected problem situations*: without anybody suspecting, enormous financial problems arise at work; without seeing it coming, you are suddenly confronted by a possible breakdown in your relationship; on the way to an important appointment, without any way of knowing, you find that the motorway has been closed. You can come up with more examples, but the characteristic of them all is that you have no idea of their nature or timing. In such situations, there is a great chance that you will not carry out your behavior intentions.

All beginnings are extra difficult

Take into account that all three change situations are most awkward when they occur at the *beginning* of a change process. There are a number of reasons for this:

♦ If you leave behind your old habits and learn new ones, this can, to begin with, give you feelings of uncertainty. This is particularly true if you make a radical change to established patterns in your life.
♦ Other people have to get used to your change and will, in certain situations, question your new behavior.
♦ You have often not yet seen any tangible results from your new behavior. Sometimes you have to wait a long while for this. That makes it difficult to adhere consistently to the choices you have made.

♦ In the past, old habits frequently resulted immediately in a good feeling, which only makes the danger of falling back into such old behaviors all the more acute.

At the heart of this section of the book is the question of how to survive in difficult change situations. To do this, we first have to be aware of what those difficult situations will be. It is sensible to list all possible situations that appear problematic to you and then to determine which of these will prove the most difficult. First list them, then select them.

Research: Anticipating change situations helps

According to the German researcher Peter Gollwitzer, it is not enough to set change goals. People who want to change should in particular prepare themselves for situations in which they will display their new behavior (the behavior that is necessary for achieving their change goals). This can be done by, among other things, defining *implementation intentions*.

Implementation intentions are mental rules such as: *if situation X occurs, then I will display behavior Y.*

According to the research of Gollwitzer and various colleagues, these mental rules can even be effective if they have been thought of just once. Mental repetition of the rules and writing them down reinforces implementation intentions.

An example: Just before the Christmas holidays, Gollwitzer asked his students to submit a report within 48 hours of Christmas Eve describing exactly how they had spent that evening. He told them he was doing research into the way people spent Christmas.

One half of the group was then asked to fill in a questionnaire. In it, they had to indicate where and when they would write their report. By doing this, they created an implementation intention. Of the group without an implementation intention, only 33 percent submitted their report within the time specified. Of the group that had filled in an implementation intention, 75 percent submitted their report to Gollwitzer within 48 hours of Christmas Eve. This research together with other experiments undertaken by Gollwitzer show that consciously anticipating difficult situations is essential in change processes.

Gollwitzer, P. M. (1999): "Implementation Intentions. Strong Effects of Simple Plans." In: American Psychologist, vol 54, no 7, 493–503, American Psychology Association.

3. Describing the most difficult situations

Once you know the most difficult change situations, describe them as clearly as possible. You can do it either formally or informally. The informal way is that you describe the situation in your own words: what can happen, where, with whom, when? What will make it difficult in such a situation to adhere to your change behavior? What will you be able to do about it?

The formal way of describing an important change situation is to break it down into antecedents (stimuli that trigger behavior), behavior, and consequences (stimuli that are triggered by our behavior). For this, you can make use of the chart later in this section.

In the *Basic Change Method*, it is not essential to make a formal analysis if you want to change certain things in your life on your own. If, however, you want to work on change with other people, certainly if this is a change in the professional or social sphere, a formal and objective analysis of difficult situations can be helpful.

In the formal approach, you should note down the following things.

◆ First of all, the desired behavior.
◆ Next, the stimuli that precede your behavior and which influence it, the antecedents.
◆ You can make a distinction between physical and social

antecedents: what happens in the environment, what do other people say and do?
◆ Finally, the stimuli that follow your behavior, the consequences.
◆ Consequences, too, can be divided into physical and social consequences.

If you want to work on several behaviors simultaneously and each of these behaviors has a number of difficult situations, the description will take quite a bit of effort. Whether you do it in a formal or informal way.

BEHAVIOR	
Every morning I will phone three customers before 11.00	
ANTECEDENTS	CONSEQUENCES
Natural change situations • Most of the email arrives in the morning • Colleagues always want to catch up on things before lunch • It is always busiest in the morning • I am determined to see things through	• I can't react as quickly to all emails • Colleagues complain that I never have any time for them • I have to catch up on my other work in the afternoon • Customers appreciate me • Long-term, I sell more
Expected problem situations • In the morning, we often have nice chats over a cup of coffee • I am determined to see things through	• I won't be able to take part in these chats • My colleagues are irritated by my absence • My colleagues talk about me behind my back • Customers appreciate me • Long-term, I sell more

Describing the most difficult change situations

139

The chance for successful change increases dramatically. Research often indicates that the chances of success will increase many times. What's more, this analysis provides the most important input for your ultimate chance plan. So you should take time doing it.

QUESTION & ANSWER

Q: Why do people show automatic behavior?
A: A few probable answers are the following. Automatic behavior relieves the brain: we are not capable of concentrating consciously on everything at the same time, so our brains do a lot of things unconsciously and automatically. These also include situations that are dangerous or which involve a high level of uncertainty. In addition, automatic behavior brings stability to our daily lives. We are to a certain degree predictable for ourselves and the people around us. In this way, we can better anticipate and react to the behavior of others.

Q: Is there any possibility of reducing the situation stimuli that work are contrary to your intentions?
A: The stronger your intention, the less grip physical and social situation stimuli will have on your behavior. Two essential mental skills can help you:

◆ the acceptance of a certain level of uncertainty;
◆ the ability to put off the thirst for reward.

The better we are in these skills, the more powerful our intentions become. As children, we had to learn all this step by step, but as adults we also need some training. The American psychologist Carl Rogers said, "You can only get true certainty by being prepared to embrace uncertainty." In addition, there is a whole range of other techniques that you can use to defend yourself against strong stimuli in the most difficult change situations. These techniques are discussed in the following chapters.

ASSIGNMENT

This part was about the influence that all sorts of situations and the stimuli in them exert on our behavior. The first thing that you must do is determine which situations will prove the most difficult in your change process and which stimuli will play a role within these situations.

◆ Take the list with the five accurately described behavior intentions that you made in the *Get Real* stage. Now for each of these behaviors think of difficult situations that you may face during your change process. Which situations concern you the most? If necessary, talk about it with your change coach.

◆ Think about difficult natural situations (*the situations in which you will have to undertake the majority of your behavior change, for example, where you work or at home*), about expected problem situations and unexpected problem situations. Think about where, when, and how your change plans could be threatened.

◆ First make a list, then make a selection. Determine now the *most difficult* situations for each of your behavior changes. Keep the number restricted. It is advisable to include the *unexpected problem situation* in your selection of difficult situations. The reason for this is that measures you devise for this can also be applied when the natural change situation or an expected change situation is *unexpectedly* more awkward than you originally imagined.

◆ Describe these change situations in your own words. Who is present, what happens, where are you, when do they occur? Which characteristics of the situation make it so difficult for starting and persisting in your behavior change? Be careful: you are talking about the characteristics of the situation, not about your characteristics.

◆ For the "unexpected problem situation," you only need describe your desired behavior. The rest will be dealt with in the following chapters.

◆ If you wish, you may also analyze the change situations in the formal way I have described in this chapter: antecedents

141

(stimuli that trigger behavior), behavior, and consequences (stimuli that are triggered by our behavior). Use the chart shown in this chapter. *On the website www.tiggelaar.nl there are several blank charts for various types of change, for example, communal change within organizations.*

Chapter 2

Investigate which stimuli in these change situations hinder starting and continuing the desired behavior

Some companies today are making use of computer software that is intended to prevent physical complaints that can arise from extensive computer use. If somebody has spent a certain amount of time in front of the computer, then a warning appears on the screen suggesting that it might be a good idea to do something else for a while.

When I first heard about this, it seemed a good idea. But unfortunately, in many cases it doesn't work. The warning on the screen has to compete with all sorts of other stimuli in the workplace.

In practice, most people simply click away the warning and then simply continue working. In addition, the nature of the activities has generally not been adapted, so the pressure to continue working is just as great as before.

What's more: if you simply continue working after the warning appears, there are no direct consequences. You don't develop physical complaints an hour after the warning appears, the computer still works, and no angry personnel manager rushes in to reprimand you.

Consequence: the next time the warning appears, you simply click it away. Within a day, this becomes automatic. Apparently, we must now wait for the first casualties to develop repetitive strain injury through constantly clicking away the warnings.

What are we going to do?

In the previous chapter, you became acquainted with the fundamental principles of behavior analysis. You now know more than many "change experts" who often only pay attention to end results and developing ingenious plans. Generally, they do not pay attention to behavior and in almost every case the influence of difficult change situations is completely ignored. If you want to change successfully – whether personally or together with others in an organization – it is essential that you have some knowledge about the way difficult change situations influence our behavior.

Behavior is the central theme of this book. And behavior is enormously influenced by direct stimuli that precede it (antecedents) and particularly by the stimuli that directly follow it (consequences). This is the ABC of change: antecedent, behavior, consequence.

In this section we will go deeper into the way the ABC of change – antecedent, behavior, consequence – actually works.

(1) **Effects of consequences.** In what way do situation stimuli that occur following our behavior influence repetition of that behavior?

(2) **Effects of antecedents.** What is the influence of situation stimuli that occur prior to our behavior?

(3) **Antecedents and consequences that hinder change.** In what way can the conflicting influence of antecedents and consequences frustrate change in behavior?

1. Effects of consequences

Consequences are the stimuli that, within a certain situation, occur *after* our behavior. We start this chapter with consequences because they have the strongest influence on behavior change.

There are two types of consequences:

◆ Physical consequences: events or things in our environment after a certain behavior.
◆ Social consequences: words or deeds by other people in our direct environment after a certain behavior.

Reinforcing behavior

When our behavior gives rise to the *appearance* of a consequence that we experience as pleasurable, the behavior pattern is *reinforced*. We call this positive reinforcement.

Example: When I type a letter on my computer, I look at the screen to see which letters appear. As long as they are the right letters, I happily carrying on typing.

Similarly, when my behavior leads to an *avoidance or removal* of a consequence that I consider *painful*, then my behavior is once again reinforced. We call this negative reinforcement. The term "negative" is somewhat confusing, but is used because a certain consequence is avoided or removed.

Example: When I notice that the battery of the laptop is getting low, I plug the computer into the mains. In this way, I avoid having to stop typing my letter.

A simple rule of thumb: if certain behavior occurs with any frequency, then it is almost certain that one of the above forms of reinforcement is active. Generally you don't have to look long or far to find it.

If, as manager of an organization, you encounter undesirable behavior, then you can be sure that somewhere in the workplace there is something that stimulates this behavior. Consequences that appear immediately and with certainty have the most influence on the repetition of behavior. Consequences that only appear later and are uncertain have some influence, but much less.

Weakening behavior

When my behavior leads to *additional* consequences that I experience as *painful* then the behavior will be weakened by this. Similarly, if my behavior results in the *loss* of something I experience as *pleasant*, then this too will weaken that behavior. The term we use for this in behavior analysis is the same in both cases: *punishment*.

Example: if by accident I place my hands incorrectly over the keyboard, then I will see the wrong letters on my screen and I will stop typing. And when I press a certain key combination, then I lose a portion of my document.

If my behavior does *not* have any consequences, the behavior is also weakened (we call this *extinction* of behavior).

Example: I am happily typing away at my computer and suddenly no letters at all appear on the screen.

If a consequence that, based on our previous experience in the past was certain to occur, does not happen, then an interesting effect arises. We repeat our behavior a number of times and become emotional. This is called *extinction eruption*. If suddenly no more letters appear on my screen, I will repeatedly try out different keys. Then I become angry. And then the behavior gradually dies down.

Do you recognize this? You must do... This is a universal occurrence that probably has something to do with the construction of the human brain. You find it in British people and in aboriginals, in Peruvians and in eskimos.

2. Effects of antecedents

Antecedents are the stimuli that occur *prior* to our behavior. There are two forms of antecedents.

◆ Physical antecedents: events or things in our environment that precede behavior.

146

◆ Social antecedents: words or deeds by other people in our environment that precede behavior.

These stimuli can cause behavior once or on several occasions.

Example: after my computer started acting up while I was typing a letter, the computer technician told me to try it again. I then tried it again.

When the behavior has no, or no negative, consequences, the antecedent will become less and less powerful in its effect on behavior.

Example: at the computer technician's request, I start typing, but no letters appear on the screen. The technician says: try it again, but after two attempts I stop altogether and tell him that the thing simply isn't working.

Antecedents can be put to excellent use for behavior change, but only if they work together with consequences. Consequences are the most important factors in behavior change. We display most of our behaviors because (consciously or unconsciously) we have learned that this behavior leads to consequences that we experience as pleasant. In particular, those consequences that follow *immediately* and *with certainty* have considerable influence.

Intentions are a type of antecedent

Perhaps you now understand why *intentions* on their own are often insufficient for a change. You could think of intentions as a kind of *mental antecedent*: thoughts in our mind that precede our behavior.

Intentions have considerable influence on trying out a new behavior, but little on its repetition. For that we have to look at the direct consequences of the behavior, or at the long-term results.

If we want to change *alone* and place considerable value on achieving a certain long-term goal, for example, because it affects our health, then, in the short term, we can tolerate some painful consequences. But, ultimately, we want positive results. That's why we do it.

If you wish to achieve change with others, then intentions are certainly insufficient on their own. In a group of people – for example, in a company – the motivation will be different from person to person. Painful consequences, feelings of uncertainty and lack of identification with the final goal can quickly frustrate a change process. Pleasant consequences that immediately follow the desired behavior can, however, help change be carried out in an effective and relatively pleasing way.

The problem with many important behavior changes is that the *long-term* results may be pleasing, but the *short-term* consequences are actually painful. Many behavior changes have a checkered start.

This explains why many attempts at change that were enthusiastically greeted to begin with are terminated before they've barely begun.

Research: the path of least resistance

How are antecedents, behavior, and consequences connected together in our heads? How does conditioning work in our minds? Researchers into brain activity have been able to let us have a little glimpse of the process. A short summary. The brain of an adult consists of billions of nerve cells called neurons. These cells have long and short "tentacles" that *almost* connect with the tentacles of other cells, but *not quite*. There are microscopic gaps between these tentacles: "synaptic spaces" is the scientific term.

The average nerve cell has between 1,000 and 10,000 such spaces where contact is *almost* made with other cells and their tentacles. This means that in the brain many thousand billion different connections can be made.

Stimuli that reach our senses from outside (light, sound, smells, touch) or that are created by our own nervous system (hunger, thirst) cause the nerve cells to send signals to each other.

This takes place by means of tiny electrical pulses. Neurospecialists call this "firing" of our brain cells. When such a fired electrical pulse reaches the tip of the tentacle of a brain cell, chemical substances are released (*neurotransmitters*) which cross the synaptic space and activate the neighboring brain cell. That neighboring cell, depending on the type of neurotransmitter, will either pass on the pulse or not, and so on. A portion of these connections come together in the brain area where millions of pulses together form conscious thoughts. Another portion sets emotional feelings in operation. And yet another portion finds its way to our muscles and causes behavior. Millions of nerve cells are involved for even the most simple thoughts, feelings, and behaviors.

Apparently when certain nerve cells regularly pass on impulses from one to another, things work more smoothly. The synaptic "connections" pass on the impulses more easily: they become "stronger" and thus create a "preferential path." Our minds literally follow the path of least resistance. In this way, we make an ever stronger connection in our mind between antecedent, behavior, and consequence. Thus, planned behavior can, step by step, develop into automatic behavior that can be triggered by one or several simple stimuli in a given situation. Neuro-researchers believe that, in general, we repeat those patterns which allow us to react most successfully to our physical and social environment. Our feeling plays an important part in this.

This repetition of patterns leads to ever better connections between the nerve cells involved. This ensures that the external stimuli that trigger certain thoughts, feelings, and behaviors have an increasing impact.

If this stimulus is absent for several weeks or longer, then the route becomes run-down and has to be partially rebuilt when the stimulus makes a new appearance.

Much behavior is thus automatically driven by situation stimuli. This is why many behavior psychologists direct their attention in behavior change at the surroundings and the stimuli these contain.

Sources include: Donahue, J. W. and Palmer, D. C. (1994). *Learning and Complex Behavior.* Needham Heights: Allyn and Bacon. Kolb, B. and Whisthaw, I. Q. (1990) *Fundamentals of Human Neuropsychology.* New York: Freeman & Company. Stein, L. and Belluzzi, J. D. (1989). "Cellular Investigations on Behavioral Reinforcement." In: *Neuroscience and Biobehavioral Reviews*, 13, 69–80.

3. Antecedents and consequences that hinder change

Many change processes are frustrated because the antecedents (stimuli that trigger behavior) and consequences (stimuli that are triggered by our behavior) that emerge in important change situations are contrary to our intentions.

Obstructive stimuli

An example. You work in a construction company where there has recently been a string of accidents. Management wants to implement a drastic increase in safety at work (*strategic aim*). For this reason, a decision has been taken that from now on everybody on the building site is required to wear a safety helmet (*behavior intention*).

The manager tells the staff that in future the wearing of a safety helmet is obligatory (*antecedent*). Everybody follows the new directive (*desired behavior*), but after a few hours the sweat starts pouring down everybody's face (*consequence*). A few people take off their helmets (*undesirable behavior* **and** *antecedent for the others*). In the following 15 minutes, everybody takes off their helmets (*undesired behavior* **and** *consequence for those who started it all*).

When the manager visits the building site the next day, he sees the helmets piled up in a corner (*antecedent*) and decides to read the riot act to the staff (*behavior intention*). But the obstinate look in the eyes of the staff (*antecedent*) makes him quickly change the subject (*undesired behavior*).

150

In nearly all change processes, desired behavior seems to be punished while undesired behavior is involuntarily reinforced. Another example: you want a new job (*strategic goal*); you have decided to write one application letter every single morning (*behavior intention*).

But the very morning you plan to start your first letter, you see an article in the paper about increasing unemployment (*antecedent*). You're distracted and writing the letter (*desired behavior*) takes more time than you'd bargained for. This in turn means you won't be able to get into town for lunch (*consequence*). What's more, that same morning a rejection letter arrives for a job you applied for the week before (*consequence*). The following morning, you don't feel like writing another letter and you decide to skip a day (*undesired behavior*). A few weeks later you realize that you haven't sent off any more letters for quite some time.

Analysis of change situations

Later in this paragraph you will find an analysis chart that will help you investigate the antecedents and consequences you may expect in the most difficult change situations.

◆ For antecedents, we have to determine whether they provoke the desired behavior or quite the opposite – undesired behavior.
◆ For consequences, we must ask ourselves whether they reinforce or punish the desired behavior.
◆ It is also important to know how strong the influence of consequences will be. Is there a weak reinforcement or strong punishment of the desired behavior?
◆ Consequences that *immediately* and *with certainty* occur have a stronger effect than consequences that occur later and are uncertain.

In the *Basic Change Method*, it is not obligatory to make this formal analysis if you are dealing with a change in your own behavior. In practice, some people find this so complex that the courage to change evaporates. If we made such an analysis compulsory, then we would be overshooting the mark. Formal analysis of difficult change situations can, however, help. If you have analyzed the most

BEHAVIOR			
Every morning I will phone three customers before 11.00			
ANTECEDENTS	+/−	CONSEQUENCES	+/−
Natural change situations • Most of the email arrives in the morning	−	• I can't react quickly to all emails	−−
• Colleagues always want to catch up on things before lunch	−−	• Colleagues complain that I never have any time for them	−−−
• It is always busiest in the morning	−	• I have to catch up on my other work in the afternoon	−−
• I am determined to see things through	+	• Customers appreciate me • Long-term, I sell more	++ +
Expected problem situations • In the morning, we often have nice chats over a cup of coffee	−−	• I won't be able to take part in these chats	−−
		• My colleagues are irritated by my absence	−−
• I am determined to see things through	+	• My colleagues talk about me behind my back	−−−
		• Customers appreciate me	++
		• Long-term, I sell more	+

Form for analyzing the most difficult change situations. What effects do the antecedents and consequences have on the desired behavior?

difficult change situations in this way and understood why at a given moment you do something you do not wish to do (anymore), then that is a big step forward in the change process. This form of awareness will, in itself, make it easier for you to exhibit the desired behavior in difficult situations.

QUESTION & ANSWER

Q: This story about conditioning seems rather far-fetched. How do you know whether it is true or not?
A: Conditioning is, at the moment, the only learning process in the

brain that can actually be biologically proven. There are possibly more learning processes, but this one has been proved. It is, however, unnecessary for you to take this sort of research, or these theories at face value. The best way to convince yourself is by carrying out a little experiment in your immediate surroundings. Select somebody near you and choose a behavior that you particularly appreciate in that person. For several days, let the person know how much you appreciate that specific behavior. Do this at moments when he or she is showing this behavior in a perfectly normal and unexaggerated way, and then see what happens.

Q: How can you distinguish between positive and negative reinforcement?
A: Positive reinforcement means that in any case *nothing goes wrong*, that there is no punishment, if the desired behavior is not exhibited. There is only reward if the behavior is actually exhibited.

Negative reinforcement has *no reward*, but the expected punishment does not occur. The fact that the punishment doesn't occur can lead to (strong) feelings of *relief* that makes it *appear* as if there has been some reward.

Smoking is a good example. Smokers light up their cigarette primarily to *avoid* the negative feeling of a lack of nicotine and the want of a certain, acquired (social) action. The anxiety that many smokers experience when they discover they have run out of cigarettes and there is no way of getting any more shows that we are here dealing with a negative reinforcement. There is a *punishment* that follows if the behavior is not exhibited.

But since lighting up a cigarette often gives the smoker a feeling of relief, he or she is more likely to *experience* the cigarette more as a small reward than as a way of avoiding punishment. Despite all the warnings on the packet.

Q: Isn't working with this "antecedent-consequence approach" far too elaborate to be of practical use?
A: If you *don't* analyze in advance what antecedents and

consequences will play a role in an important change process, there is a good chance that the desired change will be involuntarily and subconsciously frustrated. That is the reason why personal change often takes place with such difficulty, and this is also why so many costly change processes in organizations fail. Few people realize how powerful the influence of direct consequences in particular have on our behavior.

What's more: the first time you make use of this approach, the preparation will perhaps take a little more time and effort than you were used to in the past. But after some practice, it will become second nature to think in terms of antecedents and consequences. This behavior, too, will be automated. You will be able to analyze and understand both your own behavior and that of others much quicker than before.

Q: Can you also use this analysis when you tackle change with others?
A: Certainly. What is important then is that you try to place yourself in the position of the person whose behavior you are trying to influence. What effects will certain antecedents and consequences have on their behavior?

By the way, not every single person within a group will react in precisely the same way. Remember the discussion we had in the first part of this book about *change with others*. If you work with a lot of people at the same time, it can be helpful to have them make their own analysis and to participate actively in the change process.

ASSIGNMENT

In the previous chapter you determined what situations will prove the most difficult in the change you wish to achieve. Then you described these difficult situations in your own words. In most cases, that is sufficient. Perhaps you made a formal analysis. That was not obligatory, but there are several reasons for choosing to do this.

Chapter 3

Think of extra stimuli and counter-behavior that will activate the desired behavior

In the past, I carried out several assignments for a large Dutch bank. In that time, I met quite a few people who were determined to make a career for themselves in that organization. That was hardly surprising, because the bank always ended up in the top ten of the best companies to work for. And yet, some time ago, it transpired that a favorable redundancy package could persuade people to change their career plans overnight.

Since the headcount had to be reduced quite significantly, almost three-quarters of the approximately 30,000 people who worked there received a letter at their home address asking them to consider leaving the company. There was a very generous severance proposal: the number of years they had worked for the company multiplied by their current monthly salary. For those above 40 and 50, there were even more generous proposals.

The management of the bank hoped that between two and three thousand people would leave, but they had underestimated the power of the chosen reward. Within a few weeks, no fewer than 6,673 people had chosen to take advantage of the severance package. This included many entrepreneurial spirits who were able to find an alternative job or start up their own company. This enormous number of resignations caught management totally by surprise, the CEO admitted in a newspaper article. He went on to call the people who were leaving "money-grabbers." The massive exodus also created a rather strange feeling among those who remained. Had they made the right choice?

Sometimes a chosen change approach, if you choose the right stimuli, can prove altogether too successful. This was not what management had intended.

What are we going to do?

What do you now have to do with the analyses you made during the previous chapter?

First: if it is at all possible to *avoid* the most difficult change situations and the stimuli encountered in them that oppose your plan of change, then this is absolutely the best course of action during the early stages of your change plan. In practice, if your company introduces new software, it is advisable (temporarily) to restrict access to the old software.

Of course, some situation stimuli that obstruct your change are unavoidable. Because, for example, they are directly connected with the daily social environment in which you operate. If you go to work for the first time as a part-timer amid a group of full-timers, all sorts of verbal and non-verbal signals will occur, not all of which will be positive.

Although it is possible to overcome these influences, you should realize that it is never easy and that you will need help. For this, you can take advantage of three very powerful techniques that can be used to change the situation and your reaction within it. Three powerful techniques will help to climb the individual steps of your change stairway one by one:

(1) **Memory aids: working with antecedents.** *Which stimuli help you in difficult situations to carry out your behavior intentions?*

(2) **Rewards: working with consequences.** *What are the possibilities of reinforcing the desired behavior in important change situations?*

(3) **Countering: working with "extra" behavior.** *In some cases it is*

necessary to support our desired behavior with extra behavior, before or after our desired behavior.

1. Memory aids: working with antecedents

Daily life is full of all kinds of antecedents (stimuli that trigger behavior) that provoke certain behavior in us. You could compare antecedents to pressing a button on a jukebox. Each button has its own song, a certain automatic behavior:

◆ The telephone rings... we pick it up.
◆ Somebody offers his hand to greet us... we take the hand and shake it.
◆ We open the door to our house after returning from holiday... and feel ourselves at home.

It is not complicated to add conscious antecedents to important change situations. The first few times, these stimuli work as a memory aid, with which you remind yourself of your behavior intentions. After some time, these stimuli will work like the button on a jukebox – something that leads to automatic behavior. There are two types of antecedents available to you: physical and social.

Physical antecedents

Anything that will help remind you of important behavior resolutions is permissible. Here are some suggestions for using physical antecedents:

◆ Make use of your diary and its complete contents. Your diary is a good place to remind yourself daily of your life vision, your strategic goals, and your behavior intentions.
◆ Place stickers with reminders for yourself wherever you think you need one. For example, a sticker on the washing machine with the text: "Remember the environment; 40 degrees."
◆ Use posters, symbols, and pieces of equipment in your work

environment, for example, a kitchen timer for allocating a certain time to a particular meeting.

◆ Keep a note in your wallet for that moment when you find yourself in an "unexpected situation." On it, write your deepest and most honest motivation for the desired change.

Social antecedents

If you are with several people, then you can give each other verbal or non-verbal signals to remind each other of the desired behavior or to instruct each other. Social antecedents are extremely strong. We take more notice of each other than we do of "technical" signals.

◆ Make a deal with your partner that, in difficult situations, you will remind each other of a specific behavior intention with, for example, a specific word or look.

◆ Make a deal with your colleagues that you will support each other in a specific change. If you intend to ring two new clients every single day before lunch, then you can agree amongst yourselves that you will all start together at 9.30.

Some practical tips for using antecedents.

◆ Make use of words and symbols that have an emotional meaning for you. Place your own name at the top of your memory aids. This is guaranteed to make sure you read them more frequently.

◆ Use antecedents to remind yourself of your goals and the positive consequences of your change in behavior.

◆ Vary when necessary. If it transpires that the chosen antecedent doesn't work in practice and that you frequently ignore it, the time has come for a different stimulus.

2. Rewards: working with consequences

Sick leave in companies is apparently one behavior that is very sensitive to the conscious use of consequences. An example: in the refuse disposal unit in Amsterdam, annual sick leave had risen to 12 percent. Some time ago, a health premium was introduced: any employee who did not call in sick for three months was awarded a bonus of €150. Within a few months, sick leave had dropped by more than a half.

Choose positive reinforcement

In the previous chapter we dealt with the three different ways in which consequences (retrospective stimuli) influence our behavior. I will repeat them here.

◆ Positive reinforcement: the use of consequences that you or somebody else find pleasurable, so that they reinforce your behavior.
◆ Negative reinforcement: the threat of painful consequences in order to reinforce the desired behavior.
◆ Punishment: the use of consequences that you or somebody find painful, so that undesired behavior is reduced.

Positive reinforcement is by far the most effective way of stimulating desired behavior. Pleasurable consequences that immediately and with certainty follow the behavior form a powerful stimulus for desired behavior.

If you want to apply positive reinforcement for managing your own behavior and that of others it is essential, particularly in the initial stages, to be *accurate* and *consistent* when giving rewards. *Only* reward desired behavior. If the behavior does not meet the required standards, then do nothing.

Physical consequences

Tangible rewards or events that stimulate you or others to display (again) the desired behavior are called physical consequences.

159

◆ These could take the form of presents, financial rewards, more freedom at work, interesting new tasks, an evening on the town, additional days off, an afternoon shopping, a visit to a concert, buying a new book etc.

◆ Bonus points are an interesting and relatively inexpensive alternative. A large number of experiments with so-called *token economies* have shown that using bonus points can be extremely effective. This is particularly true if the bonus points can later be exchanged for (self chosen) real rewards.

The choice of rewards for others is often extremely difficult. Just think how difficult it sometimes is to choose an appropriate birthday present for somebody you don't know all that well. What the recipient likes the most is not the actual present, but the social aspect: the effort you put into finding it.

My advice is: *ask* people what they think is an attractive reward. If necessary, ask the people around you. Or research it in a different way. Beware in any case of making quick assumptions.

Social consequences

Words or deeds from (or directed at) people in our environment are known as social consequences. *Social consequences have three considerable advantages: they are free, they are extremely powerful, and you can take them with you wherever you go.* Some suggestions:

◆ Pay well-intentioned compliments, in words, gestures, or in other ways. During or immediately after the desired behavior has been displayed. Agree at work or at home that you will all do this much more regularly. Do not just use verbal compliments, but also show it non-verbally, in your body language and expression. *Make sure that others don't get the feeling that you are exaggerating: an over-the-top compliment is, for some people, a punishment, not a reward!*

◆ Evaluating together the positive effects of the desired behavior. Anticipating together achieving your goals. These consequences are applicable in both private and professional areas. If this evaluation takes place at a later date, it is important that you first of all conjure up a clear and accurate image in your mind of the displayed desired behavior. Otherwise no connection will be made between behavior and consequences.

- People often have a greater need for attention from others than you think. This is especially noticeable in children. If children do not receive enough attention by showing desired behavior, they will often try to attract attention (in many cases unconsciously and unintentionally) by undesirable behavior. Often this strategy proves extremely effective.

A problem with consequences is that in difficult change situations, nobody else is there to reward you with encouragement and compliments. The only thing to do then is to encourage and compliment *yourself*. We call this *counter-behavior* and will deal with it more fully in the following paragraph.

Research: Record sales after a friendly telephone call

The remarkable results recorded by various companies through positive reinforcement of desired behavior led four researchers in 1975 to see whether this approach would also work with customers.

The experiment took place in a jewelry shop in a small town in Texas. The customer base was first divided into three groups. The first group received a phone call with the message: *I am calling you on behalf of M&M Jewelers to thank you for being one of our customers.* The second group were also telephoned with the same message, but this time they were told that a temporary discount was being given on all sales of diamonds. The third group received no telephone call at all.

In the month following, the turnover was 27 percent higher than in the same month of the previous year. And this despite the fact that, until then, turnover had been more than 25 percent lower than the previous year. The increase in turnover lasted several months. The increased turnover was 70 percent due to those people who had received just the thank-you telephone call and only 30 percent from those who had been offered the discount. Apparently, many customers thought that the thank you in combination with the discount was too transparent, too manipulative. No additional turnover was generated by the control group.

Although some question marks can be placed over the research (the reinforcement only came for most clients weeks, months, or even years after the initial purchase), it does show that simple, unexpected pleasurable consequences can have a very strong effect. Even when involving people with whom we only have a very vague relationship.

Since 1975, technology has made enormous strides. Many companies today work with databases and make use of professional telemarketing agencies. The knowledge of human behavior, however, does not seem to have undergone a similar growth.

◆ Many telephone sales pitches take place in difficult, busy situations (much telemarketing is carried out around the time of the evening meal, the busiest time for a family).
◆ The great majority of telephone sales are made up of antecedents (*for example, asking whether you would like to buy something new or try it out*).
◆ Consciously using pleasurable consequences, for example, the social reward of getting people to tell something of themselves or their needs, hardly plays any role.

Carey, R. J., Clique, S. H., Leighton, B. A. and Milton, F. (1976). "A Test of Positive Reinforcement of Customers," in Journal of Marketing, October 1976.

3. Countering: working with "extra" behavior

If you suspect that, despite applying various antecedents and consequences in the change situation, it will still prove difficult to display the desired behavior, *countering* can be a good solution.

Countering literally means making defensive moves. It is all about defending your desired behavior from negative influences in difficult change situations with "extra behavior."

A powerful technique

Countering is a technique from behavioral analysis and is recommended by both cognitive and behavioral psychologists in behavior change. It means that in the most difficult change situations, you devise, in addition to the desired behavior, several *supporting behaviors* that help in the execution of the desired behavior. A few examples:

◆ Your goal is to achieve a better balance between work and private life. The desired behavior is that you more frequently say "no" to additional work and overtime. You have put a sticker in your diary to remind yourself of this. You are, however, concerned that, despite all your preparations, you will still say "yes" to your colleagues if they ask you to take on certain tasks. In such a case, you could formulate the following counter-behavior: *if somebody asks you to put something in your diary, first ask for a few minutes to consider the matter before you give your answer.* In this way you avoid immediately relapsing into your old pattern of behavior. In those few minutes, you can remind yourself of your goals and your behavior intentions.
◆ If you have decided that in future you are going to be a much better listener to other people, but you are worried that this won't be easy in busy, turbulent situations, then you can decide that, at the start a conversation, you sit down calmly and, during the conversation, consciously leave longer periods of silence.
◆ If you want to live more healthily and have given up smoking, it can help at moments of extreme doubt to take a nice long shower. That makes smoking rather difficult!

We can apply counter-behavior prior to our desired behavior. You can also think up counter-behavior that *follows* your desired

163

ANTECEDENT ▶	COUNTER BEHAVIOR ▶	DESIRED BEHAVIOR ◀▶	CONSEQUENCE
Most email arrives in the morning	I plan to deal with my email between 11.00 and 11.30	I plan to phone three new customers every day before 11.00	I get an order and get all my emails finished before lunch
My partner asks me about my day	I say: "you first"	I listen before I speak	My partner is pleasantly surprised

Applying counter-behavior that precedes the desired behavior: a step towards your desired behavior

behavior. You can address positive thoughts to yourself after a good performance, or consciously enjoy a good feeling after the desired behavior has been displayed.

Counter-behavior is necessary if various steps on your stairway to change are just a bit too high. You are afraid that you won't be able to carry out your behavior intention in difficult change situations.

You could look on counter-behavior as a help up to the desired

ANTECEDENT ▶	DESIRED BEHAVIOR ▶	COUNTER BEHAVIOR ◀▶	CONSEQUENCE
A colleague makes a nasty remark	I respond to negative behavior with a smile	I say to myself: "Good. I won."	My colleague stops making such remarks
It's one of those days when everything goes wrong	I focus on the YES area	In the evening, I write down everything that went well	The next day, I am better able to focus on positive matters

Using counter-behavior that follows the desired behavior

164

behavior. That is why it is essential that the counter-behavior is *easier* to carry out in difficult change situations. Easier than the desired behavior that you defined in the previous chapter. And so counter-behavior does *not* mean that you *substitute* your desired behavior with new behavior that is easier. You simply add an extra behavior that gives you an extra push towards the desired behavior.

To devise your own counter-behavior you should ask yourself the following question: *what would you be able to do successfully in difficult situations that would still promote your desired behavior?*

The same applies here as to all the creative assignments in this book: first list, then select. Develop a number of possibilities and then make a choice based on impact and feasibility.

Four forms of counter-behavior

Counter-behavior can, in common with every other behavior, appear in four different forms.

(1) Movement (motorial counter-behavior):
If certain situations make you uncertain, you can resolve to adopt an active, sporty posture. In situations that cause tension, you can consciously become calmer and take deeper breaths. This type of motorial behaviors frees the way for the desired behavior.

(2) Speaking (verbal counter-behavior):
You can address yourself out loud in difficult situations. In this way, you can consciously remind yourself of your behavior resolutions and the ultimate goal you are striving for. You can also remind yourself of the personal top achievements that you listed in the previous stage. Go ahead and say to yourself: *I can do it. I have consciously prepared myself for this moment. This will be a big step forward.* You can then reward yourself verbally if you display the desired behavior.

(3) Thinking (cognitive counter-behavior):
If you can't talk out loud to yourself, you can address yourself in

your thoughts. You can also direct your thoughts at positive images. For example, images of what it will be like when you achieve your goal. In difficult situations, you can also consciously distract yourself from awkward stimuli. Or even interpret them positively. Consider the criticism that a colleague directs at you as something that is his problem and not yours. It can also prove stimulating to reward yourself mentally for desired behavior.

(4) Feeling (emotional counter-behavior):
You can consciously induce specific feelings from the past by consciously remembering them. But also by what you think and say and how you move.

It is a well-known fact that many sports people try to counter their nervousness by inducing feelings that they remember from their very best achievements.

In the *Get Real* stage, you listed the feelings that are associated with your personal top achievements from the past and with the goals you are striving for. It can be very useful to recall these feelings at the moment you are about to give an important new performance.

Once we have selected a number of effective and attainable counter-behaviors and know which memory aids and rewards we wish to add to the most difficult change situations, we can then assemble all these elements into the chart that appears below. Such a chart describes the desired behavior, the additional antecedents and consequences, and the counter-behavior.

Counter-behavior has to be practised

Counter-behavior *must* be practised quite a lot in advance, so that, in problem situations, you do things *automatically*. This is especially true for counter-behaviors that are intended to break through existing, undesirable patterns of behavior. You can practise in your head by imagining the situations and your counter-behavior as vividly as possible. But it is even better if you ask your change coach

DESIRED BEHAVIOR		
In future, I refuse to plan any business meetings after 18.00		
ADDITIONAL ANTECEDENTS	ADDITIONAL CONSEQUENCES	COUNTER BEHAVIORS
My personal goals on a note in my wallet My behavior intentions on a yellow sticker in my diary for the week in progress	When I have refused twice in succession to make a late appointment, I will take my family out to dinner and we will enjoy together this consciously created extra free time	(before) Adopt a resolute pose, straight, before I answer/ask for some time to think before answering (after) Say to myself: "You have made the right decision"

Chart for describing additional stimuli and counter-behaviors which will promote the desired behavior in the most difficult change situations

to practise these situations and counter-behaviors with you, for example, in role play. It may also help stimulate counter-behavior if you add extra physical antecedents to the change situation: for example, a reminder of your *counter-behavior* in your diary.

A few more examples

Using counter-behavior is an *extremely powerful technique* that can play an important role in personal change processes. A big advantage is, moreover, that you always have your own behavior directly at hand (in contrast to the physical and social antecedents and consequences that you can think up for the most difficult change situations).

You can come up with all sorts of combinations of counter-behavior that can be very effective for stimulating your desired behavior in the most difficult change situations.

◆ If certain remarks that a colleague makes always make you angry or irritable, decide that you will always reply with a smile and, at the same time think: "I am master over the way I react, not her." If necessary, jot down this remark in a notebook that you use in meetings. Afterwards, pay yourself a few compliments – either verbally or mentally.

◆ If you think that you quarrel too much with your partner, decide for yourself and with you partner that in future you will take a time-out when you feel anger coming on, instead of simply going on and allowing things to escalate into a full-scale row. Compliment yourself and your partner if you succeed in inserting such a time-out.

◆ If certain situations make you feel insecure, consciously adopt an assured pose and think about positive things (your last holiday, your children, a recent achievement that you are proud of). Disrupt your feeling of insecurity by consciously doing things and thinking things that contradict this and which cause a positive feeling. Compliment yourself for the way you exude confidence.

◆ Sometimes it can be extremely beneficial to look *technically and clinically* at the situation and to think in terms of antecedents, consequences, and counter-behavior. What my manager does now is clearly an antecedent for incorrect behavior by me, but now I am going to surprise both myself and him. Let's see what the consequences are.

◆ It also helps to see the *humor* of certain difficult change situations. If necessary, make the situation even more absurd in your mind: imagine that your colleagues were in the same difficult situation, but think of them on inflatable water-horses with swimming-caps on their heads. Compliment yourself in retrospect on your sense of humor.

◆ If you want to make it a habit to concentrate on the YES area of your life instead of on the NO area, it helps if, at the end of every day, you write down something good that happened during the day.

◆ Finally: even in "unexpected situations" (*the situation that you know will come but will completely surprise you, lead to stress, and disrupt your behavior intentions*), a time-out is a good move. You are working on customer friendliness and somebody barks at you down the telephone; your are working on your relationship and your partner suddenly announces that he or she doesn't believe in it anymore; you are working on your career and your director informs you that the company has gone bankrupt... Make up your mind first to calm down (you can often do that by taking a few deep breaths and thinking about something pleasurable), and then say out loud that you would like a few minutes to think things over and use those minutes to think very vividly about your goals. In this way, you can generally protect yourself from behavior that you will later regret.

QUESTION & ANSWER

Q: Memory aids, rewards, counter-behavior... and then for every single "step" on the "stairway of change". Isn't it all too much?
A: When individual and collective change projects fail, it is almost always because we "stumble" over one of the steps. Change is not easy: you must not only really want to achieve a change, but must also make use of the appropriate techniques. The use of memory aids and rewards with the most difficult change situations and using counter-behavior are techniques that have proven their effectiveness.

Q: What consequences work best if you want to realize change either personally or collectively?
A: Behavior analytical research shows the following:

◆ *Positive reinforcement* is by far the most effective means of influencing behavior. Stimulating desired behavior through pleasurable consequences that arise immediately and with certainty, is easily the best technique at our disposal.

169

- *Negative reinforcement* is certainly a powerful tool for influencing, but only leads to behavior which allows us to avoid imminent painful consequences. Negative reinforcement will not stimulate extra efforts. Motorists will lower their speed when they see a police car and want to avoid a speeding ticket, but will accelerate again a hundred yards farther down the road. Negative reinforcement leads to behavior that is "just good enough".
- *Punishment* tells us which behavior is undesirable, but doesn't show us which one is preferable. Use punishment only to reduce behavior that will actually obstruct the desired behavior. At the same time, stimulate the desired behavior.
- *Extinction*, withholding all possible consequences of undesirable behavior so that it eventually dies out, is virtually impossible in practice. All behavior leads to one consequence or another.

Q: In the previous section you spoke about the motivating effect of real problems. Isn't that a form of negative reinforcement?
A: The start of successful change often has its origin in a confrontation with real problems. That's true. We don't need to experience the difficulties these problems cause every hour of the day when we work on change.

When I talk in this part of the book about various forms of reinforcement, then I mean the direct daily influences of patterns of behavior. We are not talking about the staircase as a whole, but rather about the various steps that one by one lead to our change goals. Positive reinforcement can help us, whether alone or collectively, to avoid or overcome major problems step by step.

Q: All these techniques seem wonderful. But surely it is all about desiring change deep down inside?
A: Even when people desperately want to change, things often go wrong. If a change process fails, it is almost always due to the influence difficult change situations exert on our behavior.

170

ASSIGNMENT

The central question in this chapter is: what can I do to ensure that I exhibit my desired behavior in the most difficult change situations, so that I can achieve my goals?

In previous assignments, you have described and analyzed the most difficult change situations. Take another look at the following five things:

◆ Devise as many memory aids as possible (in the form of antecedents) and rewards (pleasurable consequences) that can help you persevere with your desired behavior in even the most difficult change situations. Try to think of stimuli that in the past have helped promote similar behavior. Which buttons have to be pressed to stimulate in you a specific behavior?
◆ Determine the impact of each of the listed antecedents and consequences and whether it is feasible to make use of a specific stimulus.
◆ Decide now which antecedents you wish to add to the most difficult change situations and write them down in the way suggested in this chapter.
◆ Decide also which consequences you wish to add to the most difficult change situations and write them down in the same way. Decide which consequences you can introduce yourself and which can be better added by your change coach. Consider working with bonus points that can later be exchanged for an attractive reward.
◆ Determine whether it is necessary to formulate *counter-behavior* for some change situations. You can do that by asking yourself the following question: *What could I actually do in these difficult change situations that would stimulate the desired behavior?* Think up several counter-behaviors and only then select most effective and the most feasible.

Chapter 4

Make a concise step plan: warm-up and start, some intermediate steps, and a follow-up

Some time ago, I made a promise to go to the next family reunion on my bike. It meant cycling about 60 miles. In preparation, I made a list of the names of the villages I would pass on my trip so that I could cycle on without having to stop to consult the map. What's more, I had just read something about attainable intermediate steps in a plan. This seemed a perfect opportunity to put the theory to the test, so even the smallest hamlet found a place on my list.

The theory worked. It was even a bit too accurate for my liking. The day of my trip was wonderful, but I had a very strong head wind. And with such a head wind, even small steps of just a mile or so were far too long.

As I cycled, I made up for myself one intermediate stop after another: first reach that farmhouse; first get to that crossing just a little way ahead, and so on. Twenty stages of three miles on that day were far too much for me. But more than a hundred stages of a few hundred yards – I could just about manage that.

What are we going to do?

In the previous section, you formulated a number of each of the five behaviors that together can lead to the realization of one or more strategic goals. In the last three assignments you have also determined which are the most difficult change situations and have made a choice from possible antecedents, consequences, and counter-behaviors.

Using this, you can in the short term start your new behavior and persevere with it, and, in the longer term, can reach your change goals.

Now we are going to combine all these elements into a simple, concise plan, made up of three sections: the *warm-up and the start, several intermediate steps,* and *the follow-up.*

(1) **The warm-up and the start.** Accurately decide how you are going to warm up and how the first week of change is likely to proceed. Decide how you will measure your behavior.

(2) **Formulate several intermediate steps**. Change takes place step by step. Decide in advance which intermediary stations you are planning to visit.

(3) **Formulate the follow-up**. Most changes are never really finalized. There is period of maintenance necessary for every new plan.

1. The warm-up and the start

Every beginning is difficult, but without a beginning there can be no end, according to a German proverb. You frequently hear complaints about the resistance that is often encountered right at the start of any collective change. And even in personal change, people often feel uncomfortable during the first days of a change process. There are several causes for this *"begin dip."*

Causes of the begin dip

Although we generally associate stress with negative events, positive things can also lead to frustration and stress. Psychologists have shown that pleasant events such as a marriage, addition to the family, change of job, closing a mortgage, and holidays are often important causes of stress. According to some of them, this is due to change. There is also research that shows that it is actually the accumulation of small everyday frustrations, coupled with a major event, that lead to stress. Think of what it is like not to be able to find your toilet bag on the first day of your holiday, or the lack of sleep that generally goes hand in hand with an addition to the family. But there are other reasons as well: the familiarity with specific (social) situations, the stimuli within those situations and the habitual behavior that we have made automatic, are things we have to leave behind. *Every habit that leads to the avoidance of a painful feeling or the enjoyment of a pleasurable feeling is to a certain degree addictive.*

When our subconscious control system is not clear about the immediate advantage of change, it will constantly try to revert to the old behavior.

Both causes result in a negative feeling of frustration and loss that is a characteristic of the beginning stages of a change process. The illustration below shows this.

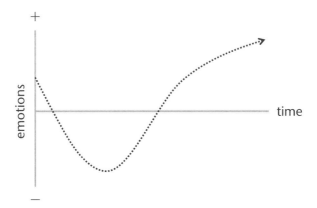

The begin dip: at the start of a change process, we frequently experience feelings of loss and frustration

Medicine to combat the begin dip

Medicine to combat the begin dip consists of five elements:

(1) A thorough warm-up, in which you carefully prepare all the materials for the most difficult situations (stickers, posters, notes, etc.) and have run through the situations on a number of occasions. In any case, you should run through them mentally, but preferably also in real life. This is particularly necessary if you are planning to use *counter-behavior* as a change technique. Remember: a good warm-up prevents injuries. And that is just as true in a change project.
(2) A strict plan for the first week, which offers security and gives you something to hold on to.
(3) Sufficient attention from our change coach and our other support troops.
(4) Sufficient positive reinforcement of our first behavior change.
(5) Daily measurements of our behavior and discussions about it with our coach: have we carried out our intentions?

The first days

It is vitally important that you carefully and precisely plan your first week of change. Try not to think of a behavior change as just something additional: completely clear your diary for at least the first day of a change process and then carefully schedule in only those things that will help you get the behavior change under way and help you persevere with it. For this you should use the situation analysis we discussed in the previous chapters and the situation stimuli that you have selected.

◆ Plan the first day from hour to hour and put everything in the service of the behavior change. A few examples: write the first three letters of application for the new job you are after; remind yourself every hour of your aim to spend more time with your children; remind yourself at every meal of your intention to say clearly to your colleagues what you want and what you don't want; plan a dinner with your partner on the first day so that your intention to spend more time together is put into practice from the very start.

◆ Plan the days of the rest of the week with a little more flexibility, but reserve enough time for matters that support your behavior change. In any case avoid appointments and activities that are likely to cause extra stress. Avoid as far as possible any situation that could make it difficult for you to display your desired behavior.

It really doesn't matter whether you are planning to stop smoking on your own, or that you are collectively, with 1,000 people in a company, planning to change over to a new way of registering hours. The first days are always difficult.

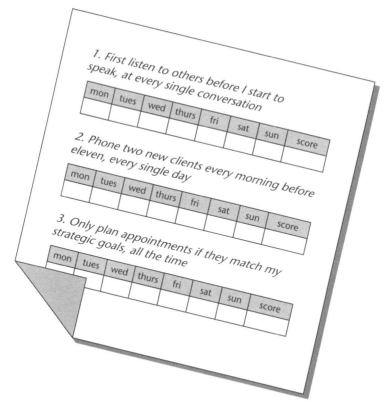

1. First listen to others before I start to speak, at every single conversation

mon	tues	wed	thurs	fri	sat	sun	score

2. Phone two new clients every morning before eleven, every single day

mon	tues	wed	thurs	fri	sat	sun	score

3. Only plan appointments if they match my strategic goals, all the time

mon	tues	wed	thurs	fri	sat	sun	score

Example of a simple form for measuring behavior

◆ Smokers have to spend their first healthy day sleeping well, eating well, and avoiding "smoking situations." Walking, swimming, cycling, showers, and early to bed. Their coach has to be on hand.

◆ People who have to learn a new computer program should make the change with their direct colleagues and immediately tackle some of the most complicated assignments. They should help each other and be able to call in the help of trainers who are standing at the ready. Only when they have overcome the first obstacles should they be allowed to tackle any other work.

Reward the first steps of change in a generous manner, but only *after* they have been successfully taken. Kick-off festivities organized by companies *before* any change has taken place are simply a waste of money. But a party at the *end* of the first successful week is extremely sensible. A reward must be felt as something that *results* from the change, otherwise there is no reinforcement of the behavior change.

Measure and measure

It is extremely important to monitor our behavior and to know for sure whether we are entitled to a reward. To do this, we have to measure every single day whether we have carried out our behavior intentions. Measuring is essential if we are to determine whether any real progress has been made. To do this, we can stick a simple form in our diary with our five behavior intentions written on it. During each work day, we can make a daily note about whether we have achieved our intentions. Discuss these measurements at the start every day with your coach and other people if necessary, for example, with people who are also working on a change.

2. Formulate several intermediate steps

The employees of the American technology concern Cisco work with personal goals that are made on a weekly basis. This may seem rather exaggerated. In many European companies, employees are only expected to work with quarterly or annual goals. And in many companies, individual employees do not have any goals at all.

But if, after a year, it transpires that the (hidden) goals have not been achieved and the company is in difficulty, whose fault is that? And who must bear the responsibility for the consequences? The Cisco approach is quite clever. Instead of one large, secretive, and imposing goal, people work on several thousand small, concrete, and incrementally attainable goals.

The advantage of intermediate steps

The *Basic Change Method* is primarily about forming new behavior habits. To do this, you *measure* in the action stage your desired intentions *daily*. We will deal with this action stage in greater detail in the next section. Actually, these are daily intermediate steps, but you can refine it further.

You can, for example, slowly increase the frequency of the desired behaviors. Suppose that, as a business man, you decide you want to talk to more customers. In the first month, you can ring one customer every day; in the second month, you can increase this to two customers a day. Or suppose that you want to start running to improve your health. You can increase the distance you run every month.

Intermediate steps have three important effects:

◆ They stimulate the self-confidence of those that are changing. Intermediate steps make change an attainable process for everybody.
◆ Intermediate steps provide the opportunity for frequent evaluation and additional support during the process. You feel good when you complete a step successfully. You can also attach an additional reward to specific intermediate steps.
◆ Sufficient intermediate steps ensure that you can progress smoothly. If you only measure the results at the very end of the

179

process you could very well induce yourself and others to put off tackling difficult tasks.

Tips for intermediate steps

◆ Be careful with the extent of the intermediate steps: if the steps are too big, they can lead to disappointment; if they are too small, they can lead to boredom and make you give up altogether.
◆ When planning intermediate steps, think in terms of days, or just a few weeks.
◆ Be careful about the interval between the steps: make sure you have sufficient time to achieve one step in full before starting on the next.
◆ Try to think of these intermediate steps not so much as a checklist, in which you have to cross off one step after another, but rather as an itinerary that helps you keep on the right road. If, on your journey, you miss a turn-off, then you will have to get back on track farther on.
◆ Whatever you do, try to ensure that you achieve several tangible results in a relatively short time, so-called *Quick Wins*. These can have a particularly powerful effect in collective change processes.
◆ Attach an evaluation with your change coach to every step.

Intermediate steps keep up the spirits during a change process. It is important to think up a number of such steps in advance, but it is certainly not forbidden to think up more during the process itself.

Research: Increased self-confidence and better performance

An assessment of our own ability is apparently an important factor in our performance. This assessment, which in daily life we generally call self-confidence, is often, in psychology, referred to as *"self efficacy."* Self efficacy influences both the level of the goals we set for ourselves and the performance we show in trying to reach these goals.

Four researchers – Locke, Frederick, Lee and Bobko – investigated the role of self efficacy in an experiment in which three groups of students (209 people in total) had to perform a brain-storming task. In one minute, they had to think up as many uses as possible for an object. For example: what can you do with a plastic cup?

This test was repeated seven times with each person, using a different object in each repetition. One group was given some training in advance intended to increase the performance level; one group was trained in such a way as to lead to a poorer performance, and the control group was given no training at all.

◆ Prior to each test, the participant was asked to assess his or her own abilities.
◆ The researchers set a goal for various tests.
◆ The participants were asked to set their own goal for various tests.
◆ Prior to each test, the participant was asked about commit-ment to the goal.

The answers to the questions and the performance of the different tests were analyzed statistically per group. This showed that the *strength of self efficacy* and the *level of the goal* were the most important influences on the performance. More important, in fact, than the measured ability or the training given.

One remarkable fact that emerged was that self efficacy, goals, and performances could apparently reinforce each other:

◆ Better performance leads to a high self efficacy.
◆ A higher self efficacy leads to setting higher goals.
◆ Higher goals and a high self efficacy together lead to a better performance.
◆ The better performance leads to higher self efficacy. And so on.

One of the conclusions that we can draw from this is that setting challenging, attainable intermediate steps in a certain task will

181

lead, step by step, to an improvement in performance, probably until a certain maximum is achieved.

Locke, E. A., Frederick, E., Lee, C. and Bobko, P. (1984). "Effect of Self Efficacy, Goals and Task Strategies on Task Performance." In: Journal of Applied Psychology, vol 69, no 2, 241–51, American Psychological Association.
Bandura, A. and Locke, E. A. (2003). "Negative Self-Efficacy and Goal Effects Revisited." In: Journal of Applied Psychology, vol 88, no 1, 87–99. American Psychological Association.

3. Formulate the follow-up

The most successful films do not have a happy ending, but have a sequel. The same is true of change plans. All plans and all new behaviors must ultimately lead to certain results in your daily lives or in your company. After all, you started the change process with a certain aim in mind. You wanted:

- a new job or your own company;
- a better balance between work and private life;
- an important improvement in your family life;
- a change in your working environment;
- to instigate a social change;
- a healthier lifestyle;
- or some similar important change.

Sometimes the aim is easily recognizable. If you have a new job, then you have achieved the most important aim in your change plan. You are enjoying the reward and you can file away your change plan for a future date.

Or can you? Sometimes, after a change process, decline can set in. You will also be able to assess this decline if you measure accurately. You wanted that new job because you expected that it would lead to certain improvements: less time traveling, higher salary, a pleasant working environment, more responsibility. And does the job actually offer all that? Even after you have been doing it for a while?

Continue measuring

It is advisable to keep measuring change processes that seem to have been completed at one-, two-, or three-month intervals. You can plan in these evaluations in advance in your diary. Each time you check your results against your life vision and your strategic aims, you plan in the next evaluation moment. It doesn't take much trouble and yet it ensures that if there is any decline you will catch it at an early stage.

Most forms of change demand ongoing maintenance. A healthy lifestyle is never "finished" and the same is true of a profitable business. These aims demand more than a one-off change. Persevering in these new habits can be difficult. Many people revert to their old habits after many months or even years. That is not just something that happens to former smokers and alcoholics. I will repeat what I said earlier: *Every habit that leads to the avoidance of a painful feeling or the enjoyment of a pleasurable feeling is to a certain degree addictive.*

Certain rules apply to these "permanent change processes."

- *Do not assume too quickly that you are somehow invulnerable.* If we are well advanced in a change process we can become over confident and backslide. Daily measurement of your behavior will help avoid backsliding.
- *Renew your change plan every year.* Every year, set new results that you want to achieve, define new behavior aims, and review once again the list of situations, antecedents (stimuli that trigger behavior), consequences (stimuli that are triggered by our behavior), and counter-behaviors.

Reducing memory aids, rewards and counter-behavior

Most people don't want to become too reliant in their change process on extra antecedents, consequences, and counter-behavior. That is generally not necessary. After a few weeks, our new behavior has, to an important degree, become automatic and the first results (the reason we started it in the first place) lead to a *natural reinforcement* of our new behavior. By that time, we no longer feel insecure in

183

displaying our new behavior. It has become routine. This is the moment that we can start reducing the use of extra stimuli and counter-behaviors. Once you are a few weeks along your path, you can start thinking of making use of these stimuli and counter-behaviors later than before, or actually skipping their use.

Literature on behavior analysis suggests that this gradual reduction has a positive effect on our ability to persevere in our new behavior. Step by step, the behavior becomes more resistant to negative influences.

Nevertheless, it is apparent that *measuring* our own behavior or the results of it remains essential. Often the frequency of such measuring can be somewhat reduced, but it is not advisable to stop this altogether.

People who have lost a lot of weight, but then don't bother to use the scales make it a lot easier for themselves to gain the weight they have lost. And anybody who has set clear financial goals for his or her company, but no longer measures them after the first year can probably forget about achieving any further growth.

QUESTION & ANSWER

Q: You should start your change carefully, or not?
A: Both are possible. But the start of your change must be very clearly marked. Small first steps have the advantage that they are easily attainable and therefore increase your motivation and self-confidence. A somewhat bigger step has the advantage of making the way back that bit more difficult.

On the first morning, it is sensible to do something that is absolutely attainable, effective, and fun. Try to be creative and choose something that suits you or the people you work with.

Some ideas:

◆ If you start a new job or a new company, ring your 20 most important clients on your first morning and tell them that you will be sending them a welcome present.

184

- If you are working on your relationship with other people, on your first morning ring three people with whom you have something to make up. Offer your apologies for what happened, listen to their side of the story, and promise that in future you will behave differently. Reward yourself by doing something pleasant that afternoon with your partner or a good friend.

Q: Is it wrong to carry on using certain antecedents and consequences that you have thought up?
A: It is just like eating, drinking, and vacuuming. Some things are necessary in our lives. Extra antecedents and consequences may, in some cases, remain essential. This is true, for example, of bonus schemes in companies. You should also never get rid of that card for *"unexpected situations."* After all, you never know for sure *when* such an unexpected situation will crop up. If you are afraid of sliding back into old habits, you should keep on working with extra stimuli or counter-behaviors. It is a way of keeping your wits about you.

But you should try to reduce step by step the frequency with which you make use of external stimuli, counter-behaviors, and measurements.

ASSIGNMENT

If we are planning to put together a bookcase from Ikea, we demand clear instructions that can be followed even by somebody with two left hands. But if we want to achieve an important change in our personal life, many people want to do it without making any plan at all and without any structure. That is not very sensible, and that is why we are going to write our own Ikea instructions. A clear, step-by-step instruction for your personal change, or the collective change you are undertaking with others.

(This is also the last major assignment in this book. From now on you will only be set smaller, less time-consuming assignments.)

185

A good plan doesn't need to be thick. For a personal change, all you really need is a couple of sides of A4. For a change in an organization, a maximum of ten pages is enough.

A good plan contains the following components:

(1) Your name and a description in a number of short phrases of your personal talents and abilities.
(2) Your life vision, in a number of short phrases.
(3) Your strategic aims for the coming years – clearly, attractively, and accurately formulated. You should also set yourself a deadline.
(4) The five behaviors that you have chosen for the coming year of change. These must be formulated in a *measurable, attainable,* and *personal* way.
(5) The name and other details of your change coach.
(6) A description of the most difficult change situations, including *"the unexpected problem situation,"* and the measures you will take in the form of *memory aids, rewards and counter-behaviors* to get through such situations successfully.
(7) A description of the way in which you are going to evaluate and measure your behavior daily. Also plan a periodical discussion of these results with your change coach.
(8) A plan for the warm-up and the start-up. When are you going to prepare yourself? On which day will you actually begin? What will you do hour by hour on your first day? What will the first week look like? Which rewards can you expect at the end of the first successful week?
(9) Several intermediate steps. How do you build up your change step by step? At which moments on the way will you make an evaluation? Are there additional rewards on the way, for example, for the first tangible results (the *quick wins*)?
(10) A follow-up for your change. In which way will you handle periodical measurements? Or is there a planning for a renewal of your change, for example, after exactly one year?

Chapter 5

Make clear agreements about the execution of the plan, both with yourself and with other people

Attention from others for our change attempts, progress, and ultimate performance is essential. I see this every week on the evening before my daughter's music lesson. Although she enjoys the lessons and the practising, she is always still a little bit apprehensive. She fanatically plays through each of her pieces of music. The following day, after all, her efforts will be carefully listened to. And if a concert is approaching, then it becomes very tense indeed. Because then dozens of people will be listening to the way the children perform.

It is amazing how little such things change throughout your life. Even some of the managers I know who are well into their fifties still get worked up if they have to present their ideas to their colleagues. Just as my daughter puts in that extra bit of practice on the day before her lesson, so they will sit at their computer deep into the night preparing for their presentation. After all, tomorrow all eyes will be on them.

Having to put up with this pressure day in day out is not a good thing. But a little of this pressure in a change that really demands something from you can be extraordinarily stimulating.

Nearly everybody is susceptible to social pressure. It is sensible to let this work for us.

What are you going to do?

A good change plan is a big step in the right direction. Certainly, if the plan contains an accurate description of new behavior and if careful consideration has been given to stimuli and counter-behaviors, that will stimulate the desired behavior in the most difficult change situations. If you've managed to do all this, then you are much farther than most people who decide to make a change.

Unfortunately, in both our private lives and our business lives, too many plans remain in the bottom drawer. Often it is support and pressure from others that get us to take the first steps.

(1) **Agreements with yourself and others.** *Make a promise to yourself and others about what you are going to do.*

(2) **The advantage of a change contract.** *Making a binding contract about change can be very effective.*

(3) **First make agreements about behavior, and then about results.** *Concentrate in change on the thing that you actually have control over: your behavior.*

1. Agreements with yourself and others

Making agreements and promises can have an interesting effect on people. If you put them down on paper, or put some other effort into them, you will get a positive feeling if you stick to your agreements and a negative one if you break them. The same is true of agreements you make with yourself. Although you can generally break such a promise without causing too much damage, most people don't like doing that.

Consistency and discipline

Our natural desire for consistency, which you have read about earlier, prevents us from too quickly abandoning our intentions and resolutions. We want to do what we promised to do and we want to do things that reflect the image we have of ourselves. This desire to be consistent can be further strengthened by publicly making agreements with other people. This is something we have known for as long as man has existed and something we consciously use. At a wedding, two people publicly promise to be faithful to each other. Many religions have a creed in which people publicly proclaim or confirm their beliefs. And even for political parties there are fundamental beliefs, a motto, or an anthem that is regularly repeated at meetings.

Although this urge for consistency can lead to all forms of self-deception, we can still take advantage of it in our change processes. People who promise the members of their family that they will control their temper in future or send e-mails to colleagues promising to meet a certain deadline will feel highly obligated to keep those promises.

This principle also has another aspect – people are often intrinsically afraid of making promises to other people. Even if they know that no physical or legal consequences will occur if they are unable to keep those promises. Apparently, the social consequences of not keeping one's word are bad enough.

Suggestions for agreements

When we have our change plans ready, we can make this consistency principle work in our favor by making agreements with ourselves and with others. These should include our change coach.

Some suggestions:

- ◆ You can tell other people the date on which your change will start and which intermediate steps you have planned. You can also give a copy of your personal change plan to other people.
- ◆ You can discuss in detail with others how you will behave in the most difficult situations that you have described. It also helps if you agree to contact your coach after each difficult situation.

189

- ◆ You can reach an agreement with others that if you find yourself in a difficult situation and are tempted to abandon your desired behavior, you will first of all telephone each other.
- ◆ Make a firm agreement about one thing: that at fixed times you discuss your behavior measurements with your change coach.
- ◆ This can also work well in organizations. Ask individual employees to explain to personal relations and customers how the change process is going to work and what they can contribute to it.

2. The advantage of a change contract

Research in the field of cognitive consistency has shown that people are more inclined to keep to opinions, agreements, and promises that have cost them some difficulty.

The social psychologist Leon Festinger, for example, suggested that people more strenuously defend both to themselves and others activities for which they receive little pay. We automatically think up arguments to justify our behavior. Contracts that are reached after tough and lengthy negotiations lead to greater satisfaction and commitment from the partners in the negotiations.

We can make use of this principle when designing behavior change in our private lives, or collectively. The *Basic Change Method* in fact makes use of this in all sorts of ways: investigating the need for change, the possibilities and desire for change; analyzing and changing specific change situations and making change plans. All these relatively minor exertions together ensure that the urge to persevere gradually increases. This principle is particularly effective when you undertake change with others, for example, in a company. In that case, let your colleagues actively work to thinking up the various behaviors that are necessary to reach a specific goal.

What is included in a change contract?

One way of being *even more* certain that your change will be a success is to draw up a change contract. You can draw up a change contract with yourself, with your change coach, or with other people.

A change contract contains a summary of a number of components in the change plan you have made. It doesn't require a lot of additional work. The most important elements of such a contract are:

(1) The name of the people entering into the contract. For example you and your change coach.
(2) A description of the proposed desired behaviors.
(3) The way in which these behaviors with be measured and rewarded.
(4) A planning for the start-up and several intermediate steps. Note down the evaluation moments that you plan with your coach.
(5) The signature of those making contract.

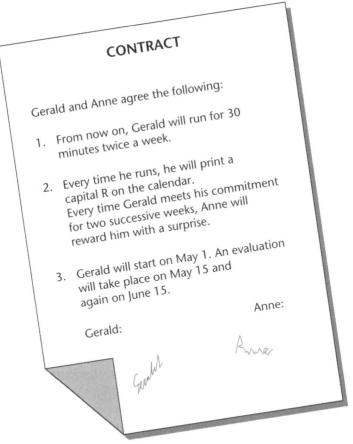

CONTRACT

Gerald and Anne agree the following:

1. From now on, Gerald will run for 30 minutes twice a week.

2. Every time he runs, he will print a capital R on the calendar. Every time Gerald meets his commitment for two successive weeks, Anne will reward him with a surprise.

3. Gerald will start on May 1. An evaluation will take place on May 15 and again on June 15.

Gerald:

Anne:

Example of a change contract

Research: Losing weight fast using a contract

How can you succeed in getting people to lose more than ten kilograms in ten weeks?

Behavior researcher Ronal Mann asked eight people to participate in research into weight loss. He offered them a legal contract in which they agreed to the following:

◆ At the start of the contract, each participant had to hand in a large number of valuable articles, such as jewels, money, and clothes.
◆ These valuables could be redeemed one by one by losing sufficient weight. One article was returned to a participant who lost one kilo.
◆ If, in addition, they achieved their goal weight at intermediate intervals of two weeks, they received a bonus: an additional item was returned to them. At the end, the participants were given back those articles they considered most valuable.
◆ For each kilogram that they gained in weight or for not meeting the intermediate goals, the participants forfeited one of their possessions. Prematurely leaving the program meant they would lose all their valuables.

The participants were allowed to choose their own diet and were weighed three times a week by the researcher. Remarkable results were achieved. In the measurement period preceding the research period, the participants gained on average 0.4 kilograms per week. At the start of the contract period, the participants lost a little more than one kilo each week. During a pause in the program, the participants gained on average 0.9 kilos per week. When the program was resumed, the participants lost on average 0.6 kilos per week.

Mann concluded that the program worked, but pointed out that the participants sometimes went to extraordinary lengths to achieve their goal weight, including taking laxatives. He concluded that in future it would be better in such programs to concentrate on desired eating habits rather than on weight loss results.

Mann, R. A. (1972). "The behavior-therapeutic use of contingency contracting to control an adult behavior problem: Weight control," In: Journal of Applied Behavior Analysis, 5. 99–109. Lawrence: Society for the Experimental Analysis of Behavior.

3. First make agreements about behavior, and then about results

Contracts, promises and agreements are not things to be taken lightly. Making agreements and promises helps you in your change process, but if used incorrectly, they can also have negative consequences.

◆ Employees can promise their customers things that ultimately they can't deliver. This can damage the relationship with the customer.
◆ Similarly, if we make agreements about change in our private life and don't keep these agreements, this can have consequences for our relationships. An important rule when making agreements is only to agree about things that are crucially important (preferably in the short term) and over which we have control. This means that you must first make agreements about behavior. Behavior is something you can contribute yourself to change and over which you have control. This is particularly true now that you know how situation stimuli work. What's more, behavior is something that plays a role in the short term; results generally only emerge later.

Be careful of agreements about results

If you really have an influence on end results, then you can make agreements about them. But if these end results are dependent on a whole range of external factors, such as cooperation with people

193

you do not know, it is not really sensible to include results in the change contract or in verbal promises that you make.

Many mistakes are made by companies in this area. Managers who only work with result-oriented goals for their employees take enormous risks.

◆ If through external circumstances the results are not achieved, this can lead to frustration and stress among employees. If this happens regularly, it can, for example, result in a rise in sick leave, but also to undesirable behavior such as simulating results. Recently, we have increasingly witnessed this phenomenon with top managers.

◆ Within a short space of time, a *who-gives-a-damn* attitude can develop among employees. This has been described by the psychologist Martin Seligman as *learned helplessness*. It can arise within just a few weeks, when people have done their very best and have reached the conclusion that the goals are quite simply beyond their control.

◆ After one or more disappointments, employees will be inclined to distance themselves from the goals and from the people who thought them up.

Managers would do well to negotiate goals with each employee individually. These negotiations can be tough, as long as they are carried out honestly and both parties ultimately commit to them. Always keep in mind that these agreements should only refer to behavior and the results over which the employee has *actual control*.

QUESTION & ANSWER

Q: Isn't working with behavior analysis a sort of manipulation? Particularly when it concerns change in others?
A: The use of positive reinforcement within companies is not only very effective, it also creates a positive relationship between everybody concerned, helps people develop self-confidence and directs attention to the present and the future, rather than

dwelling on the past. In particular, the use of social consequences that people experience as pleasurable leads to a better working environment. It is good to realize this. Behavior analysis studies natural behavior in an objective way; it studies such things as the influence of stimuli from the surroundings on behavior. This is not something that has been thought up by psychologists, but rather something that always plays a role and can be observed by everybody. In fact, we spend our time both at work and at home giving off stimuli to others. These antecedents and consequences *always* have an influence on other people.

Behavior analysis makes us *conscious* of the process and helps us to apply these positively in both our private lives and in our organization. When we use these stimuli to provoke damaging behavior then that is, of course, reprehensible. Not because of the method used, but because of the nature of the behavior it provokes.

If we are conscious of our interventions, but the person we are trying to lead is not aware of them, it can feel rather uncomfortable, even when it is about stimulating positive desired behavior.

The simplest solution is to allow others to participate in defining desired behavior, the antecedents, and the consequences. In practical collective change, many people do not pick up the terminology of behavior analysis, but do recognize the underlying principles in their daily lives.

ASSIGNMENT

The last assignment in this section of the *Basic Change Method*.

◆ Consider for yourself the possibilities you have for making agreements about your behavior change. With yourself, with your change coach, or with other people.

- ◆ Determine whether you only wish to make verbal agreements of whether you should draw up a change contract. Ask yourself why you choose the one rather than the other.
- ◆ Next make agreements about your resolutions. Include a periodical review in which you report your behavior measurements to your coach.

Part 4:
Take Action

Start, measure, and reward desired behavior

"The great aim of education is not knowledge but action," said the British philosopher Herbert Spencer. And that is what this part is all about.

The assignment facing us is: *Measure at the start the behavior and only later the results of the behavior. Ensure that for everything that goes well, there is a regular and immediate personal reward.*

If personal behavior change is like writing, directing, and performing a new play, then we have now reached the eve of the premiere. We have written the script, we have run through all the most important scenes... just a few more rehearsals and we are ready to appear before an audience.

The previous two parts of the *Basic Change Method* have probably cost you quite some time because you had to learn a number of new terms and make this way of thinking your own. (If you find the terms difficult, there is a list of them at the beginning of the most important terms in the *Basic Change Method* at the front of the book.) In the *Get Real* stage, you accurately formulated your behavior intentions. And in the *Make Plans* stage, you took a whole lot of measures to ensure that your intentions would be translated into behavior. My own experience is that this is an intensive process in which you discover a lot about yourself and your behavior. And because of this, you get a better insight into change processes that you undertake with other people.

Take Action explains what is involved in sticking to your plans and in solving change problems that occur during the process. What's more, you will find a number of very practical tips in each chapter that will help you successfully start your change and keep it on the right track. The following five steps will be handled.

I. *Ensure a daily confrontation with the most important elements of the plan.* Keep your abilities, goals, and behavior intentions clearly in mind. Do not forget in which way you will tackle the most difficult change situations with antecedents, consequences, and counter-behavior.

II. *Measure the desired behavior daily and only later include the results.* Many people are uncomfortable with measuring behavior. Measuring behavior, however, is apparently a very powerful tool in behavior change.

III. *Ensure that for everything that goes well, there is a regular and immediate personal reward.* The positive reinforcement of desired behavior is a very effective instrument in change processes. But one person's reward can be another's punishment.

IV. *Don't give up if something goes wrong, but go back one step and persevere.* Backsliding does not mean the end of the change process, but rather an important learning moment. How can we pick up the thread in the best way possible?

V. *Keep on regularly measuring behavior and its results according to your plan; make adjustments if necessary.* Most changes are never "finished". Periodic measuring and checking remains essential. If backsliding is evident, then you should measure and adapt more frequently.

Chapter 1

Ensure a daily confrontation with the most important elements of the plan

A few years ago, I had a conversation with somebody who was involved in arranging finance for new businesses. Every day, he would read a number of reports about trends in various sectors, review the business plans of starters, and hold meetings with the business people themselves.

He thought this last point was the most important: "You first have to know what sort of person you're dealing with. What type of man or woman is it? What is their drive?" Then came the business plan: "You know that many of the prognoses in it won't happen. Generally, the details are no longer valid after a few weeks. But I think it important that people are capable of making a good plan. That they have put down on paper a route for themselves. That they have a clear goal in mind."

A problem for many starters is that during the difficult and busy initial stage they lose sight of their original plan. Of course, it can soon become obvious that the plan isn't any good. But if the plan is good, you still come up against situations and uncomfortable feelings in the initial stage.

It is extremely important in that initial stage constantly to remind yourself of your goal and other important points in your plan. You shouldn't want to see immediate results, but you should want to stick to your plan.

This is not only true for people who want to start their own business, but for all changes that enterprising people think up.

What are we going to do?

When I visited New York for the very first time – and that wasn't so very long ago – I was exhausted at the end of my first day. Undoubtedly, it had something to do with jet-lag, but I am certain that it was also due to the incredible number of stimuli that bombard you every single minute in such a city. If you have no map or no destination, and simply had to rely on where the advertisements, traffic noises, and other signals would lead you, you would most probably be permanently lost in such a city. When you first embark on a process of behavior change it sometimes causes much the same feeling. You are visiting a place you have never been before. And because of all the new impressions you have to deal with, you run the risk of losing sight of your goals and forgetting your plans. This chapter therefore deals with two points.

(1) **Keep your abilities, aims, and behavior intentions in mind.** *What were your talents again? Why did you want to start this change in the first place? What was it you were you going to do in the here and now?*

(2) **Manage the most difficult situations according to your plan.** *Accurately execute your intervention. Use your memory aids, your rewards, and your counter-behavior. And measure every day.*

1. Keep your abilities, aims, and behavior intentions in mind

If we had to ask ourselves what was the aim of every single action we undertook on any given day then we'd soon become a mental wreck. But when embarking on and persevering with an important change, it is essential that we keep our aim in mind. Together with other important elements from our change plan.

I would advise you, certainly at the very beginning, to take your plan with you wherever you go, so that you can remind yourself several times a day what you are doing. Even just carrying your plan with you can provide support in awkward situations.

The most important elements from your plan – your abilities, your goals, and your behavior intentions – deserve at least a prominent place in your diary. But perhaps you can think of other places as well. Your computer desk, your screen-saver, your mouse mat? Or what about the place-mat at breakfast? Perhaps you should stick your goals to your car's dashboard. And it can help if you repeat them to yourself during your morning run.

Make sure in a creative way that you are confronted throughout the day by the most important elements of your change plan.

Your abilities

Reread what you wrote down during your very first assignment in the *Get Real* stage. What were those special actions and learning achievements of which you can still be proud? If it helps, jot down one word in your diary that regularly reminds you of your proudest achievement.

If you occasionally think back over all that you have learned in your life and realize that you still have virtually the same learning ability, you can only reach the conclusion that you have unexploited potential. Perhaps you aren't yet able to do everything you would like to do, but the chance is great that you could learn it.

Don't misunderstand what I am saying here: this is not a plea for vanity or over-achievement. It is a plea to take a realistic look at your talents.

Your goals

Goals are an essential prerequisite of all change. Without a relevant goal, change becomes irrelevant. Goals offer directions, give energy, promote perseverance and the discovery of action strategies and solutions to problems we encounter on the way, as we read in the *Get Real* section.

203

Goals are vitally important when we encounter disappointments in the change process. If the change doesn't go to plan or even fails altogether, a clearly defined *vision* in combination with transparent *strategic goals* can help us develop an alternative route. You should also realize: we are 100 percent certain of what we had yesterday and much less than 100 percent sure of what will happen tomorrow. If we do not have something inspiring and concrete to look forward to, then searching for certainty will become a search in the past and we will not make any progress at all.

Ensure that you regularly re-read your *life vision*. A manager of a large international corporation told me recently that he carried a card in his pocket with his most important aims in life. Regularly – and certainly if he faced difficult decisions or was under enormous pressure – he would, he told me, take that card from his pocket. In this way he could remind himself, in particularly stressful moments, of what he really considered important when he had been able to look at things calmly and dispassionately.

Your behavior intentions

You wrote down five behaviors. Each is *measurable, active,* and *personal* and will now help you achieve your strategic goals.

You should realize that five is quite a lot. In addition, the chance is great that in the wake of these five well-defined behaviors, other smaller behaviors will also change "by themselves." Behavior change is like building a house. If you change a wall, you will also have to change the electrical circuits and a hole will appear in the ceiling that you will also have to fix. A few examples. If you decide that in future you will take a run every morning, you will have to get up earlier. Once you have been doing this for a while, you will start feeling fitter and will have the energy to do things with your partner and children that you never did before.

The same is true at work. If you decide that in future you will not say *yes* to every single request made of you, but only take on those

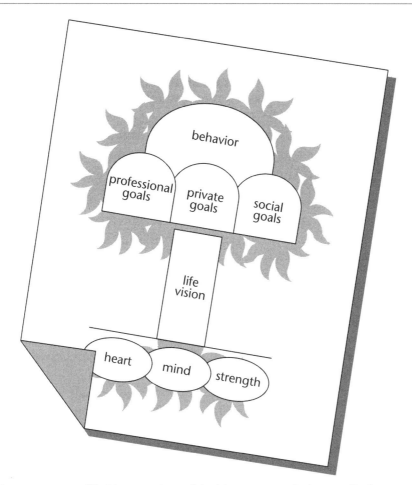

You can carry a filled-in growth model with you to remind yourself of your abilities, life vision, aims, and behavior

things that really matter, you will also have more time to do your important work well. This could lead to you gaining a reputation as a specialist in the area that appeals to you most. Many behaviors are connected with other behaviors. That is why, in a change process, you are often confronted with unexpected and less pleasant things. If you change your behavior, this can mean that your relationship with certain people will come under pressure. It is not always possible to take this into account in advance.

205

Research: Emotions and desires as start and finish of changes

Emotions and desires play a much more important role in the planning of goals and behaviors than many psychologists have assumed until now. That is the hypothesis of researchers Marco Perugini and Richard Bagozzi.

The pleasurable or painful emotions that people expect to experience when they have achieved their goal exercise considerable influence on our desires. Those desires are in turn responsible to an important degree for our intentions. And intentions (together with situations) direct our behavior. To prove that they were right, the researchers took a recognized cognitive theory about behavior (*The Theory of Planned Behavior* by Icek Aljen mentioned earlier in this book) and extended it with a number of factors including "expected emotions" and "desires."

In an initial piece of research, 108 students were extensively interviewed about their plans, ideas, and emotions relating to either their weight reduction or their weight increase. In a second piece of research, 122 students were asked the same questions about more or less study.

The statistical analysis convincingly demonstrated that the expected emotions had an important influence on the desires of the participants and that these desires had a strong influence on their behavior intentions. Thus, the hypothesis of the researchers was proven to be true.

A practical application in change processes (including those within the *Basic Change Method*): it is valuable, before *prior to* and *during* a change project consciously to anticipate the emotions you will feel when you reach your goal. What positive feelings will we experience when we achieve our goal? What negative feelings will we feel if we fail?

These expected emotions have an important influence on your intentions and your behavior.

Perugini, M. and Bagozzie, R. P. (2001). "The role of desires and anticipated emotions in goal-directed behaviors: Broadening and deepening the theory of planned behavior." In: British Journal of Social Psychology, vol 40, 79–98, British Psychological Society.

2. Manage the most difficult situations according to your plan

I repeat again: change costs an investment in attention, energy, and time. And often we don't even invest half of what is necessary to change our behavior successfully. The knowledge contained in this book can certainly help you tackle things with greater success, but that doesn't mean it suddenly becomes easy. You have to make the real investment yourself.

Some people have problems with this. If that's the way it is, then I don't want it, is how they react. They hope they will be able to find a short-cut to easy results. And when a new guru suddenly appears promising that you can change without effort, they are at the front of the queue. An easy change that is doomed to failure is, it seems, preferable to a difficult change that leads to success.

Accurately using the three behavior change techniques that we learned in the previous part – *Make Plans* – will cause some diffi- culty. I do not say this in order to discourage you, but so that you know you have to pay it sufficient attention. Memory aids, rewards, and counter-behavior are intended, it is true, to support you in diffi- cult change situations in your intended behavior, but you will have to give them considerable attention, time and effort. It is sensible to prepare these three change techniques together with your coach.

Memory aids

I would advise you to keep these memory aids as simple as possible. That is true of both the physical, tangible memory aids and social, collaborative aids that you are planning to apply. If you have decided that in future you will take a half-hour break, plan this in your diary for several weeks in advance. In addition, ensure that your mobile telephone or computer gives a signal at the chosen time.

If you need to change things in your workplace or in your home in order to remind you of your behavior change, do this during your warm-up period. Do not put this off until the moment you start your actual change. The same is true for social memory aids. Practise these during your warm-up.

Rewards

Rewards, too, can be divided into physical and social categories. Physical rewards have to be arranged in advance. It is not particularly motivating if you have decided – either with yourself or collectively – on rewards and then are unable to present the reward at the appropriate time. It can, in fact, do no harm to start rewards during the warming up. In that way you ease yourself, as it were, into the change process proper.

The same is true of social rewards. Ensure that you know what you want to say to others or what you expect from others. Do not wait until the starting pistol has gone off, but begin early in the warming up with positive reinforcement of desired behavior.

Counter-behavior

Counter-behavior is a separate subject. This *help behavior*, with which you make the way clear for *desired behavior* in the most difficult change situations, *must* be practised in advance. You can do that in your head by imagining as vividly as possible the most difficult change situations, the counter-behavior and the desired behavior this triggers. But practising "live" with your coach is even better. Think up, if necessary, additional memory aids to remind you of your counter-behaviors. Some advice for each of the four types of counter-behavior that we have identified:

(1) *Movement (motorial counter-behavior)*: Practise your posture and movements several times. If necessary, exaggerate them, so that you do not feel embarrassed at the moment you have to make use of your counter-behavior.
(2) *Speaking (verbal counter-behavior)*: Formulate the messages you

will use for yourself in the most difficult change situations as simply and clearly as possible. Practise them with a feeling for theatrics. Shout them out several times. Later, when you say your message to yourself out loud, it will seem perfectly normal.

(3) *Thinking (cognitive counter-behavior)*: Once again, formulate inner verbal messages as simply and clearly as possible. Practise them first out loud and only then say them to yourself silently. Also practise visual and other thoughts several times over. Speak aloud at first what you are seeing or hearing in your mind.

(4) *Feeling (emotional counter-behavior)*: It is absolutely essential to practise how to conjure up emotions. Probably you will have to call in the help of other forms of counter-behavior. Test the chosen movements, words, and thoughts. Check whether they really do trigger the emotion that you need in the most difficult situations.

QUESTION & ANSWER

Q: Are there better or worse moments to start the execution of your plan?
A: Periods when you are extremely busy are not particularly suitable for starting the execution of your plan. But, it is always busy and will remain busy. Then you have no choice. It is generally best to start the execution of your plan when you are not in your normal daily surroundings. A number of physical and social antecedents (stimuli that trigger behavior) and consequences (stimuli that are triggered by our behavior) are then temporarily out of the picture.

Something similar applies to companies. Don't choose the busiest period in which to start your plan. In the first days in particular, the change process demands a lot of time, energy, and attention.

Q: How should I approach the warm-up? Do you then actually start the change process or not?
A: Be as enthusiastic and serious about your warm-up as about your actual change. Make the warm-up as much fun as possible.

Practise your new behavior in as pleasant a way as possible. Couple conscious positive emotions to your new behavior, so that, later – when you actually begin – you will feel good about your behavior change. If you carry out the warm-up properly, you will quite easily push through to the actual change process.

Q: In the previous section, we discussed several different forms of working with consequences (stimuli that are triggered by our behavior). Now we are only talking about positive reinforcement. Doesn't that restrict the possibilities?
A: I would strongly recommend that you are extremely careful about applying other forms of influence – such as negative reinforcement and punishment – alongside positive reinforcement.

What's more, both negative reinforcement and punishment go hand in hand with a certain feeling of *restriction*, whereas positive reinforcement promotes a feeling of *freedom*. Punishment of others in particular can prove for educators, teachers, and other leaders a *dangerous stumbling-block*. Since others immediately stop undesired behavior when they are punished, this seems to you a form of *positive reinforcement*. You are immediately rewarded for handing out the punishment. The risk is that you then become incorrectly convinced that punishment is a desirable educational and management instrument. Rewarding desired behavior is, as we said earlier, a much more powerful instrument, despite the fact that as leader you only receive the rewards *later*. In fact, when, under similar circumstances, the other person shows the reinforced behavior. One final disadvantage of negative reinforcement and punishment is that applying these techniques in a business or a family requires you to be constantly on sentry duty. Only if there is supervision can the threat of punishment work. I can, I must admit, think of much more pleasant things for educators and managers to do.

Chapter 2

Measure daily only the desired behavior and only later include the results

A friend told me what her family had experienced during a trip to the Belgian Ardennes. One afternoon they had decided to take a walk together. After about half an hour they passed a sign which, promisingly, said "Château." The children were eager to see the castle, so the trip resumed following the direction of the signpost.

"Although the road we walked along was extremely pleasant," she told me, "we couldn't enjoy very much at all. Because after that first sign, we didn't come across any other signs at all. In fact, there wasn't really one of us who believed we would actually find the château. We all thought we had missed a turning or something like that. But finally, after walking for something like two hours, we saw the château in front of us." This story is a good illustration of how change works if you only concentrate on your ultimate goal, don't see anything pleasant on the way, and are not stimulated. The inclination to call things off is extremely powerful.

Just as on the way to a castle in the Ardennes it is nice to enjoy the walk, the surroundings, and each other's company (and occasionally to come across a sign that tells you that you are on the right road), it is important during a change process to pay sufficient attention to the steps that have to be taken one after another.

x

What are we going to do?

In this book we have used a whole lot of metaphors for change. We have compared change to climbing a staircase, step by step. A while ago, I climbed with my children to the top of the Dom Tower in Utrecht. That was an extremely good exercise in climbing a long staircase. The steps in the tower are quite different from the ones I am used to at home. Narrow, steep spiral staircases, with extremely high steps that were also badly lit and worn away.

Each time we moved up a storey – after a short explanation by our guide – I had to make sure where I put my feet so that I didn't stumble and fall. It always took about ten steps before I got the knack and was able to move up faster.

The metaphor of the staircase is quite apt. Of course you want to get to the top, but every single step is an achievement in itself and requires your attention. The first steps in particular are often difficult. If at the bottom you want to run up the steps as quickly as possible, you'll most probably fall flat on your face. And that's why we say: first behavior, then the results.

(1) **Measuring behavior.** *Keep a record from the very first day how much you invest with your behavior in your strategic goals.*

(2) **Measuring results.** *Measure after a time what the results are of your change efforts.*

1. Measuring behavior

I can imagine that this is a subject that worries you a little. Perhaps you think: *I really want to change, but that measuring is just a bit too much of a good thing for me. I'm not going to do it!*

Let us first of all take a look at something else. Recent years have seen a growth in the number of people investing in stocks and shares. Not always with success, but often with dedication and attention.

The media has immediately seen an opportunity: there is a whole range of investment magazines, investment websites, the newspapers have expanded their economic sections, and there is a lot of attention given daily on radio and television to the share index.

This enormous amount of stock exchange news is very interesting for a large number of people. It says something about the development of the economy and the development of their own financial reserves. In fact, we think it perfectly normal that investors are interested in daily news about stocks and shares.

Personal life results

Now back to our subject. *In change processes, you invest your behavior in your personal future life results.* What the yield will be at the end is determined by the course of behavior you take today.

And while at the stock exchange you have to watch the rise and fall of the shares with your hands tied behind your back, when you invest in change you have the key to better results in your hand.

I would dare to state that your personal change news is far more important than the average exchange news. With your change efforts, you invest in your personal development, in the relationship with your partner, in your children, in your career, in your company, in your society. It is all about your personal happiness and that of the people you hold most dear.

If the newspaper carried a daily column entitled *"The personal happiness of Mr Tiggelaar and his family,"* I would be waiting at the front door for the paper to arrive. Well, you can write this daily column yourself, and it will only take you two minutes. Write down every morning whether or not you achieved your resolutions yesterday. Think about the scores for a moment, and then set to work. Nothing more, nothing less.

Don't make it complicated by using percentages or other formulae;

simply write down whether you achieved your resolutions yesterday or not. Yesterday, did you:

◆ spend at least one hour in which you gave your attention exclusively to your children?
◆ take a time-out *every time* a moment of irritation arose?
◆ run your three miles?
◆ compliment your partner at every moment when that was justified?
◆ ring two new clients before 11 o'clock?
◆ spend two hours studying?

I would not make such a point of this if I did not, after countless behavior researches *and* based on my own experience, know with 100 percent certainty how important it is.

Measuring stimulates commitment to and perseverance in our change behavior in a very powerful way. And behavior is and remains the link between nice plans and final results. Incidentally, you can only accurately apply *positive reinforcement* if you measure. You can only inform your *change coach* about your progress if you measure. If you don't measure, then you've done a lot of your preparation for nothing. What's more, if you don't measure, then you will have to rely solely on your change intentions. And unfortunately they make up less than half of what you need for a successful change.

Research: Measuring behavior improves sporting performance

The competition swimmers of the Canadian *Shannon Height Sharks* had considerable difficulty with disciplined training. The 32 boys and girls between the ages of nine and 16 regularly missed training, arrived late or left early. And *during* the training, when they were waiting for their next instructions, the coach was too busy keeping order to pay attention to improving the swimming performance of his pupils. Even though he had dressed them down on several occasions, their behavior had not improved.

Researchers Thomas McKenzie and Brent Rushall suggested placing a board on which the swimmers had to mark down their presence. Only if they were present and had arrived on time and stayed to the end could they place a cross by their name for that particular training. If one of these conditions was not met, all the crosses by his or her name were rubbed out, and he or she had to start all over again.

During this first experiment, the absentee rate fell by 45 percent, late arrival by 63 percent, and early departure by 100 percent. In a second experiment, this method of *self-monitoring* was also applied during the training. Instead of waiting for instructions, the swimmers could follow a program themselves. Each time they finished a part of the training, they could indicate this by placing a cross by their name on a second board. On average, 27 percent more time was spent on actual swimming. And the results followed, too. In several months, the club climbed from sixth place to second in the Canadian province of Nova Scotia. Eleven of the swimmers made it through to the provincial trials instead of just two before the experiment.

McKenzie, T. I. and Rushall, B. S. (1974). "Effects of self-recording on attendance and performance in a competitive swimming training environ-ment." In: Journal of Applied Behavior Analysis, vol 7, 199–206. Lawrence: Society for the Experimental Analysis of Behavior.

2. Measuring results

The ultimate results that you are aiming for with a change process often take a long time coming. That is why we first have to look at behavior. But that doesn't mean that in the beginning we won't see any results at all.

In the previous section I advocated carrying out change in a creative, energetic way. That leads, in any case, to a feeling of satisfaction – the feeling that you have achieved something. And our feelings are an important factor in our change desires. You know that by now.

In addition, it is possible that a first big push, dependent on the sort of change, immediately leads to some results. If you send a gift to 500 important customers on the day you start your company, there's a good chance you will be able to note down a number of appointments in your diary. By ringing them all up, one by one, you further increase your chances.

The first results

In addition, you may have formulated among your intermediate steps a *Quick Win*. A first result can be achieved without too much effort. In companies, people often speak of "low-hanging fruit:" results that you can easily reach and are so ripe that they almost fall off into your hands. Quick Wins have an extremely motivating character.

One of the first results that you will notice in a real change is the emotional "dip" that we have spoken about. A feeling of nostalgia for old habits that do not cost us any energy. Or sometimes even worse: the feeling that that you have to *kick* a behavior habit that was almost literally *addictive*. All behaviors have something addictive about them. They offer structure and a feeling of security that we do not willingly give up. Even if the habit in itself is harmful.

We can complain about this dip, but we can also take advantage of it. If at the start of your change process you are confronted by a certain pain, a feeling of loss, then you know you are on the right path. It is a good idea to reward yourself at such moments.

If you have been undertaking your change process for some time, you will notice a rather remarkable phenomenon. The things that you first did reluctantly become routine and themselves cause a feeling of deprivation if you fail to do them. Your new behavior is beginning to become addictive. Anybody who starts running or doing any other sport will, in the first weeks, have to force themselves to keep up the new behavior. But if you persevere for a few weeks, you will no longer want to miss the training because this makes you feel bad. If you interrupt your new behavior pattern, you become restless, feel guilty, and often don't even know why. First, you use your will to change your behavior, and then the behavior changes your will.

QUESTION & ANSWER

Q: Does measuring always work positively? Even in companies, for example?
A: Certainly not. Measuring is only effective if it is used as the basis for positive reinforcement. It is a cardinal sin for change managers to use measurement of employees in a company for punishment or negative reinforcement. In such cases, you turn the measurement instrument into something worthless, because employees will immediately look for ways of disrupting the measuring. If in a company there is *resistance* to the measuring of behavior or results, then you can say with virtual certainty that the results were or are used for something other than positive reinforcement.

Q: Don't new habits simply keep themselves going, after a certain time?
A: If after a given time we experience results that we personally consider important, this can work as a natural reinforcement of our behavior. From that moment, we can gradually reduce the use of extra antecedents (stimuli that trigger behavior), conse-quences (stimuli that are triggered by our behavior), and counter-behavior. You will find more about this in the previous section. Measuring behavior often needs to be continued for quite some time or even indefinitely. We will return to this later in this section.

Q: Do all habits form themselves as quickly as others?
A: No. The speed with which our habits are formed varies from person to person and from behavior to behavior. Some behaviors quickly lead to natural consequences that are important in our lives. Other habits take longer and forming a habit that remains intact without outside help takes more time.

Chapter 3

Ensure that for everything that goes well, there is a regular and immediate personal reward

My first full-time job was as editor for a weekly magazine. On the day before going to press, everybody worked very hard to gather the very last snippets of news. Every news fact that a journalist was able to uncover was greeted with enormous enthusiasm by his or her colleagues. In one way or another, everybody seemed to think that they were doing something very important on that day (I won't comment on whether that was really the case, but it was certainly the feeling that we all shared). I generally went home feeling very satisfied, The following morning was a different story altogether. The weekly editorial meeting would take place in which we would discuss the previous week's issue. There was little trace of the dogged investigative energy of the day before. The discussions took place in a rather complaining tone. There was always something bad to be said about everybody. The enthusiasm that had been carefully built up the day before, was now calculatedly and professionally demolished.

What are we going to do?

The Vietnamese monk Thich Nhat Hanh wrote something rather beautiful about the importance of positive reinforcement. I will paraphrase it here. *If a plant does not grow, do not blame the plant. You should find out why it does not grow. Perhaps it needs fertilizers, more water, or less sun. But when we have a problem with other people, we generally place the blame on them. Alas that never has a positive effect. Just as it has no effect to try to convince another person with arguments and threats. Only if you understand the other and show this can something change.*

You do not need to be a monk to recognize the wisdom hidden in this statement. Quantitative behavior analysis also shows that reward is far more effective than punishment or the threat of punishment. In addition, rewards promote our feeling of freedom and self-esteem, while punishments give us the feeling that we are being coerced or belittled. More than enough reasons to be generous with rewards in a change project. But they should meet strict conditions.

(1) **When should you reward?** *Rewards should be frequent and immediate following the desired behavior.*

(2) **Personal rewards.** *If a reward doesn't reinforce a person's behavior, they will not look on it as a reward. A reward is only a reward is this is seen as such.*

1. When should you reward?

Ensure that for everything that goes well, there is a regular and immediate personal reward is the title of this chapter. Nicely put, but I would agree that it is not always easy.

First, this rule demands that we are strict and consistent. Only if the desired behavior is displayed do we or the other people with whom we are undertaking the change process deserve a reward.

In this stage, we do not pay attention to any other behavior, except that which obviously obstructs the desired behavior. Second, we must apply the reinforcement *immediately* following the behavior. That is much easier for individual change than it is for collective change.

As manager, you will have to spend a lot of time encouraging your people – particularly at the start of the process. You should set aside several days for this. It is extremely unwise to ration your time and attention at this stage. There is a good chance that *insufficient positive reinforcement* at the start will make all the investment done until then worthless!

By the way, it is an excellent idea to let employees monitor and coach each other. Ensure that they have clear instructions on this.

Rewarding too late can mean that we reward the wrong behavior in ourselves, or in other people. If an employee receives a bonus in December for something he did in May, he will more likely associate it with something he is doing at that specific moment. That can be anything: being aggressive during an evaluation meeting, wearing a new suit, anything you like. It is essential that there is a *direct connection* between reward and behavior, and that works best by giving the reward *immediately* after the behavior has been shown. If there is nothing else to do but reward or thank somebody later, then you should specifically state the reason for doing it: Thank you for helping me get that pile of books from the library last week. If you have only seen the result, ask the other person how he achieved it. Then express your appreciation for the behavior he or she describes.

Should we always reward, or do it irregularly

Another question is whether we should *always* reward desired behavior, or just *occasionally*.

The most effective approach, according to behavior researchers, is to reward new behavior very frequently at the start of the process and then occasionally later on. Once the behavior has been displayed on a large number of occasions, we can gradually adopt an alternate reward schedule. Psychologist Burrhus Frederic Skinner said in an interview: "Look at a hall of people playing bingo. They sit there for hours on end, listening with utter concentration to numbers that are called, and place crosses on their paper with great accuracy. Any employer would give his eye teeth if every single person in his company would work as hard and as accurately."

The commitment people show when playing games such as bingo – but also gambling games such as roulette and blackjack – has, according to researchers, to do with the *variable reward ratio*.

In general, positive reinforcement apparently works better if there is a degree of unpredictability about the reward. I suppose we think that is more exciting. Rewarding yourself is not particularly unpredictable. It helps in this stage if you ask your change coach or somebody else to confer the reward on you.

Be careful: you have to make sure it is *certain* that the reward can be earned and that it is *directly* connected to the desired behavior. When a reward is given at every single instance of the desired behavior being displayed, a certain element of boredom apparently creeps in.

If we don't only want the goal of our change to be attractive but also the road leading to it, we should vary the rewards that are given along the way. This is particularly important in collective change. Make sure that there are sufficient surprises: do not always give out rewards, but reinforce the behavior after a certain time more irregularly. In addition, use different rewards or let others occasionally choose the reward they would like to receive.

Research: Positive reinforcement on the work floor of Emery Air Freight

A classic case study in the field of positive reinforcement in work environments is the story of Emery Air Freight. Emery was and is a freight company that works worldwide. The company currently belongs to Menlo Worldwide and has more than 500 offices in 200 countries.

At the end of 1960, Edward Feeney, one of the company's directors, decided to apply positive reinforcement within Emery; he had been inspired by the publications of the behavior psychologist Skinner. He followed precisely the steps laid down by Skinner:

◆ Identify the situations on the work floor where improvement seems possible.
◆ Research the level of current performance and the stimuli that influence it.

- An accurate specification of the desired behavior and the goals that should be met.
- An accurate measurement of the behavior (in most cases by the employees themselves).
- In the beginning, very frequent positive reinforcement by the management, immediately following the desired behavior.
- Later, less frequent reinforcement by the managers, so that natural reinforcement (for example, higher job satisfaction or other tangible results) can take over.

Even simply investigating performance in advance often leads to remarkable results. Managers are apparently less capable of assessing this than they assume.

They estimated, for example, that containers were, by combining small shipments, filled to a capacity of 90 percent; in fact, the research showed that this on average was only 45 percent. A behavior program that was developed for this achieved remarkable results in just one day: at most Emery locations, on average, containers were filled to 95 percent of their capacity. This resulted in an annual cost reduction of $ 650,000 (and this in the early 1970s).

That the behavior program was responsible for the result was shown when the behavior measurements (because of a change of management) were no longer carried out. The filling of the containers then averaged 50 percent. When the measurements were resumed, the required norm of 95 percent was once again achieved.

The application of behavior analysis also led to considerable improvements in other areas, such as reporting faults and returning customers' calls in the service department. Several Emery managers considered the approach that rested largely on positive reinforcement unworkable. Particularly for those people who, in their eyes, were problem cases. Several of them left the company because of their dissatisfaction with the program.

"At Emery Air Freight: Positive Reinforcement Boosts Performance," in Organizational Dynamics, winter 1973, 41–50.

2. Personal rewards

We said earlier: what one person considers a reward, another person can consider a punishment. Just think of "Employee of the Month" boards that some companies use. Some employees are proud of having their name up there. For others, it is a punishment to have their picture published on the boards. This creates some remarkable effects: some employees who want to make the board, but miss out on it for several months will see this as a punishment and perhaps lose their motivation. Others who do their work well but want to avoid having their portraits on the board may actually under-perform. In addition, reward programs that have people competing against each other frequently have negative consequences. Rating lists in companies and competitions result in one winner and a whole lot of losers. One person enjoys positive reinforcement, the rest receive a punishment.

Programs that only have one type of reward, that have employees competing against each other, and above all reflect the reward preferences of the boss, should be immediately terminated.

Perhaps the managers who think up such programs believe they are offering *positive reinforcement*. In fact, many of the stimuli that are created by such programs are experienced as *punishment*.

A reward, or a punishment – it remains a personal matter. In collective change processes, you will always have to consult the person involved if you are to understand which stimuli will reinforce the desired behavior for him or her personally.

◆ You can do this simply by asking them.
◆ You can also ask people in their environment, which allows for the element of surprise that we discussed earlier.
◆ In addition, we can observe the person concerned: what does the person do when he or she has a choice, what hobbies do they have?

You decide. It will make a bigger impression if a manager offers an avid water-sports lover a day sailing on a classic four-master than if he were to offer a gift voucher for the equivalent amount of money. The personal attention involved in the first present makes the reward (without any additional costs) far greater.

Don't be afraid of rewarding

One of the things you will have to overcome in order to manage change is the reluctance to reinforce yourself and others. Many people think it "exaggerated" to reward "normal" behavior. Employers often think that their staff should "simply" do what they are paid for. Only when "abnormal" behavior occurs will management react. The same is often true in bringing up children. Normal behavior is tacitly accepted and a reaction only follows abnormal behavior. Generally, a punishment. The disadvantage of this approach is that it is *not* clear to the other person what we expect of them. In child-raising, you can descend into a negative spiral of "abnormal" behavior followed by punishment, another abnormal behavior, another punishment, and so on.

In many companies, this means that people work at avoiding mistakes and punishment. And all the time, management complains that employees show so little initiative.

QUESTION & ANSWER

Q: Doesn't this shower of rewards mean that people will ultimately never do anything of their own accord?
A: In psychology there has been much discussion about the use of *extrinsic motivation* compared to *intrinsic motivation.*

External motivation, for example aided by giving rewards, *can*, under certain circumstances, reduce internal motivation, the free will to undertake something. This phenomenon is called over justification. Various research programs into the strength and nature of this phenomenon have given conflicting results.

According to the researchers Carol Sansone and Judith Harackiewicz, two experts in this field, the reduction of intrinsic motivation occurs when self-chosen voluntary behavior is subjected to extra forms of reinforcement. In particular, reinforcement that exerts considerable control over behavior (such as negative reinforcement) and the use of physical consequences are particularly undermining.

This effect does not occur when extra consequences do not occur constantly but sporadically, and when these consequences have a feedback or information function (*how well am I actually doing this?*) *and* when they are social forms of positive reinforcement.

At the start of a change, it is virtually always necessary to use positive reinforcement. But when, after a time, the first results have been achieved and natural reinforcers start to emerge, it is good to reduce where possible the extra antecedents and consequences.

By the way, measurement of behavior should carry on as before. Positive feedback of behavior apparently has a stimulating effect on intrinsic motivation.

Q: It is sometimes essential to correct and criticize things. How do I do that?
A: Stimulation and encouragement work better in changes than pressure and criticism. Always ask yourself whether it is really necessary to voice your criticism about yourself or others. Avoid automatic behavior. If you really must be critical, don't use the obligatory sandwich formula: *You are doing very well... BUT...* Most people think of this as manipulative and don't take your positive feedback seriously. Make use instead of a more positive formula: *You're doing very well. May I give you some tips to help you improve your performance even more?*

By the way, if you have been chosen for self-monitoring by those involved in the change process, then criticism is generally not necessary. Employees can see from their own measurements when they deviate from the behavior goals.

Chapter 4

Don't give up if something goes wrong, but go back one step and persevere

Change demands more than just willpower. If it had just depended on my willpower, I would never have been able to stop smoking, lose weight, or get fitter.

In all three cases, I experienced major and less significant moments of backsliding. Moments in which I was totally convinced that I couldn't change things, that they were anchored in some inaccessible place, in my youth, or elsewhere.

Only by thinking in small steps have I finally managed to become reasonably fit, to lose two stone, and to banish smoking permanently from my life. Of course, backsliding isn't very nice. Of course you throw away a very large investment if, after a few months of healthy living, you take up smoking again. With one cigarette, you trigger an old habit pattern that is so strong that it immediately wants to take control of your life. And it is not particularly sensible, after a few weeks of healthy eating, to indulge yourself in some restaurant or other.

There is something else: if you have succeeded in overcoming an old habit for several weeks or months and replace it with new behavior, then you can do it again. And the second time you will probably do even better.

View backsliding as a learning experience. If, when you are halfway up the staircase, you trip and fall to the bottom, that doesn't mean that that is where you belong. It just means that when you climb the stairs the next time, you have to pay extra attention to that one loose step.

What are we going to do?

Some change experts maintain that as long as you *believe* that you can do something, you can *really* do it. That doesn't only sound too good to be true, it *is* too good to be true. Our human abilities are certainly greater than we think, but they still have their natural restrictions.

The reverse is also true. If we believe that we *can't* do something, we *won't* be able to do it. Simply because we will never make a start on it. This principle makes backsliding in change processes such a difficult phenomenon. Backsliding can seriously damage our self-confidence. We thought we were doing quite well, we believed in it. And then... then it all went wrong.

Backsliding is inextricably linked to change. Whether that is personal change or corporate transformations: it's all about "if at first you don't succeed... " If something goes wrong along the way, we have to take it seriously, but we mustn't throw in the towel. It is best to decide in advance that you will learn from it and then just persevere. This chapter offers such suggestions for this.

(1) **A step back.** *What do we do if something goes wrong along our road of change?*

(2) **Persevere.** *How can we pick up the thread once we have rectified any mistakes in our plan?*

1. A step back

An important change is like a long drive home. You could get a puncture on the way, or even be involved in an accident. In the former, it means doing a repair at the side of the road, in the latter it may mean arranging a replacement car. One thing is certain: you will eventually get home.

In a change process, a variety of things can go wrong. If we look at things very closely, we can identify three types of problems:

A one-off case of backsliding

The *first* type of problem is when you encounter a *single case* of backsliding. For example, for one meal you deviate from your diet. It is important that you do not justify the behavior or in any other way reinforce it. This inclination is found in many people, and also frequently plays a role in groups. We want to be rid as quickly as possible of that nasty feeling that comes with backsliding. But if we too casually accept it, the chances are that the next time the backsliding will be more serious.

It is better to ask yourself how you can prevent backsliding the next time. Did it occur in a situation for which you had prepared yourself? Then it is a good idea to prepare yourself even better for such situations and, for example, add extra stimuli. If it occurred in a situation for which you had not prepared yourself, make sure that you now prepare yourself for such situations. Otherwise there is a good change that the next time you backslide it will be more serious. And, during the week after that first case of backsliding, ensure that you give extra reinforcement to the desired behavior.

Increasing and total backsliding

The *second* type of problem is an *increasing and ultimately total backsliding* in behavior. You no longer display the desired behavior, but a conflicting behavior.

An example. After a number of attempts, the customers of a company decide to return to ordering everything by telephone rather than on the new website. If this happens, even though you had accurately applied reinforcing stimuli in the most difficult change situations, the *conflicting* behavior (for example, using the telephone instead of the website) has a greater reinforcing character than you originally suspected.

You can now take various measures:

(1) *First of all, you can ensure even stronger reinforcement of the desired behavior.* You could, for example, introduce a lottery for those who use the website. Every order placed on the website is good for one

lot that is entered in a draw at the end of each week or month. Anybody who orders via the telephone does not participate.

(2) *Another approach is that you track down the reinforcing factors in the conflicting behavior and where possible use them for the desired behavior.* If the customers continue using the telephone because they enjoy the social contact, have the telephone operators only phone those customers that order on the website. Orders by telephone will only be handled by a voice-response system. Once the measure is introduced, the telephone operator will first be used to phone all the customers who order on the website and thank them for making use of the site. After some time, the operator can telephone occasionally to check whether the customer is satisfied with the service offered.

(3) *A final alternative – if the other measures fail – is to punish the conflicting behavior.* This is an approach that would not be effective in the example we have used, since in most cases the customers would simply decide to take their business elsewhere.

No results

A *third* type of problem occurs when the desired behavior is displayed, but the *results are not, or only partially, achieved.* In that case there are two possibilities. The desired behavior has been correctly chosen, but is *not* being correctly displayed. Or the behavior is being correctly displayed, but has been *incorrectly* chosen: ultimately there is no causal effect between the chosen behavior and the desired results.

In the first case, additional training can help, or a more accurate execution of the desired behavior. *Only* when the behavior is correctly displayed should reinforcement follow.

In the second case, you have to take a step back in the change process. You will than have to take a closer look at the chosen behavior. That sounds more dramatic than it is. Often, slight adjustments prove to be more than sufficient. Perhaps the chosen behavior demands too great a step all at once, and you will have to choose instead to first take a number of smaller steps. In the day-to-day application of behavior analysis, people often discover that, during the change process, the desired behavior has to be adjusted or formulated more clearly. A final word: beware, when you back-slide, of the questions to ask yourself. Do not ask: "Why am I here?" but rather "How did I get here?"

Do not ask: "Why does this always happen to me?" but rather "How can I achieve my goal despite this setback?"

Research: Self-defense against stress and against backsliding

Stressful situations are frequently the cause of backsliding in change processes, Often stress has to do with conflicts between intentions and/or situation stimuli:

- Think of somebody who enthusiastically works on improvement plans for his or her department, but realizes that this could lead to some colleagues losing their jobs.
- Think of the shop assistant who has just attended a course on customer-friendliness, but whose boss refuses to allow her to exchange an article, while the customer stands at the counter and gets increasingly annoyed.

These are typical moments to hang up your good resolutions and to revert to behavior that has always stood you in good stead in the past. Although it is preferable to let change intentions and various situation stimuli to work hand-in-hand, this sometimes proves difficult. Life is full of major and minor disappointments. For this reason, various behavior researchers have thought up methods for controlling *stress reactions* to inevitable adversities. In this way, possible backsliding can be prevented. Often it is a combination of anticipating stressful situations and practising counter-behaviors that combat the stress.

A much-used *physical* form of self-defense against stress is prac-tising relaxation exercises in advance. These include concentrating on taking several deep breaths before reacting in stressful moments. This is often combined with (internal) verbal self-instructions which have also been practised in advance. You say to yourself in your head: *Okay, this is going to be a stressful situation. Remember: breathe deeply and don't let yourself get worked up.*

231

A technique that has proven successful in several research programs is Meichenbaum's *stress inoculation training*. This approach, which is generally undertaken under the guidance of a therapist, consists of three stages.

(1) *Conceptualization*: in this stage, you investigate alone or together with others which situations and which stimuli within them can lead to stress.
(2) *Skill training:* you practise a number of techniques that help reduce stress reactions. Such as relaxation exercises and self-instruction. You also practise confronting stressful stimuli, in which the strength of the stimuli is gradually increased.
(3) *Application and perseverance:* now you put the theory into practice. Often you start with some "home work," in which you consciously seek out (moderately) stressful situations. During this stage, there is generally a certain degree of supervision.

This approach is partly similar to the preparations we discussed in the previous section, but becomes even more important if we are anxious about backsliding, or after backsliding to pick up where we left off.

Beehr, T. A., Jex, S. M. and Ghosh, P. (2001). "The Management of Occupational Stress." In: Handbook of Organizational Performance (New York: The Haworth Press); Meichenbaum, D. (1977). Cognitive-behavior Modification: An Integrated Approach. New York: Plenum Press. Sarafino, E. P. (1966). Principles of Behavior Change. New York: John Wiley & Sons.

2. Persevere

"Reasonable people choose to adapt to the world around them. Unreasonable people choose to adapt the world around them to themselves. That is why progress is due to unreasonable people," wrote the Irish dramatist George Bernard Shaw.

Perseverance is an important quality for people who want to change something. Whether in their own lives or in the lives of others. Perseverance is not just a matter of willpower, but is also about how you consider backsliding. Four tips for making it easier to persevere after backsliding.

(1) *See backsliding as a learning moment.* Analyze what went wrong in a professional way. Don't descend into self-recrimination, but ask yourself how you can avoid this the next time it occurs. The approach outlined in the previous paragraph helps you with this. Realize that you will most probably have to set aside more time, space, and energy for your change than you have until now. Free up extra space in your diary and in your head.

(2) *Prepare yourself even better for difficult, stressful situations.* Virtually all backsliding occurs in difficult, stressful situations for which you are insufficiently prepared. If that is the problem in your case, use the lessons in the previous section and in the research sections in this book to prepare yourself even more thoroughly for these situations. Consciously controlling your stress reactions in difficult situations helps prevent backsliding. Extra and other forms of counter-behavior can also be of help.

(3) *Make persevering fun.* Just as the very start of the change process has to be fun, the second start – after backsliding – should also be worthwhile. Measure every single day, evaluate every single day, and ensure once again that you have sufficient positive reinforcement during your first week. Check your original plan and, once again, make agreements about it with your coach. Do not start reducing your positive reinforcement of the desired behavior until at least a week after your restart.

(4) *Also look at the advantages.* Overcoming problems and difficult situations is something that people have to grow into. This is also true when you want to resume your change process after backsliding. When, after a few months, you look back at this difficult period, you will be glad that you persevered. The famous inventor Thomas Edison was famous for his positive attitude to failed experiments. "Every time we fail, we eliminate yet another way that doesn't work."

QUESTION & ANSWER

Q: Apparently there are all sorts of stimuli that can conflict with each other in a change process. Isn't this all just a bit too complex?
A: Change, managing yourself, and managing others: that is indeed complex, and will always be complex.

That was why I insisted, right at the start, that you ask yourself whether you are working towards a real goal and a real solution, because otherwise it will all be a waste of energy.

If you do not investigate situation stimuli prior to and, if necessary, during the change process then there is a very big chance that various stimuli will continue to conflict with each other and that the change attempt will deliver for management and those involved in the change nothing but frustration. If, however, you have developed some knowledge about how positive reinforcement and other forms of conditioning work, you will be better able to judge whether your goal is attainable, how that goal should be achieved, and how you can stimulate yourself and others towards this end.

Q: What do you do if a real calamity strikes? An accident, for example, or an illness?
A: Some calamities do not, in themselves, obstruct the change process. They only cause additional stress and uncertainty. In such cases, follow your plan for dealing with "unexpected problem situations" and apply stress management. When calamity strikes, (for example, a serious illness), some people backslide into old, bad habits that they have sometimes done without for many years, such as smoking or other unhealthy behavior. It is perhaps understandable that it happens, but in fact it simply multiplies your problem.

If a calamity *really* makes it impossible for you to continue your change, then set a date for resuming your change process. Perhaps you will then also have to start right from the beginning by setting new goals.

Remember that the experience you have gained with any change process will always stand you in good stead. And that includes the way you deal with unexpected, major catastrophes.

Chapter 5

Keep on regularly measuring behavior and its results according to your plan; make adjustments if necessary

People often say that measuring means knowing. And that's true. The trouble is that measuring often reveals things that you would rather not know. That is why we consciously and unconsciously avoid those measurements that could prove unpleasant for us. We prefer self-deception to hard truth. That starts when we are children. Often in such a transparent way that as adults we can laugh about it. "You don't need to check. I really have cleaned my teeth. Honest." "How did my test go? Oh, good, I think. Yes, it went well."

As we grow older, the problems we try to hide become (a little) more serious and the excuses (a little) more refined. "I really don't need to see the doctor. This cough is perfectly normal. My father always had it, and he lived to 85." "Things are really going well in the business. Financially, we're a little bit behind, but on the other hand we are right in the middle of developing new products and we are on the look-out for new premises."

It helps if you make a habit of measuring and evaluating your behavior. Just as some people have a regular medical check-up so that they can catch major problems in the bud.

Regularly reflecting on your life vision, your strategic goals, and your behavior (of last month, last week, or yesterday) may be confrontational, but it helps you intervene as early as possible if problems arise.

What are we going to do?

Our minds are a factory in which stories are constantly being manufactured. Stories that help us tackle the problems and challenges of everyday life. This factory works day and night and the stories produced are often magnificent. But if the factory is not supplied with the right raw materials, the quality of the goods suffers. The stories may still sound wonderful, but if we ask one or two critical questions, we discover that they have little depth to them.

Of course, the factory in our head can get on for a time without the supply of raw materials. After all, we carry a whole lot of information in our memories. But the interruption must not last too long. As the reality around us changes, the value of our information decreases. Often faster than we would wish. It is important that we maintain and, where necessary, revitalize our new behavior. We have to measure now and again whether our resolutions still match the world around us.

The last step in the Basic Change Method revolves around two things:

(1) **Keep on measuring.** *Even if we think we have achieved our results, it is still important to measure at regular intervals. To prevent inadvertent backsliding.*

(2) **Renew according to plan *and* if you backslide.** *When we undertake a planned revitalization of our plan or when we backslide, it is important to mine once more our knowledge of change.*

1. Keep on measuring

Ernest Hemingway said that he kept a tally of the number of words he wrote everyday on large sheets of cardboard. If he felt like fishing, he would set himself the task of writing twice as many words as usual the day before he took the time off. Hemingway told his friends that he kept a running total so that he couldn't deceive himself.

If you have arrived at the final stage of your change plan and you have achieved certain results, there is a danger that a certain familiarity will creep in and you start deceiving yourself. This is what is known as *habituation* (see also the second part, the chapter about self-deception). Because of this we no longer perceive how positive the realized changes have been for us. We no longer notice every day just how great our family is, how well we are doing at work, and how healthy we are feeling. Without a certain degree of variation and stimuli, we can start thinking of our happy existence as routine and dull. That isn't perhaps nice, but it's the way people are.

Open-ended changes

Various sorts of changes, both in your personal life and in companies, can never reach a finishing line. The change does not end with a result that can be cashed in. That is true, for example, of losing weight or working on physical fitness. Often a permanent change of lifestyle is necessary in order to maintain your desired weight or your fitness.

In companies, you see the same thing when working on goals such a customer satisfaction or safety. These changes are never "finished". They are not about results that you can pick up and take home under your arm. What is *essential* in these types of changes is that every year you draw up a new change plan.

Whether your plan has a clear end result or is more open-ended, it is still best in both cases to keep on measuring the results. For change programs with a clear end result, you should do this monthly or quarterly. Jot down in your diary your measuring and evaluation moments some time in advance and on the day, spend a few minutes on the measurement. In other change programs, daily measurement is essential. There is a risk that, after a time, we may start neglecting things. This is certainly dangerous if there is a delay between behavior and results.

In many cases, stopping measurement is followed by a gradual decline in your behavior and your results. Because you have stopped measuring, you will only notice this when it is too late. An external signal will be needed to confront you with your decline.

◆ It is possible that others will point out your decline to you. This demands a certain courage and directness. It is not socially easy to say:
  – Hi, I see you've got problems with your weight again...? or
  – Business is terrible in that company of yours, I've heard?
◆ It can happen that once you cross a certain critical point you will notice your own decline. If you no longer make those daily phone calls to customers, the turnover of your company will gradually decline. If your bank account goes into the red, you will notice for yourself that something is wrong.

Don't stop measuring

In both personal change and organizational changes that have *unstable results*, we often see the so-called yo-yo effect. We are satisfied with a certain result and do not realize that it is only temporary. Next, we become more lax in measuring, after which the results largely evaporate. Only when others or circumstances draw attention to it, do we suddenly wake up and understand what has happened.

Perhaps you are thinking: must I continue measuring my behavior and my results for the rest of my life? The answer is actually another question. How awful would that be if it were the only way to exchange undesired behavior and undesired results for desired behavior and desired results? Think back to the metaphor of the stock exchange: your strategic goals and life vision are surely just as important as the FTSE index.

Now I fully understand that nobody wants to spend their whole life daily measuring their behavior and results. Therefore, you should choose a frequency that seems reasonable and attainable. The most important thing is that you give yourself the chance of adjusting where necessary as soon as possible. It is better to measure once a month than not to measure at all. It will soon become clear when weekly or daily measurements are once again called for.

Research: Do rewards still work after ten years?

Does rewarding desired behavior work in the long term? To answer this question, the results of reward programs in Wyoming and Arizona for safe behavior were monitored carefully, for a period of ten years. This took place in two mines. Mining is one of the most dangerous fields of industrial activity. In 1985, more than 500 people lost their lives in the US alone; there were, in addition, 40,000 injuries that resulted in one or more days of sick leave.

Despite obligatory, intensive information and training programs, the absentee levels in the two mines involved in the research as a result of injury was frighteningly high. In the mine in Wyoming the figure was eight times the national average and in Arizona, three times.

In the early 1970s, a so-called *token economy* was established in both mines. Employees were able to earn monthly points in three ways.

(1) If, during one complete month, they did not sustain any injury, they were awarded several hundred points.
(2) If their team as a whole did not sustain any injury during one complete month, they received several hundred additional points.
(3) If individual employees made usable suggestions to improve safety or had prevented wounds or damage to vehicles, then several hundred, or even several thousand additional points were awarded.

If they did not meet any of these conditions, then no points were awarded. If intentionally no report was made of cases of injury, points were also withheld.

The points could be exchanged for articles at a whole range of shops in the area and through a post-order catalogue. A double-bed could be purchased for 7,600 points, and with 20,400 points you could become the proud owner of an aluminum, gas-fueled luxury barbecue.

The results were remarkable. The annual absentee level as a result of injury dropped in Wyoming by on average 89 percent and in Arizona on average 98 percent. And this brought the mines up to the fourth and twelfth place respectively based on the national average.

The costs of accidents and injuries (before the introduction, these were running at several hundred thousand dollars a year) dropped in both mines by on average 90 percent during the research period, which seemed to show that the introduction of a *token economy* proved to be a very *profitable investment*.

The researchers discovered that the program remained powerful throughout its life time. What's more, they heard from the employees and members of the family that the program was highly appreciated.

Fox, D. K., Hopkins, B. L., and Kent Anger, W. (1987). "The long-term effects of a token economy on safety performance in open-pit mining." In: Journal of Applied Behavior Analysis, vol 20, 215–24. Lawrence: Society for the Experimental Analysis of Behavior.

2. Renew according to plan and if you backslide

For changes that are never completed, such as a new lifestyle or further development of your company, you should renew your plan every year.

Decide every year which results you should strive for, define new behavior goals, and review once more the list with difficult change situations, memory aids, rewards, and counter-behavior. Raise the bar every year.

Although after a while extra antecedents and consequences become less important, Emery Air Freight (see "Research" in the previous chapter) showed that even after several years, most employees cannot do without *daily measurement* of their own behavior.

Apparently, measurement of your own behavior in many cases is not only a prerequisite for consciously applying *extra* consequences, but also for the growth of *natural* consequences. We only have a good feeling about our behavior if we first know that we have actually done well. In addition, a measurable score also leads more quickly to social reinforcement of behavior.

A new plan

We have also seen that for changes that *do* seem to have an end, there can still be the need for a new plan.

If you receive signals from your own measurements or from your environment that your results are declining, then the time has come to take action. Apparently there is a need to reapply certain situation stimuli and we must once again start measuring daily.

If no major changes have taken place in your desire, or in your living circumstances, then you can most probably make do with a new version of your original plan.

Making a new plan is often not the biggest problem. It will only take you at the most a couple of hours if you stay close to your old plan. And if you decide to make a new plan, the experience you have now gained will help you complete it a lot faster than you did the first plan.

Similarly, the implementation of this new plan does not need to be boring: after all, we aim to make change as pleasant as possible.

What is more difficult is that when faced with such disappointments, people become depressed and adopt a defensive attitude: *You see! Two years doing my best, and it's all been for nothing!*

This is a dangerous form of self-deception. The time that we actually spent doing our best, carrying out our plan, measuring our behavior, and applying positive reinforcement has brought us the right results. It is our own laxity in measuring our behavior and results that has caused the decline. Not a very nice conclusion, but the right one.

Attention points for renewal

When we resume or toughen up our plan, it is good to remember a few factors that are essential in the *Basic Change Method*:

◆ Run through your goals. Do you still stand by them? What do you *feel* about the proposed end result?
◆ Is the desired behavior simple and attainable? Is it precisely defined? Is it *Measurable, Active, and Personal*?
◆ Check your goals and behavior intentions very carefully. Is there any hint of self-deception?
◆ Is the list of important situations still accurate? What situations led us to ignore measuring our behavior? What antecedents and consequences could you add to prevent this happening a second time?
◆ Have you included in your plan the need regularly to check your actions with somebody else?
◆ Search for a new coach, or contact the person who previously acted as a sounding-board for you. Tell others that you are once again starting a change project. Incidentally, it is almost inevitable that this renewal will lead to growth. This is illustrated by a quotation from the American poet Oliver Wendell Holmes: *The mind, once expanded to the dimensions of larger ideas, never returns to its original size.* Once you have tasted the things that you can change, alone or with others, you will begin the next change process with greater ambition and greater self-confidence.

QUESTION & ANSWER

Q: Using conditioning techniques on myself isn't such a problem. But using them on others, such as that research in the US dealing with the mines, gives me a Big Brother feeling.
A: This discussion will always dog the use of conditioning. In itself, that's a good thing, since applying this technique, particularly with others, needs to be done carefully and responsibly.

If there is clearly a win-win effect, as occurred in the miners' case, few employees will object to the practical use of these techniques. What's more – and I will repeat it again – there is little point in objecting to conditioning, since this learning process takes place all the time and everywhere. At most, we can object to the conscious use of conditioning techniques.

In the early 1970s, there was much discussion between psychologists and corporate consultants about the use of stimuli and conditioning in the workplace.

This discussion was not about whether or not the approach worked. Countless clinical research programs and applied behavior analysis had already demonstrated that they had a strong to very strong effect. Various research cases included in this book show this.

The primary fear was literally that the use of positive reinforcement in the working environment may prove *too* effective and that employees could, perhaps, become addicted to rewards in their jobs.

For this reason, the leading business writer Peter Drucker was, at the time, an outspoken opponent of the use of conditioning. Some people also thought it rather scary that this sort of influencing took place outside the free will of the employees. In recent years, I have frequently been confronted with these old objections to positive reinforcement in the workplace. A participant in a training session who had experimented in his working environment with the use of antecedents and consequences remarked: *You have to be careful with it. It is much more powerful than you think (...) I found it, to be honest, rather frightening.*

That positive reinforcement has such a strong effect makes clear demands on the responsibility of management in organizations. I personally believe that in collective changes people should be strongly involved in discussions about *both* the development of *behavior intentions* and the planning and application of *change situations*.

Subjects such as corporate philosophy and ethics become more important when we use effective management methods. The behavioral psychologist Skinner has regularly maintained that it is not the *technique of conditioning* that has led to problems, but rather the fact that it has got into the wrong hands. Too many leaders in companies and social institutions use their power and influence for their personal gain.

Part 5:
Working with the
Basic Change
Method

Change is not easy. It demands attention, energy, and time. These are the words we used at the very start of our joint trip of discovery into behavior and change.

If you have read the previous chapters about the *Basic Change Method*, you have already invested a lot of attention, energy, and time in understanding behavior change. More than many people will ever do. This is certainly true if you have carried out some or perhaps all of the assignments.

You are now familiar with the fundamental principles of human behavior change; these apply to both change within a company and change within your personal life; and they apply to change you undertake individually and change you undertake collectively with other people.

Not every change will, of course, run its course without encountering problems, but your ability to change has greatly increased since you started this book. What's more, the things you have learned here will no longer have to be learned experimentally in practice.

Right at the start you read the three demands I placed on the *Basic Change Method*. The method must be:

(1) extremely effective;
(2) simple to use for everybody;
(3) based on accepted scientific research.

This last part of this book is primarily aimed at the second of these principles: translating theory to practice.

You will therefore find examples, tips, and pieces of advice that will help you apply the principles discussed in the first section in realizing change either in your private life or collectively with other people.

The two chapters in this final section are:

I. *Personal change in practice.* We first look at individual changes in different areas: private life, professional life, and society.

II. *Collective change in practice.* Then we look at collective change, in which we concentrate on the professional area, but do not forget change in private life or society.

Chapter 1
Personal change in practice

You often learn important things in passing – between two meetings, during a coffee break. That was the case with FDNT.

An elderly manager that I sometimes worked with told me that he had worked with FDNT for many years. And with considerable pleasure. FDNT stands for: First Do Nasty Tasks, and it works like this: (1) In the morning, make a list of the tasks that have not (yet) been planned into your diary, but which have to be done: telephone calls you have to make, forms that you have to fill it. (2) Give each of these tasks a grade, from least enjoyable 1 to most enjoyable 10. (3) Reward yourself with a cup of coffee once you have completed the list, and then get started with the nasty tasks. (4) Cross out each job you do with a pen (I think this is extremely satisfying, and reason enough to do it on paper, rather than with an electronic organizer or on your computer) and work, step by step, towards the more enjoyable tasks.

Result: each subsequent task is a reward for the one just completed. The day starts with the least enjoyable tasks and ends with the most enjoyable one. Even if it is late in the evening, it is often enjoyable to complete the list.

I now know that this is a practical "time management" application of positive reinforcement and that psychologist David Premack thought up this method more than 40 years ago and that it is called "the Premack Principle". But if you don't mind, I will keep on referring to it as FDNT.

What are we going to do?

It is almost a law of nature that individual change precedes collective change. If you are aiming for change in your family, in your company, or in the street where you live, you will have to take the initiative yourself and inspire other people by what you do and say.

What's more: if you know what it is like to change your own behavior, you will better understand what is involved in achieving collective change.

In this chapter we will look at two subjects:

(1) **Applying the Basic Change Method**. *Get Real, Make Plans, Take Action... Two illustrations of the application of this approach to change.*

(2) **Personal change in different areas.** *A number of practical suggestions for changes in professional, social, and private areas.*

1. Applying the Basic Change Method

In this paragraph, I would like to share a number of change experiences with you. They are meant both to illustrate and to inspire. I will not constantly refer back to the previous chapters, but will deal with the examples on the basis of the three stages in the *Basic Change Method*:

- *Get Real*: formulate goal-directed objectives and tangible behavior intentions.
- *Make Plans*: thoroughly prepare for the most difficult change situations.
- *Take Action*: begin, measure, and reward desired behavior.

Family and overcoming awkward habits

Following an article about change in a magazine, I received a letter from David. He asked whether he could phone me for help with a number of problems he was wrestling with.

Although I generally do not do this sort of thing, I agreed with him

250

that we would try out several of the techniques I had been studying for this book.

Get Real... What David wanted was a better relationship with members of his family, more social contacts, and particularly that he addressed problems which resulted from his defensive, sometimes negative attitude towards other people.

I think there are quite a few people like David: mentally healthy, don't feel like visiting a shrink, and yet wrestling with matters that are a hindrance to themselves and to others. During a number of telephone calls and e-mail exchanges, we translated his aims into three tangible behavior intentions:

◆ Always listen first and put yourself in the other person's place, and only then say something, particularly in contacts with family members.
◆ In all contacts with other people, always consciously concentrate on things that are going well and not on things that are going badly.
◆ Every time you feel as though you are about to lose your cool, take a step back and ask yourself, with a touch of humor: *Does the other person really wish me ill, or is that just something in my head?*

Make Plans... David and I discussed all sorts of situations that could prove difficult. We visualized how he could give a positive twist to these situations with his new behavior. David decided to keep a list for himself on which he could give himself marks for all the resolutions that he carried out. When he reached a certain number of points, he would take an afternoon off, go into town, buy himself a new book, and spend at least an hour drinking coffee. That was something he normally could not do without feeling guilty about it, but now he could honestly "earn" it.

Take Action... For several months, David and I would speak to each other on the telephone and discuss his behavior measurements together and to list the points of attention for the coming days.

After a few months, we were able to evaluate each other. By this time, David had bought himself quite a few books and had spent many hours drinking coffee in town. But what was more important: the most important family relationships had been repaired, David had joined a church (he had wanted to do this for some time, but was extremely apprehensive about taking the first step), and finally he had mastered the ability to drive out negative thoughts and behaviors with a few positive and humorous self-instructions.

David and I were amazed at the relatively simply way in which he had achieved these results. What did become obvious, however, was that regularly measuring his behavior, even after several months, was still essential.

More time for important matters, without financial sacrifices

One change that has had major consequences in my own life is that, once every six months, I now set myself new tangible goals and adjust my existing goals for my work and evaluate my work behavior. If I were asked to make an estimate, then I would say that this saves me at least half a day's work each week and annually makes a substantial financial contribution to my business. Not that this is my main priority. I simply mention it to show that working less does not necessarily lead to lesser results.

I am, of course, quite aware that as an independent business man, I can permit myself more freedom than people who work for a boss. But I think this story will also provide people on a salary with some good tips. Let me explain how I now work, using the stages of the *Basic Change Method.*

Get Real... I thoroughly review my work goals every summer and Christmas holiday. I ask myself what my ambitions were, what I am actually working for, and whether or not I am deceiving myself. Often this process takes several days. I make notes in a small notebook that I generally carry around with me, cross out things and sometimes write them down again using exactly the same wording. I also ask myself what behavior is required in the coming months to bring me closer to my goals. In order to arm myself against self-deception, I look through my diary for the previous months and check my income. In this way, I know which activities were financially attractive and which were not. When I first started doing this, I came to the conclusion that I frequently agreed to appointments, meetings, and activities that did not bring me closer to my personal goals *and* did not generate any income. I had consciously to say "no" more often.

The most important behavior intention that I formulated for my work (and still follow) was: *Determine in advance whether each appointment and activity contributes to your goals.*

Make Plans... Situations in which I feel a social pressure to say "yes" remain the most difficult. There are so many nice people who wish to make appointments for rather vague reasons. Before I know it, I have my diary in my hand, even though this is not what I really want. That is why I searched for a solution *in* my diary. First with notes written here and there throughout my diary, and now with self-made pages for my diary.

The diary pages contain my goals and my resolution not to write in just "any" appointment and activity, but first to take a timeout and to ask myself whether this is really useful. In addition, for the last few years, I have resolutely blocked out in my diary parts of the day that are consciously intended for my family. I know many active and well-meaning men and women who only put business appointments in their diaries, assuming that the rest of the time is for their families. Unfortunately, that "rest" is often extremely limited.

Take Action... During the last few years I have frequently said no to things that I would previously have done. Often it is enough on the telephone to say that it "simply isn't possible" to be somewhere and sometimes you have to say honestly that you are currently focusing on other things.

Weekly, I check my diary against my goals. Sometimes this means that I have to adjust my planning. In the beginning, I sometimes had to cancel appointments that I had made. That is painful, but it teaches you in future to think more carefully *beforehand*.

Now that I have been doing this for several years, I can make up a provisional balance, and it is without doubt positive. I am no longer concerned about *how many* things I have in my diary, but whether they are the *right* things. This is not so much a matter of willpower, but rather the use of a number of simple techniques.

Research: What do people really want?

Perhaps you have been walking around for some time with a few ideas in your mind about things you would like to change. But do you also know *why* you want these changes?

For several decades, psychologists have been asking themselves what motivates people, what they *really want, deep down inside*. What are our congenital universal urges, desires, and needs that direct our emotions, our thoughts, and our behavior? It was not the first motivation theory to be developed, but it has certainly become the best known: the hierarchy of need, developed in the 1950s by Abraham Maslow. According to Maslow, people first have to have their physical needs satisfied – such as food and safety. Next, their social needs: interaction with other people and gaining respect. And finally, people want to have their individual spiritual needs satisfied, such as curiosity, enjoying beautiful things, and ultimately self-fulfillment. According to Maslow, the "lower" needs are prerequisites for satisfying the "higher" needs.

Several years ago, the American researcher Steven Reiss published a new motivation theory, based on interviews with more than 6,000 people. Reiss identified 16 basic desires that everybody has to some degree or other. In random order:

(1) *power: the desire to influence others*
(2) *independence: the desire to put trust in yourself*
(3) *curiosity: the will to obtain knowledge*
(4) *acceptance: the desire to belong*

(5) *order: the desire for transparency and organization*
(6) *save: the desire to collect things*
(7) *honor: wanting to be faithful to your parents and your country*
(8) *idealism: the desire for social justice*
(9) *social contact: the desire for companionship*
(10) *family: the desire to raise your own children*
(11) *status: the need for social prestige*
(12) *revenge: the desire to get even*
(13) *romance: the need for sexuality and beauty*
(14) *eating: the need for food*
(15) *physical activity: the need to use your body*
(16) *peace of mind: the desire for emotional tranquility.*

Paul Lawrence and Nitin Nohria, both professors at Harvard University, published results of their investigation into basic motives soon after the appearance of Reiss's research. They arrived at a much simpler and thus more elegant model. According to Lawrence and Nohria, there are only four genetically determined drives (D1 to D4).

◆ *(D1) The drive to acquire:* collecting material and immaterial things that we consider valuable.
◆ *(D2) The drive to connect:* the desire for relationships with other people.
◆ *(D3) The drive to learn:* the desire to explore our physical and mental environment.
◆ *(D4) The drive to defend:* the desire to protect the material and immaterial things that we possess.

The researchers' conviction was that, ultimately, people look for activities that satisfy these four motives. If we allow ourselves to give too much attention to acquisition (M1), we may damage our relationships with other people (M2). And if we are too concerned with defending what we know, believe, and possess (M4), we will not learn (M3).

A frequently expressed criticism of such motivation theories is that they are all very "earthly." They lack a spiritual dimension, yet 85 percent of the world's population is religious. Non-believers will suggest that this religious search is inspired by earthly motives. And many believers will argue that much earthly searching arises from a spiritual vacuum.

Gross, R. (1996). Psychology. The Science of Mind and Behavior. London: Hodder & Stoughton. Reiss, S. (2000). Who am I?: The 16 Basic Desires that Motivate Our Behavior and Define Our Personality. Los Angeles: J. P. Tarcher. Lawrence, P. R. and Nohria, N. (2002). Driven. How Human Nature Shapes Our Choices. San Francisco: Jossey-Bass. CIA (2002). The World Factbook 2002. https://www.cia.gov/library/publications/download/download-2002/factbook2002.zip

2. Personal change in various areas

The fundamental principles of human behavior change are the same in all areas of life. But each area has specific characteristics. That is why we give a few tips for applying the *Basic Change Method* within different environments.

The professional environment

The work environment is a source of behavior stimuli. Managers, colleagues, customers, e-mail, telephone, the workplace, the reward system: all influence your behavior whether you like it or not.

If you do not have a clear plan for the way you deal with work, your professional life will be decided by others. That is not always favorable. Many people are dissatisfied with their work and the number of burn-outs has drastically increased in recent years. Feelings of impotence and working far too many hours with too few results play an important role in this.

Several years ago, *Scientific American* catalogued a number of frightening research reports about people (particularly men) who lost themselves in their work:

◆ Japanese research shows that men who work more than 11 hours a day have 2.4 times the chance of dying from a heart attack than men who work seven to nine hours a day. The Japanese have their own word for this – *Karoshi*. Death by overwork.

◆ Swedish research shows that men who have little control over the demands made by their work run 1.8 times the chance of dying from a heart condition than men who have greater control over their work.

◆ Men who receive little social support from their colleagues have 2.6 times the chance of a fatal heart attack than men who do have this.

◆ Italian research shows that increased authority coupled with decreased physical activity significantly increases the chances of heart disease.

The conclusion is simple: do not work more than seven to nine hours a day, spend your free time on relaxing activities, and make sure you take enough exercise. The typical reaction from most hard-working people is equally predictable: *That may be fine for others, but I simply can't change things. Things are just too busy.*

A few suggestions:

◆ *Make sure your work doesn't take you over, but that you are in control.* Plan an evening once every six months in which you evaluate and plan your working life. Use the *Basic Change Method* to determine what you really consider important and especially to translate this into your daily behavior.

◆ *Build up a healthy resistance to the influence of all types of situation stimuli.* Consciously anticipate difficult change situations in your working environment. Work with your own situation stimuli and counter-behavior. Plan, for example, a specific time each day for making telephone calls and answering your e-mails. If you have your e-mail program open and your mobile switched on all day long, you will be constantly interrupted and won't be able to finish anything.

◆ *Plan your day carefully. Make time for this in the morning.* This time will pay itself back time and again during the day. Give your full attention to planning the things that are related to your goals and only then plan in the rest. Work with FDRT.

257

◆ *Avoid too much traveling and traffic.* Do as much as you can by e-mail, and by telephone. You save the time you would otherwise spend traveling *and* more. Conference calls always work faster and more effectively than physical meetings.

Private life

Personal changes in your private life are closely connected to changes in your professional life. Many people struggle with a bad balance between work and private life. They want to change things in their private lives, but they simply do not have either the energy or the time because these are gobbled up by work.

During a recent study among managers, more than 90 percent indicated that they regularly experienced a lack of balance between their work and private lives. One in three said that this led to conflicts at home.

Fernando Bartolome and Paul Evens studied the conditions that allowed people to experience a good balance between work and private life. They interviewed 2,000 managers and their partners. The results showed that problems at work often had repercussions in family life. Work-related concerns, stress, and frustrations are taken home and cause problems there. There are also managers who feel comfortable in both work and home without any pronounced tiredness, tension, and distraction. According to the researchers, these people have three things in common.

(1) *They are able to deal well with changes at work:* they openly discuss decisions about their career – both in advance and as it progresses – with their partners and together they weigh the risks involved.
(2) *They choose appropriate work:* they choose work that matches their competencies, that they enjoy doing, and that reflects their (moral) convictions. Wrong choices, according to the researchers, are often the result of: financial and other attractive rewards and external pressure. One essential for a right choice is

sufficient self-insight: why am I doing this? Because I enjoy doing it and am good at it, or because of factors such as money, status, and power?

(3) *The ability to handle disappointments in work:* they look disappointment honestly in the face. They analyze their emotions and try consciously to learn and make new choices.

A number of additional practical suggestions for a better balance:

◆ If you are required to think a lot at work, or are involved in knowledge work it is essential that you *plan your thinking time.* Many people just allow their minds to wander over all sorts of things in an unplanned way. Often you may be "physically" at home, but "mentally" still in the office. Plan in advance when you are going to think about a certain matter.

◆ *Set aside five minutes each day to round off your work.* Finish your work by writing down matters you must not forget and then put everything out of your head. On your way home, resolve to give your partner and children the attention they deserve.

◆ *Avoid black holes.* Black holes are the activities that cost time, attention, and energy, but don't give anything back in return. Not even a few pleasant memories. A few typical black holes: watching an excessive amount of TV; all sorts of thoughts about things that went wrong in the past; thoughts about things over which you have no control; thoughts about and discussions with people with whom you have no real relationship.

◆ *Consciously begin each day with a few positive thoughts.* Every morning, spend one minute writing down things you are grateful for: your health, your partner, your family... anything. No time to write? Say it out loud, in the shower, while you jog, behind the wheel of your car.

The social area

I can understand that personal changes in the social area may be of least interest to you. Most people I meet during seminars and workshops want to invest in their private life and their career. But when people start talking about the social area, the discussion usually turns to the behavior of other people. *Other people are so rude; other people drive so fast in our street; other people's children destroy our things.*

And yet it is very relevant to take a closer look at the way you function in society. It says a lot about your progress on the path of personal development. By looking at the way you treat people you do not know, you can measure the level of your inner refinement.

How, for example, do you treat people who are lower down the social ladder than you? How do you react to the shortcomings of others? What do you do if the checkout person in the supermarket is rude to you? Do you become angry and let it show?

Let me speak for myself: too often, I allow my social behavior to be determined by that of other people. For example, I become too easily irritated in traffic. The social stimuli that occur in such situations trigger behavior in me of which (generally only a few minutes later) I am not especially proud. Every time something like that happens, I conclude that I still have a lot to learn.

If we are unable react in such social situations with the same friendliness and thoughtfulness we show in difficult situations in our work or private life, there is still much to improve in our behavior and our character.

In your work and private life, you profit directly from patient, friendly, and resolute behavior. But in the social field, you will never pluck the fruits of your behavior yourself. We have to content ourselves in this area with the inner conviction that patient, friendly, and resolute behavior is, in the long run, in everybody's interests. Our self-control has to defeat direct external stimuli. That victory is a characteristic of true civilization.

Developing the sort of self-control that can profit other people can take a whole lifetime. The American writer Stephen Covey maintains that people go through two stages of development in their lives, both of which cost considerable time, attention, and energy.

◆ We start our lives being *dependent* on others. But there comes a time when we have to learn to walk on our own two feet and have to struggle for *independence*.

◆ As we develop further, we discover that *mutual dependency* offers the best results. We need the cooperation of others to achieve our goals and find happiness.

QUESTION & ANSWER

Q: Do you always have to start right at the beginning of the Basic Change Method?
A: The *Basic Change Method* is constructed in such a way that all the various change insights and techniques that it contains reinforce each other as much as possible. But that doesn't mean that these techniques won't work on their own.

Anybody who wants to experiment with behavior change could, for example, begin by measuring behavior daily, as described in the *Take Action* stage. Daily measurement and reinforcement of desired behavior can also, without the two previous stages, lead to results. Anybody who knows exactly what behavior he or she wants to change, but notices that this cannot be achieved with will power alone, would find the techniques described in the *Make Plans* stage very beneficial. These techniques help you persevere with change in the most difficult circumstances.

Anybody who doesn't really know what he or she would like to change would do well – perhaps after a little experimentation – to start at the beginning with the *Get Real* stage.

Q: Can you really approach change in professional life with the same method as in your private life or in your social functioning? Surely there are considerable differences?
A: There are all sorts of differences between the professional, social, and private areas. These differences, however, are basically social influences and other factors in the specific environment.

> The way we *mentally deal* with these influences is the *same* in all three areas. And that is what the *Basic Change Method* is really all about.

What now?

If you are an individual who wants to start a change process, then you can begin the *Basic Change Method* at any time you like. It isn't difficult. You look at the *Get Real, Make Plans,* and *Take Action* stages and follow the steps described. But perhaps you are feeling uncertain about the impact this could have? Perhaps you are hesitant about undertaking a change process that could cost weeks or months? Perhaps you would first like to try out some of the techniques?

In that case, I would advise you to try something small from the *Basic Change Method*.

Some suggestions:

◆ Concentrate for a period of two weeks consciously on possibilities and not on impossibilities, on the YES area instead of the NO area. You will notice that even using this simple technique will make you feel better and allow you to perform better.
◆ You may have had certain behavior resolutions in mind for some time. If so, develop a number of *counter-behaviors*: simple support behavior that will help you display the desired behavior. Then put your resolutions in practice just once, and evaluate what happened. You will probably discover that you are capable of more than you think.
◆ Measure for a week one or more behaviors that you consider relevant. Every morning, note down your measurement for the day before. You will notice that this simple act of measurement can have an effect on your behavior.

Chapter 2

Collective change in practice

A few good friends of mine have worked for some years at a large mail-order company. A little while ago they told me that big changes were afoot. Management wanted to give people on the work floor more personal responsibility. In future, people would decide as a team on things such as shifts, holidays, and other operational matters.

I can imagine what management thought of this decision: "Finally something that our employees will appreciate: making decisions themselves, taking responsibility, empowerment!"

Unfortunately for the management, the employees I spoke to didn't see it that way. One suspected an underhand attempt to economize. "In future, we have to do the work of management as well." Another was undecided, it couldn't be true: "Years on end, they've never asked us about anything, and now, all of a sudden, we have to decide everything ourselves. I think it's fishy."

The change was ultimately implemented and, it seems, without too much trouble. But the reactions of the employees highlight a problem that is encountered in many organizations. Employees who have been with the company for quite some time, no longer trust the intentions of management. They are tired of all the reorganizations and from all those consultations that never produced any tangible results; they relapse into apathy. There is not really any resistance, but neither is there any real enthusiasm.

The change that is really necessary is breaking down the walls of miscommunication. Good intentions are not sufficient for this. Employees must experience that this time management means what it says. A matter of doing!

What are we going to do?

"Experience and reason teach that things that depend on many seldom succeed," wrote the Italian philosopher Ludovico Guidcciardini in the sixteenth century. The collective realization of change is not easy. In this chapter we will look at collective change in work, private life, and social environments. Two points to note:

(1) **Application of the Basic Change Method.** *Three examples to illustrate how successful collective change can be approached.*

(2) **Collective change in various areas.** *A number of practical suggestions for change in the professional, social, and private areas.*

1. Application of the Basic Change Method

We will look at a few examples of collective changes. Each time we will use the three stages from the *Basic Change Method*. I will repeat them here:

(1) *Get Real*: formulate goal-oriented and concrete behavior intentions.
(2) *Make Plans*: thoroughly prepare the most difficult change situations.
(3) *Take Action*: start, measure, and reward desired behavior.

Permanent change in a department

During a seminar, I met Peter. A man in his forties, he was head of a project management department of an international company. In previous weeks, he had been confronted by increased pressure from his head-office in London. The market was in recession, and a whole range of company processes had to be adapted in record time. The goal was a total cost reduction of 20 percent in one year.

Get Real... Peter realized that it was absolutely essential to measure all his processes frequently and accurately, so that he could intervene on time. There was an existing agreement that the nine project managers would hand in their progress reports every Friday before the end of the day. But as the years went on, things became lax; in fact, nobody ever met the deadline. That had to change.

Make Plans... Peter arranged a meeting with his project leaders in which they could openly and honestly discuss the problem of the missing progress reports. At first he only asked questions and let his project leaders talk. From this, he learned a number of things.

◆ The project leaders wanted to discuss their progress verbally with Peter personally. They enjoyed that contact. And apparently, Peter unintentionally stimulated this undesirable way of working with his jovial attitude.
◆ The project leaders had the impression that nothing useful was ever done with their reports. They never heard anything from Peter about them once they had been discussed.
◆ All of them considered Peter's new interest in their progress as a form of "meddling."

At the end of the meeting, Peter explained the necessity of the progress reports to them. He told his project leaders about the economy drive instigated by head office. He also discussed with them how the process could be made more useful and attractive. Ultimately, they decided together that in future they would hand in their progress reports by noon on Friday and that at the end of the day Peter would produce a handy total summary. (The project leaders saw this as a reward for their efforts.) From this summary, which Peter needed in any case to do his work properly, the project leaders could easily see whether their projects were interfering with each other, for example, due to duplication of effort.

This total summary would, in future, also form the basis for the project review meeting on Monday morning. Anybody who didn't hand in their report would not be allowed to participate in the discussion on Monday. Finally, Peter resolved for himself in future to thank everybody directly by e-mail for delivering their reports.

265

Take Action... The first week, Peter sent everybody an e-mail, thanking them for delivering their reports. But he had not kept sufficient time free in his diary to make the total summary.

During the meeting on Monday morning, Peter apologized to the others and promised that next week he would do what had been agreed. The next Friday, everybody again handed in their reports before noon, and this time Peter succeeded in keeping his promise. In the months that followed, during which I occasionally spoke to him, he managed – with one exception – to get all reports in on time and to produce the total summary. Partly as a result of this, his department was able to meet virtually all its goals. Peter later sent me an e-mail: This approach works, but it is essential, as manager, to be consistent and strictly keep all your promises. That demands a considerable change in the way you work.

A year of change within a world company

Jack Welch – the top manager who spent his whole working life at General Electric and made this one of the largest companies in the world – related in his biography and in a number of interviews how, in the 1990s, he helped his company into the Internet era. A good example of a successful large-scale change operation.

Get Real... Welch tells how, when he was 63, he became interested in the Internet during a vacation with his wife in Mexico. She had taken her laptop with her so that she could check her e-mails and follow the news. Welch had given little attention to computers until his wife told him that on several sites, people were speculating about his successor at GE and a possible share split of GE shares.

Several months later, during a visit to one of his directors in London, Welch learned that this 36-year-old man had an Internet-coach of 23 who, on several occasions, coached him in e-mail, the web, and chatting. This was the translation into behavior that Welch needed.

Make Plans... Within a few weeks, Welch ensured that the top 500 managers in GE had all chosen their own personal mentor. Welch asked them to look for somebody within the company under the age of 30 and handy with computers, to provide them with three to four hours' hands-on training every week. During the same period, the situation in a large number of GE offices was changed. So-called "parallel information paths" were closed. If certain information was distributed both digitally *and* on paper, the paper version was discontinued. In this way, employees and managers without any digital knowledge could no longer survive.

Take Action... All managers had to report their progress in the digital field. Following the introduction with the top 500, Welch extended the plan to the top 3,000 people in the concern. Within one year, GE had a large number of internet activities in operation. These were both externally directed, such as online auctions, and internally directed, such as streamlining administrative processes.

The idea of Internet mentors within GE had an important side effect. Young people who had just started working were, for a few hours each week, the teachers of the very highest managers in the concern. According to Welch, this initiative turned the company upside down in just a few months.

A national change in just one day

Social changes can be found in all sorts and sizes. One very remarkable change took place on Sunday September 3, 1967 in Sweden. Within one day, the country changed over from driving on the left to driving on the right.

Get Real... Discussion had raged about this for many years in Sweden. All the neighboring countries drove on the right, only Sweden drove on the left. It had been introduced in 1734, but nobody could really remember why. Driving on the left frequently caused problems, particularly along the border with its neighbor Norway. Strangely enough, most Swedish cars were fitted with a left-hand drive, which was intended for cars driving on the right. Although 85 percent of the population who voted in a referendum held in 1955, were against any change, the government decided in 1963 that, in future, traffic would drive on the right.

Make Plans... The change was prepared with military precision for four years. Every possible problem situation was taken into account. All Swedish households received a 30-page booklet, explaining the new traffic regulations. The change-over would take place on Sunday morning at 05:00. In most areas, no traffic was allowed between 01:00 and 06:00. In the major cities, no traffic at all was permitted for the whole day.

Take Action... On the appointed day, thousands of civil servants and military personnel changed all the traffic signs throughout Sweden in just a few hours.

The change-over to driving on the right was accompanied by a lowering of the speed limit. In the period following, the speed limit was raised gradually step-by-step. In this way, the Swedish population could get used to the new situation without any chaos.

Research: Participation essential in change management

According to organizational researchers Nigel King and Neil Anderson, one of the greatest problems in change management is the *illusion of management*, or the illusion that change is easy to manage. According to them, much change management literature intentionally exaggerates (in order to attract more readers) the influence management has on organizational change.

This illusion of manageability consists, according to King and Anderson, of three contributory illusions:

◆ The illusion of linearity: organizational change always runs neatly in a number of strict stages.
◆ The illusion of predictability: organizational change is a process that can be managed.
◆ The illusion of controllability: managers are in control of change. If anything goes wrong, this must be due to something beyond their control.

If many changes do not allow themselves to be controlled by a *top-down* approach, then an alternative must be found. Several classic research studies in the field of change management, which are also referred to by King and Anderson, show that employee participation in the definition of change is generally essential. After all, nobody offers resistance to plans that he or she has developed themselves. In the 1940s, Lester Coch and John French Jr. conducted one of the first studies into organizational change. The researchers discovered all sorts of resistance in the American *Harwood Manufacturing Corporation* and advised using group briefings and group participation. This reduced the resistance and cleared way for the introduction for new work methods. Paul Lawrence, too, offered the same advice based on his research at the end of the 1960s: he suggested that more attention be given to employee participation in the developing of changes. Something new was his attention to the impact of changes on individual relationships in the workplace. According to Lawrence, a lot of resistance arises from this. Technical and other innovations are, according to Lawrence, more easily accepted as long as the social relationships remain unaffected. This was, he suggested, true at all levels of the organization.

Lawrence's contemporary Herbert A. Shephard determined that most, and the best, applicable new ideas came from people who had to do the job themselves. This is generally not the top of the organization. But because, according to Shephard, new ideas are generally considered disruptive, they are generally eliminated in the *bottom-up* communication. And without help from the top, it is generally not possible to implement change. Sensible managers would thus do well to guarantee free, open bottom-up communication.

Coch, L. and French Jr., J. R. P. (1948). "Overcoming Resistance to Change," in Human Relations, no 2, 512–32. King, N. and Anderson, N. (1995). Innovation and Change in Organizations (London: Routledge). Lawrence, P. R. (1969). "How to deal with resistance to change." In: Harvard Business Review, January–February, 115–22; Shephard, H. A. (1967). "Innovation-resisting and innovation-producing organizations." In: Journal of Business, no 40, 470–77.

2. Collective change in various areas

Although the fundamental principles of human behavior change are the same in all life areas, each of these areas has its own characteristics. For this reason, we give here a number of points that require attention when applying the *Basic Change Method* in different environments.

The professional area

Organization change is a profession with its own jargon: *reengineering, right-sizing, empowerment, turnaround management, self-directing teams, customer-oriented teams* and so on and so on.

Whatever we like to call it, ultimately it is all about operations that *demand* a change in behavior and that must *lead* to a change in behavior. A change of behavior in one of the three groups that are most important for an organization: customers, employers, and financiers.

A few years ago, I carried out a study into the introduction of ICT innovations in more than 100 Dutch companies. This showed that *the way the change was approached* was one of the essential success factors. There are four elements that, *even during the very first preparations*, determine to a significant degree whether the change will ultimately succeed or fail:

These four factors are, in order of importance:

(1) *Good cooperation between those people who will lead the change*: do you really pay attention to what others in the change team propose; do you really listen to their opinions? And do they listen carefully to each other? Is there an underlying trust in each other?
(2) *Decisions by people who have influence in the organization*: do the leaders involved actually speak out? Do they really commit themselves to the change process? These can be both informal leaders (people who enjoy respect in a certain group) and formal leaders (those with a position of authority).

(3) *Good communication with the people who will have to execute the change*: have the people who will actually have to execute the change had a real chance to give their input? Have they been listened to for long enough and with real attention?

(4) *Agreement about what should happen*: even if the three previous requirements have been met, things can still go wrong. It often transpires that the various people involved have different ideas about the ultimate goals of the change and of the steps needed to achieve it. Always check whether those involved in the change process can explain in their own words what the change is all about. These conditions apply when you have, in a company, decided together that change is necessary. Before this conclusion is reached, quite a lot has to happen. Organizations are a good breeding ground for unfortunate habits that are difficult to change and all forms of self-deception.

When successful top managers are confronted with sweeping changes in the outside world, they have, according to Harvard professor Donald Sull, the inclination to cling even tighter to the "success formula" that made their company so successful in the past. For this reason, important changes are often put off for far too long.

Researcher Sydney Finkelstein suggested that a large number of disasters in corporate life, in which wrong decisions (almost) resulted in the company's destruction, can be explained by various types of self-deception.

◆ There is often a lack of a realistic picture of the world outside, because management prefers not to hear bad news.
◆ This sort of news often doesn't even reach the top, because subordinates do not want to pass it on.
◆ Top managers are inclined to believe too long and too resolutely in their own infallibility.

Entrepreneurs and managers would be better at change if they cherished their self-confidence, but made sure that this did not develop into pride. Two pieces of practical advice:

◆ As manager, ask for regular (anonymous) critical feedback, so that you occasionally hear the bad news about yourself. This can be extremely painful, but at the same time very educative.

◆ Periodically look resolutely for bad news about the company and about information that undermines the current standpoints. Beware of the risks of *group think* (*see chapter 3 from Part 1: How change really works*). Perhaps you may now be thinking: I was supposed to concentrate on my YES area, on the things I am good at? That's true, but if there are things in the NO area that obstruct further growth, then these must be eliminated. Real knowledge of behavior change is missing in many organizations. During recent years, management and employees have paid considerable attention to tricks that can help you get other people to do something quickly. Books and seminars about slyness, politics, power, manipulation, and conspiracy enjoy a growing popularity.

Perhaps this is an indication of frustration, perhaps people in companies think: *Now it's my turn – if I can't get things done honestly, let's try some dishonesty*. Whatever the explanation, this interest will virtually always have a negative, destructive motivation. Leaving aside the moral objections to such approaches, they also lead to a considerable loss of energy, time, and attention within organizations. Political power games often result in destroying what somebody else has built up. This does not serve the interests of the organization and its customers, but only the interests of the individual involved.

This obsession with power and manipulation often results in *more than a half of the people* spending *more than half their time* talking about their colleagues. We all know that such organizations exist; but tell me honestly, would you really like to work in one?

The private area

Collective change within the private area is a precarious matter. Everybody has their own idea how you can best work on a relationship. And magazines are filled each week with how to bring up your children. Can a general approach such as the *Basic Change Method* add anything to all this?

I think it can. A few years ago, I came across a study by Bernard Murstein. He suggested that in a long-term relationship, such as a marriage, three stages could be identified:

(1) *The stimulus stage:* in the very beginning of a relationship, people pay considerable attention to external characteristics, such as the physical attractiveness of the other person.
(2) *The value stage:* if, after the initial meeting, a relationship develops, people spend a lot of time exploring each other's values and other opinions.
(3) *The role stage:* once a relationship has a more permanent character, the individual roles become important. Who fulfils which role in a relationship, and how do these complement each other?

My own experience matches that which Murstein and other researchers have shown. Being able to communicate openly about various roles is one of the most important ways of maintaining a long-term relationship.

I think that many families require a new, more balanced distribution of roles. A well-known fact: in families where both parents work, the woman still carries out the majority of household duties and takes responsibility for the upbringing and care of the children. This remains true if both husband and wife have a full-time job.

There is a simple way of working on a redistribution of roles:

◆ *Do not wait until dissatisfaction turns into open hostility.* Agree to discuss the various roles openly every six months. Plan this in your diary. Try to do this as professionally as possible. Avoid recriminations and accusations, listen patiently to each other and make firm agreements for the coming months.
◆ *Use the approach outlined in the Get Real stage.* Review together the

273

good things, express your goals, and translate them into behavior. Avoid self-deception and coach each other in these changes.

The social area

You could write a whole book about social change. I am convinced that the *Basic Change Method* – thanks to its fundamental character – can work well in stimulating change in the population at large. But we should not close our eyes to the complexity facing local government. Two thoughts about this. First of all, government, particularly at a national level, is more concerned about reducing the NO area and less about increasing the YES area. This is a result of the social choices we have to face in most Western countries. Government takes a back seat and only intervenes when things go wrong.

A troubling consequence of this is that governments make use of instruments of influence that are less effective than they would like. Governments are more focused on punishing undesired behavior than on stimulating desired behavior. This does, of course, restrict really dangerous developments, but does not move society in a direction that we consider valuable. Second, governments have to play on a very complicated field. There are many different interests in society that have to be considered. Many more than in an average company. Developing a policy in which citizens have a high level of participation (that, in itself, is just as important here as in corporate life) often leads to lengthy procedures, in which it is simply impossible to please all parties concerned. There will always be large groups of people who *have* participated, but are *not* satisfied with the final decisions.

A few possible questions for the governmental administrator who wishes to use the *Basic Change Method* for changes of social behavior.

◆ What positive social goal are you aiming for?

- What behavior – measurable, active, personal – from citizens must be stimulated for this?
- How can you, as government, change both the situation and the intentions of these people, in order to stimulate that behavior?
- How can you make use for this of effective change techniques, such as stimulating the desired behavior?

QUESTION & ANSWER

Q: If I read all this, then I get the impression that 90 percent of all organizations are badly managed. This isn't possible, is it?
A: Most organizations are, of course, not mismanaged at every moment in every single situation. But it is a fact that in many organizations, the most important change rules, such as organizing a serious dialog between the initiators and the people who must do things, are totally ignored. What's more, the (social and physical) situation stimuli often conflict with the aims of management and employees. This results in sub-optimal performance and leads to frustration and stress.

Q: Does a collective change require the same feeling of urgency among all participants?
A: Change specialists are divided in their opinion about this. It does, however, help: if employees in a company are convinced that there is a real problem and that it requires them to work together on a real solution, the chance of a strong behavior intention is much greater than when they simply follow orders from management. In the *Get Real* stage, we mentioned the research of Kahneman that shows that problems are twice as motivating as opportunities. Because of this, conflicting situation stimuli will much more easily be overcome. This is also true of collective change in the private and social areas.

Q: Is involvement always necessary in changes?
A: You could think of exceptions. In crisis situations, it may be necessary for a manager to work top-down for a clearly prescribed and defined period. This can be true in:

- a financial crisis;
- a crisis in the relationship with customers and investors;
- a crisis involving the product or processes;
- a crisis in relation to (some) employees.

Incidentally, it is still advisable, even in these cases, to obtain the advice of specialists within the organization.

What now?

The *way* collective change is approached has a major bearing on its success. You should therefore be extremely careful how you introduce the *Basic Change Method* to other people. Do not immediately make this way of working an obligation, but first give people the chance of familiarizing themselves with one or more techniques:

- You could think of working with *Measurable, Active, Personal* behavior intentions that the employees formulate for themselves. Try this out for a few months with a group of colleagues or employees. During the half-yearly evaluation, translate one important goal into one or two very clear behavior intentions.
- Consciously anticipate with others difficult change situations and help them develop measures that ensure they will persevere doing what they really want. The victory that this ensures can free the way for a more professional application of behavior change.
- Strive to ensure that as many environments as possible make use of positive reinforcement. Focus yourself primarily on stimulating desired behavior. At your work, in your family, and in your contacts with other people. You will notice that this, in most environments, is highly "contagious."

A personal note

According to the British writer C. S. Lewis: Most people will, if they really look deep in their hearts, know that what they desire is something that

276

cannot be had in this world. It is offered to you by everything in this world, but the promises are never kept. Life is, for most people, a search for security, for stability. Unfortunately, most earthly securities are temporary. A job, a house, a relationship… Everything comes to an end, and frequently sooner than we would like. This search for security explains both our need for and resistance to change. According to C. S. Lewis, we ultimately have to look higher. And I agree with him. I consider people the writers, directors, and leading actors in their own lives, and God as the producer who makes everything possible.

I believe that we, as people, have been given the assignment of doing something meaningful with the talents we have been given. Both for others and for ourselves. That is true in our family, but also in our work: creating value always precedes making profit.

Of course, it is never possible for us mere mortals to keep these resolutions every hour, every day, or even every week. But it is an ambition that, in itself, is extremely valuable.

A scientific basis for behavior change

The aim of this book is to give as many people as possible an accessible and practical change method that, when used properly, is very effective. Personally, I think it valuable that such important matters should have a good foundation. This is why I have included here a short justification for the various building-bricks that are used in the Basic Change Method. The position I propose in this book is, in psychological circles, called an interactionist standpoint. I do not believe that we can only explain our behavior through our conscious resolutions. And I do not believe that we can solely explain our behavior by the stimuli from the surroundings. I believe in a dynamic balance between the influence of our intentions and the situations in which we act.

This conviction has it roots in the studying of a great number of both cognitive-oriented studies and behavioral studies. I examined these both during previous study and research projects, and during

277

my specific preparations for writing this book. But there is also a pragmatic foundation: my own experience in coaching, training, and consultancy work has taught me that interventions that have *both* a cognitive *and* a behavioral component work better than interventions based on one or other of these approaches. And this is certainly true when forming new behavior habits. For me, a goal-oriented combination of theories and techniques from both schools of thought is preferable.

The combination of cognitive and behavior change processes

There have, of course, been people who have proposed a combined approach. Kurt Lewin's *Field Theory* (1951) was one of the first theories in which the effects of intentions by a person and effects from the situation in which that person was operating were combined in a dynamically balanced way.

Lewin postulated B=f(P,E). In words: *Behavior = a function of (the interaction of Personal Characteristics with Environmental Factors).* He adopted this approach in a wide range of areas: intimate relationships, work situations, and situations in society.

We also find the combination of cognitive theory and behaviorism in therapeutic circles, where they are often applied under the name cognitive behavioral therapy (see, for example, Corsini and Auerbach, 1996). The founder of cognitive therapy, Albert Ellis, made use of behavior change processes such as *counter-behavior* in his treatments in the 1950s.

The *Transtheoretic Model* of Prochaska and Norcross (1999) and the *Stages of Change Model* of Prochaska, Norcross and DiClemente (1992; 1994) (two names for virtually the same approach) integrate ten different change processes from different psychological schools that can be characterized as more cognitive oriented (particularly used during the *preparation* of a change according for Prochaska *et al*) or more behavioral oriented (largely applied *during* the change).

278

These ten processes have all found a place in the *Basic Change Method*.

These techniques are:

(1) Consciousness-raising: gathering information about yourself and the problems confronting you.
(2) Dramatic relief/Emotional arousal: experiencing and expressing emotions connected with the problem and the solution.
(3) Self-re-evaluation: reflecting on how you think and feel about yourself in relation to the problem.
(4) Environmental re-evaluation: reflecting on the effects of the problem on the environment.
(5) Self-liberation/Commitment: choosing for and believing in your own abilities to change; committing yourself to these changes.
(6) Social liberation: searching for and finding possibilities in the (social) environment to bring problematic behavior under control.
(7) Counter-conditioning/Countering: replacing dysfunctional behavior responses with responses that promote the desired change.
(8) Stimulus control/Environment control: modifying the behavior situations in order to promote the desired behavior.
(9) Contingency management/Reinforcement management/Reward: rewarding desired behavior and punishing undesired behavior.
(10) Helping relationships: important people who help in a change process by offering support, care, understanding, and acceptance.

In addition, there are examples of the very effective application of a combination of cognitive and behavioral insights in the work environment. An example is the study by Frayne and Latham (1987) in which absenteeism in a governmental organization was reduced by:

◆ on the one hand, setting specific goals;
◆ on the other hand, analyzing environmental factors that could either help or hinder the achieving of these goals;
◆ and finally, rewarding progress and punishing backsliding.

More recent studies, such as the meta-analysis that Ouelette and Wood (1998) made of predictable behavior theories, show that these combined approaches can be very fruitful, particularly when applied to the development of new habit behavior. They write:

"(…) understanding of habits has practical use; it enables social scientists to devise more effective strategies to help people initiate new behavior and change existing behavior. Altering frequently performed behavior in constant contexts requires conscious decision making to devise and implement new responses and to suppress or divert any well-practised behavior that might be cued by the environment.

"(…) The most effective change strategies are likely to be ones that impede performance of established behavior while facilitating formation of new behaviors into habits.

"(…) To maintain intentions to adopt a healthier lifestyle, change strategies should ensure that some immediate, positive consequences emerge from the new healthy behavior. In addition, effective strategies should provide the opportunity for repetition of the new behavior in a stable supporting environment. Frequent performance of the desired behavior in such contexts is especially likely to yield new habits that can themselves proceed relatively automatically."

Theoretical building blocks for the Basic Change Method

The *Basic Change Method* is the result of an ongoing interaction between the study of change theory and the testing of ideas from this in the daily practice of coaching, training, and management. In addition, other methods that used a practical combination of various change techniques were investigated. The *Basic Change Method* makes use of the following theories and models in the fields of teaching and change as building blocks; these are arranged in alphabetical order:

(1) *Azjen: Theory of Planned Behavior.* As support for the various building blocks that are necessary for forming a behavior intention and for the importance of a behavior intention for ultimate behavior.

(2) *Bagozzi and Perugini: Model of Goal-Directed Behavior.* As support for the importance of emotions and desires in forming behavior intentions.

(3) *Bandura: Social Learning Theory.* As support for the importance of learning from others and for the influence of *self-effectiveness* on the setting of goals and performance.

(4) *Gollwitzer: Implementation Intentions.* As support for the importance of the cognitive anticipation of change situations.

(5) *Green and Kreuter: Precede-Proceed Model.* As support for the combination of cognitive and behavioral psychological elements in a practical approach and as support for *beginning at the end*: first formulate the end results and then work back to the actions required today and the way to influence them.

(6) *Locke: Goal setting theory.* As support for the setting of specific, ambitious end goals and specific attainable intermediate steps and for formulating intermediate steps – in collective change with others – by the people executing the change.

(7) *Prochaska, Norcross and DiClemente: Stages of Change Model.* As support for a clear process of open-ended stages and for combining change techniques from various psychological directions into one workable, practical approach.

(8) *Rogers: Diffusion of Innovations.* As support for the notion that group change is the sum of individual change.

(9) *Skinner: Operant Conditioning.* As support for the use of situation stimuli to develop new behavior.

What's new?

The Basic Change Method as a practical step-plan for behavior change, can best be compared with the integral, prescriptive approach of Green and Kreuter and of Prochaska, Norcross and DiClemente. The question is, of course, "what's new"? I will list here five innovations that I think are important:

(1) *The development of personal measurable behavior goals in combination with a preceding conscious stimulation of self-effectiveness.* This is not done by either Prochaska *et al* or Green and Kreuter.

(2) *The inventory in advance and an analysis of difficult change situations.* This is not part of the processes suggested by either Prochaska *et al* or Green and Kreuter.

(3) *The conscious involvement at various moments in the approach of emotions and desires.* Green and Kreuter do not pay any attention to this; Prochaska *et al* do;

(4) *Explicitly involving automatic behavior and conditioning in the approach.* This is under-exposed, particularly in Green and Kreuter;

(5) *The broad application area and the positive approach, the emphasis lies on what we wish to achieve, not what we wish to avoid.* The work of Prochaska *et al* is mainly directed at independently vanquishing bad social and health-related habits, and Green and Kreuter concentrate solely on influencing the health-related behavior of others.

Literature

During the research process that preceded the writing of this book, some books and articles sprang out and strongly influenced my thinking. In writing this book, I have been considerably inspired by books, reference material, and articles by *Ajzen; Ajzen and Fishbein; Cooper, Heron and Herward; Daniels; DuBrin; Gollwitzer; Green and Kreuter; Bross; Johnson, Redmon and Mawhinney; Kin and Anderson; Locke and Latham; Mintzberg; Prochaska, Norcross and DiClemente; Ouelette and Woods; Rogers, Sarafino; Skinner;* and a whole range of articles from the *Journal of Applied Behavior Analysis.*

I have also enjoyed many popular publications about change, such as the books by: *Steven Covey, Anthony Robbins,* and *Leslie Wilk-Bracksick.* Some of the tips included in this book are inspired by the practical and immediate approach. I have *not*, however, based any factual assertions about human behavior and psychology on these works.

I have arranged here the most important literature used in this book into categories, so that you can learn more about the various subjects yourself. The sources used for the various inserts on Research are not repeated here.

Intentions and behavior

Ajzen, I. (1988). Attitudes, Personality and Behavior. Chicago: The Dorsey Press.
Ajzen, I. (1991). The theory of planned behavior. Organizational behavior and human decision processes, 50, 179–211.
Ajzen, I. and Fishbein, M. (1980). Understanding Attitudes and Predicting Social Behavior. Upper Saddle River: Prentice-Hall.
Armitage, C. J. and Conner M. (2001). Efficacy of the theory of planned

behavior. A meta-analytic review. British Journal of Social Psychology.

Bagozzi, R. P. and Kimmel, S. K. (1995). A comparison of leading theories for the prediction of goal-directed behaviors. In: British Journal of Social Psychology, 34: 437–61. London: The British Psychological Society.

Bandura, A. (1977). Self-efficacy: Toward a unifying theory of behavioral change. Psychological Review, 84, 191–215.

Bandura, A. and Locke, E. A. (2003). Negative self-efficacy and goal effects revisited. In: Journal of Applied Psychology, vol. 88, no 1, 87–99. American Psychological Association.

Davidson, A. R. and Jaccard, J. J. (1979). Variables that moderate the atti-tude–behavior relation: results of a longitudinal survey. In: Journal of Personality and Social Psychology, 37, 1364–76.

Donahoe, J. W. and Palmer, D. C. (1994). Learning and Complex Behavior. Needham Heights: Allyn & Bacon.

LaPiere, R. T. (1934). Attitudes versus action. In: Social Forces, 13, 230–37.

Locke, E. A. and Latham, G. P. (2002). Building a practically useful theory of goal setting and task motivation. In: American Psychologist, vol 57, no 9, 705–17. American Psychological Association.

Locke, E. A., Frederick, E., Lee, C. and Bobko, P. (1984). Effect of self-effi-cacy, goals and task strategies on task performance. In: Journal of Applied Psychology, vol 69, no 2, 241–51. American Psychological Association.

Perugini, M. and Bagozzi, R. P. (2001). The role of desires and anticipated emotions in goal-directed behaviors: Broadening and deepening the theory of planned behavior. In: British Journal of Social Psychology, vol 40, 79–98. British Psychological Society.

Petty, R. E. and Cacioppo, J. T. (1996). Attitudes and Persuasion: Classic and Contemporary Approaches. Boulder: Westview Press.

Wicker, A. W. (1969). Attitudes vs. actions: The relationship of verbal and overt behavioral responses to attitude objects. Journal of Social Issues, 1969, 25: 41–78.

Situation and behavior

Bakker-de Pree, B. J. (1987). Constructionele Gedragstherapie. Nijmegen: Dekker and Van de Vegt.

Beek, E. van de (2002). Prikkels maken gezond. In: Elsevier, 21 September 2002. Amsterdam: Reed Elsevier.

Carey, R. J., Clicque, S. H., Leighton, B. A. and Milton, F. (1976) A test of positive reinforcement of customers. In: Journal of Marketing, October 1976.

Daniels, A. C. (1999). Bringing out the best in People. New York: McGraw-Hill.

Fox, D. K., Hopkins, B. L. and Kent Anger, W. (1987). The long-term effects of a token economy on safety performance in open-pit mining. In: Journal of Applied Behavior Analysis, vol 20, 215–24. Lawrence: Society for the Experimental Analysis of Behavior.

Grant, L., and Evans, A. (1994). Principles of behavior analysis. New York: Harper Collins.

Iwata, B. A. e. a. (red.) (2000). Methodological and conceptual issues in applied behavior analysis. From the Journal of Applied Behavior Analysis. (2nd edition). Lawrence: Society for the Experimental Analysis of Behavior.

Mann, R. A. (1972). The behavior-therapeutic use of contingency contracting to control an adult behavior problem: weight control. In the Journal of Applied Behavior Analysis. 5, 99–109. Lawrence: Society for the Experimental Analysis of Behavior.

McKenzie, T. L. and Rushall, B. S. (1974). Effects of self-recording on attendance and performance in a competitive swimming training environment. Journal of Applied Behavior Analysis, vol 7, 199–206. Lawrence: Society for the Experimental Analysis of Behavior.

Onbekend. (1973). At Emery Air Freight: Positive Reinforcement Boosts Performance. In: Organizational Dynamics, Winter 1973, 41–50.

Premack, D. (1959). Toward empirical behavior laws: I. Positive reinforcement. In: Psychological Reviews, 66: 219–33.

Skinner, B. F. (1953). Science and Human Behavior. New York: MacMillan.

Skinner, B. R. (1971). Beyond Freedom and Dignity. Indianapolis: Hackett.

Skinner, B. F. (1974). About Behaviorism. New York: Random House.

Stein, L. and Belluzzi, J. D. (1989). Cellular investigations on behavioral reinforcement. Neuroscience and Biobehavioral Reviews, 13, 69–80.

Thompson, R. and Iwata, B. (2000). "Response acquisition under direct and indirect contingencies of reinforcement." Journal of Applied Behavior Analysis, vol 33, 1.

Vollmer, T. R. e.a. (red.). (2000). Behavior analysis: applications and extensions. From the Journal of Applied Behavior Analysis. (2nd edition). Lawrence: Society for the Experimental Analysis of Behavior.

Situation, intention, and behavior

Frayne, C. A. and Latham, G. P. (1987). The application of social learning theory to employee self-management of attendance. In: Journal of Applied Psychology, 72, 387–92.

Gollwitzer, P. M. (1999). Implementation intentions. Strong effects of simple plans. In: American Psychologist, vol 54, no 7, 493–503. American Psychological Association.

Lewin, K. (1951). Field Theory in Social Science. New York: Harper and Row.

Ouellette, J. A. and Wood, W. (1998). Habit and intention in everyday life: The multiple processes by which past behavior predicts future behavior. Psychological Bulletin, vol 124, no 1, 54–74.

Meichenbaum, D. (1977). Cognitive-behavior modification: An integrated approach. New York: Plenum Press.

Sarafino, E. P. (1996). Principles of Behavior Change. New York: John Wiley and Sons.

Prochaska, J. O., DiClemente, C. C. and Norcross, J. C. (1992). In search of how people change. Applications to Addictive Behaviors. In: American Psychologist, vol 47, no 9, 1102–14.

American Psychological Association.

Change with others

Bunt, P. A. E. van de (1995). Management van verandering: Interactie van omgeving, strategie, structuur en cultuur. Deventer: Kluwer.

Caluwé, L. I. A. de and Vermaak, H. (1999). Leren veranderen. Een handboek voor de veranderkundige. Alphen aan den Rijn: Samsom.

Coch, L. and French Jr., J. R. P. (1948). Overcoming resistance to change. In: Human Relations no 2, 512–32.

Egmond, C. (2000). De kunst van het programmeren. Een systematische methode om veranderingen te programmeren. Utrecht: Novem (interne uitgave).

Greer, H., Jonkers, R., Smits, A., Görts, C., Papadopoulou, K. and Begley, S. (2000). The Guide to Change. Energy Related Behavior. Best: Aeneas.

Festinger, L., Riecken, H. W. and Schachter, S. (1956) When Prophecy Fails. New York: Harper & Row.

Janis, Irving (1972). Victims of Groupthink: psychological study of foreign-policy decisions and fiascoes (2nd edition). Boston: Houghton Mifflin.

Lawrence, P. R. (1969). How to deal with resistance to change, In: Harvard Business Review, Jan–Feb, 115–22.

Mastenbroek, W. F. G. (1997). Verandermanagement. Heemstede: Holland Business Publications.

Murstein, B. I. (1987). A clarification and extension of the SVR theory of dyadic pairing. Journal of Marriage and the Family, vol 49, 929–33.

Shephard, H. A. (1967). Innovation-resisting and innovation producing organizations. In: Journal of Business, no 40, 470–77.

Wilder D A (1977) Perception of groups, size of opposition, and social influence Journal of Experimental Social Psychology 13: 253–68.

Manuals

Antonides, G. (1996). Psychology in Economics and Business (2nd edition). Dordrecht: Kluwer Academic Publishers.

Aronson, E. (1999). The Social Animal (8th edition). New York: Worth Publishers.

Aronson, E. (red.). (1999). Readings about the Social Animal. New York: Worth Publishers.

Boudon, R. (1981). De logica van het sociale. Alphen a/d Rijn: Samsom.

Brown, R. (2000). Group Processes. Malden: Blackwell.

Cialdini, R. (1988). Influence. Science & Practice. (2nd ed.). New York: Harper Collins.

Collins, B. E. (1970). Social Psychology. Reading: Addison-Wesley.

Cooper, J. O., Heron, T. E. and Heward, W. L. (1987). Applied Behavior Analysis. Upper Saddle River: Prentice Hall.

Corsini, R. J. and Auerbach, A. J. (redactie) (1996). Concise Encyclopedia of Psychology (2nd edition). New York: John Wiley & Sons.

Dipboye, R. L., Smith, C. S. and Howell, W. C. (1994). Understanding Industrial and Organizational Psychology. Fort Worth: Harcourt Brace.

Drenth, P. J. D., Thierry, Hk. and Wolff, Ch. J. de (red.) (1997). Nieuw Handboek Arbeids- en Organisatiepsychologie. Houten/Diegem: Bohn Stafleu Van Loghum.

DuBrin, J. (1974). Fundamentals of Organizational Behavior: An Applied Perspective. New York: Pergamon Press.

Engel, J. F., Blackwell, R. D. and Miniard, P. W. (1990) Consumer Behavior (sixth ed.). Chicago etc: The Dryden Press.

Forsyth, D. R. (1999). Group Dynamics (3rd edition). Belmont: Wadsworth.

Garfield, S. L. and Bergin, A. E. (1986). Handbook of Psychotherapy and Behavior Change (3rd edition). New York: John Wiley & Sons.

Green, L. W. and Kreuter, M. W. (1991). Health Promotion Planning: an Educational and Environmental Approach. Mountain View, Mayfield Publishing Company.

Gross, R. (1996). Psychology. The Science of Mind and Behavior. London: Hodder & Stoughton.

Handy, C. (1993). Understanding Organizations (4th edition). Oxford: Oxford University Press.

Huczynski, A. and Buchanan, D. (2001). Organizational Behavior (4th edition). Harlow: Financial Times – Prentice Hall.

Johnson, C. M. e. a. (2001). Handbook of Organizational Performance. Behavior Analysis and Management. New York: The Haworth Press.

King, N. and Anderson, N. (1995). Innovation and Change in Organizations. London: Routledge.

Kolb, B. and Whishaw, I. Q. (1990). Fundamentals of Human Neuropsychology. New York: Freeman & Company.

Kotter, J. P. (1996). Leading Change. Boston: Harvard Business School Press.

Orlemans, J. W. G.; Brinkman, W., Eelen, P., Haaijman, W. P. and Zwaan, E.J. (red.). (1993).

Handboek voor gedragstherapie. Houten: Bohn Stafleu van Loghum.

Leavitt, H. J. e.a. (red.) (1989). Readings in Managerial Psychology (4th edition). Chicago: The University of Chicago Press.

Mietzel, G. (1996). Wegwijs in de Psychologie. Zutphen: Thieme.

Prochaska, J. O. and Norcross, J. C. (1999). Systems of Psychotherapy. A Transtheoretical Analysis. Pacific Grove: Brooks/Cole Publishing.

Rogers, E. M. (1995). Diffusion of Innovations (fourth edition). New York: The Free Press.

Rollinson, D. (2002). Organizational Behavior and Analysis (2nd edition). Harlow: Financial Times – Prentice Hall.

Sadava, S. W. and McCreary, D. R. (red.) (1997). Applied Social Psychology. Upper Saddle River: Prentice Hall.

Sarafino, E. P. (1996). Principles of Behavior Change. New York: John Wiley & Sons.

Scroggs, J. R. (1997). Persoon en persoonlijkheid. Rotterdam: Ad. Donker.

Severin, W. J. and Tankard, J. W. (1988). Communication Theories (2nd edition). New York, London: Longman.

Warr, P. (red.). (2002). Psychology at Work (5th edition). London: Penguin.

Other publications

Bailey, J. S. and Burch, M. R. (2002). Research Methods in Applied Behavior Analysis. Thousand Oaks: Sage.

Bartolome, F. and Evans, P. A. L. (1980). Must Success Cost So Much? In: Harvard Business Review, March–Apr, no 61, 137–48. Cambridge: Harvard Business Publishing.

Beehr, T. A., Jex, S. M. and Ghosh, P. (2001). The Management of Occupational Stress. In: Handbook of Organizational Performance. New York: The Haworth Press.

Bradbury, T. N. and Fincham, F. D. (1992). Attributions and Behavior in

Marital Interaction. In: Journal of Personality and Social Psychology, vol 63, no 4, 613–28.

Brehm, S. S. (1991). Intimate Relationships. New York: McGraw-Hill.

CIA (2002). The World Factbook 2002. www.odci.gov/cia/publications/ factbook

Cornelis, A. (1997). Logica van het gevoel. Middelburg: Essence.

Finkelstein, S. (2003). Why Smart Executives Fail: And What You Can Learn from Their Mistakes. New York: Portfolio.

Ford, C. V. (1996). Lies! Lies!! Lies!!! The Psychology of Deceit. Washington: American Psychiatric Press.

Frölke, V. (2002). Psycholoog en winnaar van de Nobelprijs voor economie Danny Kahneman: Wees sceptisch, doe weinig en heb geduld. In: NRC Handelsblad, 8 Dec. 2002. Amsterdam: PCM.

Goldratt. E. M. (1986). Het doel. Utrecht: Het Spectrum. Kaplan, R. S. and Norton, D. P. (1992). The balanced scorecard – measures that drive performance. In: Harvard Business Review, Jan–Feb 1992. Boston: Harvard Business School Publishing.

Lawrence, P. R. and Nohria, N. (2002). Driven. How Human Nature Shapes Our Choices. San Francisco: Jossey-Bass.

Mintzberg, H. (1990). The manager's job: folklore and fact. In: Harvard Business Review, March–April 1990.

Mintzberg, H. (1973). The Nature of Managerial Work. New York: Harper & Row.

Myers, D. G. (2002). Intuition. Its Powers and Perils. New Haven: Yale University Press.

Porter, M. E. (1996). What is strategy? In: Harvard Business Review, Nov–Dec 1996. Boston: Harvard Business School Publishing.

Quinn, R. E., Faerman, S. R., Thompson, M. P. and McGrath, M. R. (1997). Handboek Managementvaardigheden (tweede editie). Schoonhoven: Academic Service.

Reiss, S. (2000). Who Am I?: The 16 Basic Desires that Motivate Our Behavior and Define Our Personality. Los Angeles: J. P. Tarcher.

Sansone, C. and Harackiewicz, J. M. (2000). Intrinsic and Extrinsic Motivation. San Diego: Academic Press.

Simon, H. B. (1999). Can work kill? In: Scientific American, vol 10, no 2. New York: Scientific American.

Sprenger, R. K. (2001). De motivatiemythe. Amsterdam: Prentice Hall/Pearson Education.

Sternberg, R. J. (red.) (2002). Why Smart People Can Be So Stupid. New Haven: Yale University Press.

Sull, D. N. (2003). Revival of the Fittest: Why Good Companies Go Bad and

How Great Managers Remake Them. Boston: Harvard Business School Press.

Swanborn, P. G. (1987). Methoden van sociaalwetenschappelijk onderzoek: nieuwe editie. Meppel etc.: Boom.

Velde, M. E. G.; Jansen, P. G. W. and Telting, I. A. (2000). Bedrijfswetenschappelijk onderzoek. Van probleemstelling tot presentatie. Baarn: Nelissen.

Vroon, P. (1998) Tranen van een krokodil. Amsterdam: Flamingo.

Popular publications on behavior, change and growth

The Arbinger Institute (2001). Leiderschap en Zelfbedrog. Velp: TFC Trainingsmedia.

Bandler, R. (1985). Using Your Brain for a Change. Moab: Real People Press.

Covey, S. R. (1989). The Seven Habits of Highly Effective People. Powerful Lessons in Personal Change. New York: Simon & Schuster.

Covey, S. R. (1990). Principle Centered Leadership. New York: Simon & Schuster.

Covey, S. R., Merill, A. R. and Merill, R. R. (1994). First Things First. To Live, to Love, to Learn, to Leave a Legacy. New York: Simon & Schuster.

Crabb, L. (1993). Van binnenuit. Driebergen: Navigator boeken. Daniels, A. C. (2001). Other People's Habits. New York: McGraw-Hill.

Dryden, W. (2001). Reason to Change. A Rational Emotive Therapy Workbook. Philadelphia: Taylor & Francis.

Frankl, V. E. (1985). Man's Search for Meaning. New York: Washington Square Press.

Ginneken, J. van (1992). Waarom doet u dat?! Amsterdam: Swets & Zeitlinger.

Goleman, D. (1998). Liegen om te leven. De strategie van zelfbedrog. Amsterdam: Contact.

Goleman, D. (2000). Emotionele intelligentie + Emotionele intelligentie in de praktijk. Amsterdam: Contact.

Grinder, J. and Bandler, R. (1976). The Structure of Magic II. Palo Alto: Science and Behavior Books.

Hollander, J. and Wijnberg, J. (2002). Provocatief Coachen. Utrecht: Kosmos – Z&K.

Lewis, C. S. (1999). Onversneden Christendom. Baarn: Ten Have.

Luijk, F. van (2002). Hoe krijg ik ze zover? Amsterdam: Nieuwezijds.

McCormick, E. W. (2002). Change for the Better. Self-help through Practical Psychotherapy. New York: Continuum.

Peck, M. S. (1978). The Road Less Traveled. New York: Simon & Schuster.
Prochaska, J. O., DiClemente, C. C. and Norcross, J. C. (1994). Changing for Good. New York: Avon Books.
Quinn, R. E. (2000). Verander de wereld. Schoonhoven: Academic Service.
Robbins, A. (1988). Je ongekende vermogens. Utrecht: Kosmos – Z&K.
Seligman, M. E. P. (2002). Authentic Happiness. New York: Free Press.
Smith, H. W. (2001). What Matters Most. Amsterdam: Contact.
Welch, J. (2001). Waar het om gaat. Utrecht: Het Spectrum.
Wijnberg, J. (2000). Als je zegt wat je denkt. Utrecht: Kosmos – Z&K.
Wilk Braksick, L. (2000). Unlock Behavior, Unleash Profits. New York: McGraw-Hill.

Photo: Corb!no

Ben Tiggelaar is an independent researcher, trainer, and publicist. He is one of the best-read management book authors in the Netherlands. He also lectures at several business schools in and outside of the Netherlands.

Ben can be contacted via *www.bentiggelaar.com* or *www.tiggelaar.nl*